Material Objects in Confucian and Aristotelian Metaphysics

Also available from Bloomsbury

Cultivating a Good Life in Early Chinese and Ancient Greek Philosophy, edited by Karyn Lai, Rick Benitez, and Hyun Jin Kim

Nonexistent Objects in Buddhist Philosophy, by Zhihua Yao

Interpreting Chinese Philosophy, by Jana S. Rošker

Transcendence and Non-Naturalism in Early Chinese Thought, by Alexus McLeod and Joshua R. Brown

Material Objects in Confucian and Aristotelian Metaphysics

The Inevitability of Hylomorphism

James Dominic Rooney, OP
倪佳道明

BLOOMSBURY ACADEMIC
LONDON • NEW YORK • OXFORD • NEW DELHI • SYDNEY

BLOOMSBURY ACADEMIC
Bloomsbury Publishing Plc
50 Bedford Square, London, WC1B 3DP, UK
1385 Broadway, New York, NY 10018, USA
29 Earlsfort Terrace, Dublin 2, Ireland

BLOOMSBURY, BLOOMSBURY ACADEMIC and the Diana logo are
trademarks of Bloomsbury Publishing Plc

First published in Great Britain 2022
This paperback edition published 2023

Copyright © James Dominic Rooney, 2022

James Dominic Rooney has asserted his right under the Copyright, Designs and
Patents Act, 1988, to be identified as Author of this work.

For legal purposes the Acknowledgments on p. vii constitute an
extension of this copyright page.

Cover image © Utagawa Hiroshige 歌川 広重. A Red Plum Branch against the
Summer Moon, c. mid–1840s. The Art Institute of Chicago.

All rights reserved. No part of this publication may be reproduced or transmitted
in any form or by any means, electronic or mechanical, including photocopying,
recording, or any information storage or retrieval system, without
prior permission in writing from the publishers.

Bloomsbury Publishing Plc does not have any control over, or responsibility for, any
third-party websites referred to or in this book. All internet addresses given in this
book were correct at the time of going to press. The author and publisher regret
any inconvenience caused if addresses have changed or sites have ceased
to exist, but can accept no responsibility for any such changes.

A catalogue record for this book is available from the British Library.

A catalog record for this book is available from the Library of Congress.

ISBN: HB: 978-1-3502-7634-5
PB: 978-1-3502-7638-3
ePDF: 978-1-3502-7635-2
eBook: 978-1-3502-7636-9

Typeset by Integra Software Services Pvt. Ltd.

To find out more about our authors and books visit www.bloomsbury.com
and sign up for our newsletters.

Contents

Acknowledgments	vii
Introduction	1
1 Structural Hylomorphism	7
Kit Fine	13
Kathrin Koslicki	20
William Jaworski	27
2 Structural Deterioration	33
The Substance-Part Principle in Detail	35
A Grounding Problem for SPP	39
Structures as Property-Powers	46
Structures as Proper Parts/Relations	53
Conclusion: Rejecting SPP	61
3 From Structure to Substantial Forms	63
Part I: Substantial Forms in Aquinas	65
A Primary Approach to "Prime Matter"	66
Actual Substances	69
Substantial Forms as *Essentially* Actuality	71
Matter, Material Parts, and Property Bearers	76
Form Is an Actuality *of* Matter	80
Part II: A Controversial Thomistic Thesis	82
Being a Part of a Thomistic Substance	84
The Puzzle of Parts	85
Conclusion: Forms as Metaphysical Parts	91
4 Zhu Xi's Metaphysics of Material Objects	97
The Metaphysical Landscape Painted by Zhu Xi	98
The "Priority" of *Li* to *Qi*	99
Li: Part/Universal, One/Many?	103
Radical Monism	104

Qi Alone as "Difference Maker" in a Relational Ontology	106
Li as Unitary Universal or Collection of Universals	109
Li as a Metaphysical Part	114
"Participation" Metaphysics and Hylomorphism	118
Conclusion: Confucian Hylomorphic Metaphysics	123
5 Forms Matter	**125**
Kit Fine's Theory of Things and Their Parts	129
Why Forms Matter	131
Making Restrictions on Composition Meaningful	132
Identity, in Two Flavors	137
Identity as Composition, a Transitive Relation	141
Identity as Contingently Transitive: Huayan Buddhism and Zhu Xi	146
All Coherent Restricted Theories of Composition are Hylomorphic	157
Conclusion: The Significance of Hylomorphism	163
Notes	168
Bibliography	194
Index	203

Acknowledgments

I would particularly like to thank Drs. Eleonore Stump, Bryan Van Norden, Jonathan Jacobs, and John Heil for their solicitude and care in helping bring this project to fruition.

In addition, William Dunaway and John McGinnis gave much-appreciated feedback on the individual chapters, as did those at Wuhan University—particularly Zheng Zemian, Li Yong, and Matthew Lutz. Further, I would also thank my colleagues Jonathan Nebel, Alexandra Romanyshyn, Matthew Shea, Audra Goodnight, James Kintz, and all the members of the dissertation group for their conversations and feedback that deeply influenced the outcome. Patrick Zoll and Jeremy Skrzypek were exceptionally helpful in shaping the final form of the book through helpful comments.

Lastly, I owe a debt of gratitude to Justin Tiwald, who very graciously shared materials, and to those who corrected and reviewed my translations: Nan Hu with classical Chinese and Adrian McCaffery, O.P., with Latin.

Soli Deo Gloria;
all faults being attributable to the author.

Introduction

A Chinese poet living in the Song dynasty wrote these lines:

A plum tree without snow does not shine forth;
Snow, without poetry, is overly common;
At sunset, a poem finished, heaven again brings snow;
Together with the plum trees, spring is then fully complete.[1]

Many people believe there are material objects: cats, quarks, protons, pieces of gold, human beings, chairs, and tables. Many might also count such things as plum trees and snow. But what is generally *not* taken for granted is that the poet's final line should be taken to mean that "spring" formed *one material object* composed of the poem, the plum, and the snow as its parts. If someone thought the poet was talking about a special sort of material thing, a "poem-plum-snow thing," such a person might be taken to have a very unnatural reading of the poem. There is something strange about thinking the plum is a part of the moon, because the plum is (of course) on earth and the moon quite far away. And even putting those two closely together, pulling the moon down right next to the plum tree, does not seem to many people to make those things *one* material thing.

Explaining what it is that sets apart the plum tree as a "genuine" material object, but not the plum-moon-spring-snow object, or saying what makes the plum tree's leaves or flowers its parts (but not the moon), nevertheless, is a complicated task. Peter van Inwagen, in his book *Material Beings*, famously called attention to the way in many of our puzzles about how material things can change parts over time, the best known of which is the puzzle of the Ship of Theseus, all centrally involve assumptions about what it is for one thing to be a part of another. He formulated what he called the "Special Composition Question" (SCQ) to get to the heart of the matter—"in what circumstances is a thing a (proper) part of something?"[2]—where the SCQ is a general question centered around when some things compose a material object rather than, for example, being a heap of things merely close together.

Depending on the answer one gives to the SCQ, what counts as a composite material object can be radically different. If we hold the view that there are *no* limits on how or when parts come to compose objects, for example, our world will be densely populated with lots of odd objects we ordinarily do not recognize as objects; anything could be quite literally a part of any other thing. There would then be a material object literally composed of the plum tree, snow, and moon. Or, conversely, on another extreme view, if there are no situations under which things compose anything (i.e., objects never have any parts at all), there will be *no* composite objects. And so, there would be no spring composed of plums and snow, but also no plums or snow or poems. Rather, on such a view, there would only be simple, part-less objects (maybe electrons or the like). Each would presumably require a significant shift in how we understand the world, assuming that the radical nature of the called-for revision does not incline us to reject these theories.

The aforementioned extreme views on the SCQ are generally not held by ordinary folk. Instead, many hold a "moderate" view that there are things like cats and plum trees, but that it is not the case that any old set of things compose a material object—there is no material object composed of three random pages of this book and your ear, for example. I will not be defending these "moderate" views of material composition but rather argue that, *if* they were true, all of these moderate answers to the SCQ would be variations on a very old account of how material objects are unified. This classical account is known as "hylomorphism."

"Hylomorphism" derives from the metaphysics of Aristotle (although it is not, as I will show, a uniquely Aristotelian view), where material objects are composed of matter (*hyle*) and form (*morphe*).[3] A survey of prominent names reveals not only that there are quite a few able defenders of the hylomorphism, but also that there are equally many different ways to understand and defend the theory.[4] I will be arguing that if you are among those who hold that there *are* such material objects as plums and snow, but not the other weird material objects of the extreme answers to the SCQ (including poem-snow-plum-moon objects), you are going to be committed to a fundamentally hylomorphic way of thinking about material objects. That is, you are going to hold that something playing the role of a *form* is what makes it the case that some set of material parts all compose one thing.

To set the stage, however, I will begin by dealing directly with only one broad camp among hylomorphists, which has been called "structural hylomorphism."[5] These views may broadly be described as a variant of hylomorphic theory that conceptualizes "form" as a kind of "structure." As we will see, there are various accounts of the nature of structure and its role in constituting material objects.

And all are going to agree that the thing playing the role of form—structure—is what makes something *one* material object. Yet exploring these theories can help us understand possible ways in which hylomorphism generally can resolve some of the puzzles of material composition and parthood, because not all of these authors I will survey agree on *the way in which* structure resolves these puzzles.

Thus, in the recent rise of interest in Aristotelian or neo-Aristotelian metaphysics, this kind of structural hylomorphism has been a prominent neo-Aristotelian view. Nevertheless, the various kinds of structural hylomorphism on offer span an array of metaphysical commitments. In particular, I will discuss three proponents of hylomorphism, Kit Fine, Kathrin Koslicki, and William Jaworski, who understand "structure" to function in significantly different metaphysical roles. In addition, while each claims that hylomorphism can help resolve problems in specific areas of philosophy (e.g., Jaworski utilizes hylomorphism to resolve issues in metaphysics of mind), all of these three thinkers explicitly propose hylomorphism as a satisfactory answer to van Inwagen's aforementioned "Special Composition Question." This makes their brands of hylomorphism particularly interesting avenues through which to consider the way in which hylomorphism interacts with contemporary mereology.

In what follows, I also show that there is a problem that affects each of these views. Despite the way in which Fine, Koslicki, and Jaworski differ in many particulars, all three accept a common principle that the parts of a substance can include things that are substances in their own right while they are part of the whole substance (i.e., a substance can have "substance-parts"). This principle characterizes, I propose, a uniquely "structural" aspect of structural hylomorphism, because it treats "form" as a kind of structuring of preexisting material objects.

In the second chapter, I argue that if "structure" answers the questions we had about what it is for some things to compose *one* substance, then it is not clear how there can be many such structures in one substance. Either structure makes something *one* a material object or it doesn't. If some things can continue to exist as substances while they compose other substances as parts, and each such substance retains its "structure" even while composing another as a part, then it seems as if structure really doesn't make something *one* material object. Rather, structure makes something *one* according to some other measure of oneness. I will show that, on these neo-Aristotelian versions of hylomorphism, there are too many cooks in the kitchen. If we go this way, hylomorphism is either incoherent or contradicts the assumption that a "moderate" view of composition is true.

By contrast, in other classical hylomorphic theories, what accounts for the unity of a material object does not function in this way. Instead, a material part will undergo a substantial change when it becomes a part of a substance; this is because the way that a form accounts for the unity of an object, on these views, is by being something like the *particular nature* of that substance and its parts. For this reason, there cannot be multiple substances composing one whole substance as parts—one cannot be an individual material composite "many times over." My third chapter motivates the classical view. Yet a chief reason people are hesitant to accept such classical hylomorphic theories is that they appear committed to absurd analyses of change either of objects or their parts. I respond to those worries by appeal to one such version of classical hylomorphism that strikes me as plausible and coherent: Thomas Aquinas' version of hylomorphism. In addition, Aquinas' account brings us to be able to characterize "hylomorphism" in a general way, and to present a functional account of what Aquinas calls "substantial forms."

The characterization of form I derive from Aquinas allows me to begin, positively, to press toward my main conclusion. In the fourth chapter, I begin to apply that characterization of form to argue that a medieval Chinese Confucian philosopher, Zhu Xi, embraces an independent non-Aristotelian metaphysics that parallels in important ways the Aristotelian hylomorphic tradition. In particular, Zhu Xi's metaphysics of material objects requires (and posits) substantial forms and therefore is a version of hylomorphism – one remarkably close to that of Thomas Aquinas. While it is true that Zhu Xi's account of material objects demonstrates a cross-cultural recognition that restricted theories of material composition need to be hylomorphic, the point is not primarily historical. Zhu Xi's account of material objects is dialectically well-placed for demonstrating that if composition were as the "moderate" views require it to be (i.e., the material composites are not such that any two or more things compose them necessarily), and there are no such things as substance-parts, then all these "moderate" views of composition entail the existence of substantial forms.

Finally, in the fifth chapter, I conclude by showing why it is the case that many theories of material composition are committed to substantial forms. To this end, I begin by showing that any theory of material objects that holds that there are facts about the composition of material objects, such that these facts are objective or mind-independent, is plausibly committed to entities in virtue of which a set of material parts all compose one object. Then, utilizing Zhu Xi's position against his Buddhist contemporaries as an illustration, I propose a generalized argument that all the moderate theories of material composition (even those that might hold nonstandard views about the relationship between identity and composition) are committed to entities like substantial forms.[6] If my argument is correct, any theory of material objects that accepts certain assumptions about the nature of composition should be committed to the hylomorphic metaphysical principles I outline or that theory risks incoherence. Not only then is hylomorphism a plausible theory that offers to resolve problems of material composition, but hylomorphism is the necessary framework for constructing *any* consistent, restrictive theory of material composition.

1

Structural Hylomorphism

In this chapter, I will be examining the differing metaphysics of material objects and their parts proposed by three neo-Aristotelian thinkers: Kit Fine, Kathrin Koslicki, and William Jaworski. My goals are, first, to lay out the problems or puzzles associated with van Inwagen's Special Composition Question (SCQ)—these will help us see the *desiderata* for any hylomorphic account of composition. Second, I will show how these aforementioned contemporary theories endorse different versions of hylomorphism as offering an answer to the SCQ. Finally, I will show that these neo-Aristotelians all endorse a problematic thesis, which, I will argue in the next chapter, undermines the possibility of these kinds of hylomorphism satisfactorily resolving problems of material composition.

van Inwagen's SCQ does not concern any kind of thing at all, such as sets or mathematical objects, but only the nature of *material* objects extended in space and time. Specifically, the question is intended to help focus questions about the unity and persistence of material objects through change.[1] van Inwagen was able to address these questions in a unified and principled way by showing that many puzzles about change all involve how it is that objects are composed of parts.[2] As noted earlier, the Ship of Theseus gives us an example: the planks of Theseus' ship are replaced piecemeal over time, and then the original parts come to compose a second ship. Is Theseus' ship identical to the reassembled original parts or the gradually repaired ship? The persistence conditions of the planks clearly differ from those of the ship: the planks can continue in existence even if the Ship of Theseus has ceased to be, and apparently vice-versa. So, the parts of the ship can be replaced and it is a common intuition that the ship was not destroyed in the process.

Three concrete problems of material composition can help focus on the ways in which we might be puzzled about the composition of material objects and, by contrast, what problems a good answer to the SCQ might help us resolve.

First, there is the case of Goliath and Lumpl (first proposed by Allan Gibbard). A sculptor brings together three pieces of clay to sculpt a statue of

Goliath, shaping its features and so forth. At the moment the sculptor puts together and shapes Goliath, the statue, he also brings into existence a new lump of clay, Lumpl, which is the exact amount of all the clay that composes Goliath.[3] In this case, it seems Goliath, the statue, can be destroyed, flattened, and yet Lumpl will survive the change. Similarly, Goliath does not seem to require this lump of clay, Lumpl, to exist—Goliath could have been made of another lump of clay. Further, if Goliath's finger were destroyed, Goliath will persist after such a change (albeit fingerless), whereas Lumpl would thereby cease to be. This is often referred to as the Grounding Problem, because one needs to account for how two different sets of properties—the properties of Goliath and those of Lumpl—can be appropriately grounded even though the objects Goliath and Lumpl share all their proper parts.[4] The first case illustrates how many puzzles about the identity of material objects typically arise when a certain object x and an object y share all of their parts but differ in regard to some modal properties.[5] In this first case, Goliath is not able to be squashed and continue to exist, but Lumpl can persist through such a change.

Consider a second case. Typically, a lot of problems with material composition involve differing persistence conditions of parts and wholes: object x persists over some kinds of changes, but object y does not. These kinds of changes take on another level of complexity when we consider biological organisms. Biological organisms come to be composed of different material parts (even entirely different parts) yet seem to be able to persist as the same organism or person. A debtor, for example, points out that she is composed of micro-physical particles. We don't want to say there are *both* the particles and the person in the same place at the same time. But then the debtor excuses herself from paying her debts, noting that, at the time she took out the debt in question, there was a distinct set of particles from the ones that are currently in her physical location. The new, entirely different, set of particles should no longer be responsible for the debt.[6] Obviously, "debtors" only exist within a socially constituted realm of money and debts. The salient point here is rather that the human person, who is the debtor, can undergo a change of her particles over time and remain the same person. With organisms or persons, like the debtor, we will need to explain the relation between the particles composing the organism and the organism.

A final example brings out these modal problems clearly. Consider the cases of Tibbles. Tibbles is a normal cat, but undergoes an accident in losing her tail. Initially, Tibbles is composed of her tail and her torso. Call her torso "Body-minus" (her body minus the tail). Before the accident, Body-minus is a proper part of Tibbles. Yet Tibbles, while composed of Body-minus as one of her parts, has at least one other part aside from Body-minus: her tail. Nevertheless, after the accident, Tibbles comes to be composed only of Body-minus. We might want to say Tibbles is identical to Body-minus, but then it seems like we have two identical objects in the same place and time. And they have different modal properties. It seems hard to think Tibbles could exist without Body-minus—she wouldn't be a cat if she was only a tail. But Body-minus underwent no change when the tail was lost. So it seems like we need to explain what the relations are between Tibbles and Body-minus.[7]

It is helpful, at this point, to present a few technical elements of how Peter van Inwagen set up the problem before proceeding further. The official formulation of the SCQ in *Material Beings* was: "When is it true that ∃y the xs compose y?"[8] In slightly more plain language, "when is it true that there is some y, some material whole, such that the xs, some material parts, compose it?" But this characterization of the problem requires that we specify what kind of "parts" we are talking about. Here it has become typical in contemporary mereology to distinguish two senses of "part": "proper" versus "improper" parts. Proper and improper parts are distinguished insofar as a part either does not or does *share a common part* with other parts; i.e., whether they "overlap." Thus, we can informally define x as a "proper part" of y if and only if that part x is a part of y, which overlaps no other part of y (and $x \neq y$). In characterizing what it is for the xs to compose a y as proper parts of y, van Inwagen proposes that: some things (x) are proper parts of a whole (y) if "the xs are all parts of y and no two of the xs overlap and every part of y overlaps at least one of the xs."[9] Overlapping parts are here excluded as proper parts of any object because they do not uniquely divide the parts of that object. "Improper parts" are those parts that do overlap, such as the upper two-thirds of an object and the lower half; additionally, the whole y can also be considered an improper part of itself. (These initial distinctions carry no significant ontological weight; we are at this point merely clarifying our terminology.)

While the case of Tibbles is not a problem that apparently involves biology to any significant extent, it helps us see that the puzzles of material composition might be dissolved by taking various stands on when some things compose a material object as *proper parts*. First, we could say that Tibbles *never* existed because *nothing* is composed of parts. van Inwagen called this first extreme position in regard to the SCQ "Nihilism" because it holds that there are no circumstances under which the xs compose any y. Nihilism holds all that exist are "simples," entities without any proper parts at all.[10] Whether these simples are quarks, for example, or some other yet-to-be-discovered fundamental item, the Nihilist would hold the only things that exist are those fundamental items and they have no parts. Nihilists then have an easy answer to these problems of material composition: there is no Tibbles, or Goliath/Lumpl, or Ship of Theseus, and consequently no problems about their unity or persistence over time.

On the other hand, we could think that Tibbles' tail does compose Tibbles, but that there are as many (actual composite) objects as there are things to be parts. Then it turns out Tibbles and Body-minus are objects that exist in the same time and place. In fact, there are an infinite number of objects that *all* exist alongside Tibbles—her left ear and her paws compose one object, her right ear and the Eifel Tower another, and so on. Given that any particular set of things compose an object as it were "automatically," and the existence of these objects is in no way affected by (for example) the arrangement of those things that are their parts, then we can dissolve many of the apparent problems. On this view, we would take Tibbles to be nothing more than the precise set of the cat's current parts: head, body, paws, tail. But Tibbles the set is still one material object even if all those parts (head, body, etc.) individually move to separate sides of universe. Only if his tail were strictly annihilated does that particular set of the parts (that is, Tibbles) cease to exist. In other words, an object exists necessarily just whenever the parts that compose it exist. This other position, what van Inwagen termed "Universalism," holds that there are no circumstances under which the xs do not compose some y. In formal mereology, this involves acceptance of a principle of "unrestricted composition," which formally expresses the view of the Universalist as a thesis that any two or more (nonoverlapping) things necessarily form a material object.[11] What Universalism gains in a certain kind of simplicity in dealing with composite objects, it loses in holding that there are necessarily infinite numbers of strange mereological composites. For instance, a famous example of such an odd composite is "the mereological fusion of the front half of a trout plus the back half of a turkey,"[12] which, according to Universalism, currently form a unique material object: a trout-turkey.

Echoing the sentiment that the strange kinds of composites proposed by Universalism seem ridiculous, van Inwagen noted that Universalism is difficult to reconcile with our ordinary notion of parthood: "Though I think that the color blue and the key of C-sharp and I all exist, I am unable to form a sufficiently general conception of parthood to be able to conceive of an object that has these three rather diverse things as parts."[13] For these reasons, van Inwagen notes, Universalism does not seem to "force itself upon the mind as true."[14] Further, Universalism contradicts what van Inwagen calls a set of plausible theses about the world, which we already saw with Tibbles.

Consider that I both exist now and that I existed ten years ago. The atoms that composed me ten years ago, which no longer compose me at present, still exist. Yet: "If Universalism is true, then the *x*s cannot ever compose two objects … either simultaneously or successively."[15] If Universalism were true, van Inwagen argues, the *same* *x*s cannot compose two different objects simultaneously or successively. If the *x*s are particles A, B, and C, and only these three, then Universalism holds that they compose one unique object—the object composed of A, B, and C. Shifting around A, B, and C does not involve creating some new object because the object exists as long as its parts do. While A, B, or C could individually compose some other object (e.g., the object that is the fusion of A and B), the same pieces taken as a set would together only compose the object of A, B, and C. So Universalism seems to rule out the existence of objects, like organisms, which persist through time. Yet that seems contrary to experience.

Nihilism, too, appears manifestly contrary to appearances. It seems apparent that human beings, you and I, are composite objects with parts. But, if so, Nihilism is false.[16] Neither Nihilism nor Universalism seems to match our ordinary intuitions about material objects, or even necessarily our best scientific theories about the world (e.g., physics seems to involve talk of parts).[17] Nihilism, for example, denies that you or I exist and—to paraphrase van Inwagen's objection—we can be surer that we exist than we are of any argument the Nihilist could give us to convince us that we do not.

van Inwagen therefore proposed a moderate view that avoided both of these extremes. He holds that composition happens (against Nihilism) and that there are not as many composite objects as there are potential sets of objects (against Universalism). Instead, he argued that only *sometimes,* when the circumstances are right, is it true that some parts compose a whole. As there are some restricted set of circumstances under which the *x*s come to compose *y*, any view similar in this respect to van Inwagen's proposal holds that material composition is *restricted* because it does not accept the Universalist's thesis that composition occurs "automatically" or without restriction. Hylomorphism falls under such restricted accounts of material composition because it will offer a set of restricted conditions to questions such as the following: "Suppose one had certain (nonoverlapping) objects, the *x*s, at one's disposal; what would one have to do—what *could* one do—to get the *x*s to compose something?"[18]

Hylomorphists will all agree on an answer: you take the *x*s and give them a *form*. By virtue of the form that the *x*s possess, the *x*s will compose an object, a *y*; or, similarly, if and only if the *x*s have a form do they come to compose an object *y*. In the above situations, for example, the debtor is one whole material object composed of their particles because those particles have one *form* (the form of the debtor). The respective properties of Goliath and Lumpl, just like Tibbles, and the facts about their parts changing over time, would be explained by their forms, if they have them.[19] Appeal to a form is generally appeal to a restriction on composition, but, if everything *did* have a form, hylomorphism would not quite be a standard kind of Universalism. As I will show in regard to Kit Fine's account of material composition, having a form or structure does not function in the same way as being a member of an arbitrary set. The restrictions on material composition then can be quite broad, in principle, but (as I will argue in the fifth chapter) there are good reasons for hylomorphism to be less plausible the less restrictive that it is.

We could get much more technical in laying out further assumptions of standard mereology. For example, it is also a core assumption of standard mereology that the relation of parthood is reflexive, transitive, and antisymmetric. This is to say that everything is an (improper) part of itself [reflexive], any part of any part of a thing is itself part of that thing [transitive], and two distinct things cannot be (proper) parts of each other [antisymmetric].[20] Nevertheless, neither I nor the authors I will review will bring these characterizations of parthood relations into dispute, so I will not introduce any further technical terminology in this regard. In addition, some specifications of mereological relations or principles can carry ontological weight insofar as they specify under which circumstances or how material composition can occur.[21] For instance, what are called "supplementation" principles relate to how we can decompose a whole into its parts. These decomposition principles are intended to capture the intuition that decomposing a whole into its parts results in more than just a single proper part. (Similarly, principles that go the other way—composition principles—indicate at what bounds a set of things come to compose an object.) But which such principles we should accept are debatable (Koslicki, as we will see below, accepts a controversial decomposition principle—"Weak Supplementation" (WS)).

For my purposes, further technical complications will distract, however, from the goal of understanding whether and how hylomorphism can resolve the problems associated with material composition. At this point, consequently, I will turn to the particular theories of material composition proposed by Kit Fine, Kathrin Koslicki, and William Jaworski. Each of these contemporary metaphysicians appeals to "structure" as that in virtue of which some parts compose a material substance. Thus, these three are useful because they each explicitly argue that hylomorphism has unique resources for addressing van Inwagen's question about composition.

Yet each offers a very different analysis of the way in which structure does so. In particular, in addition to outlining various ways that structures can account for the unity of material objects or substances, I will show that these contemporary theories accept a very particular sense in which it is possible that substances can compose others as parts. All formulate their hylomorphic theories of composition to explicitly address van Inwagen's SCQ, which makes them dialectically useful for my overall argument. Nevertheless, we need to get more detail about each view in order to grasp how each aims to resolve the problems of material composition.

Kit Fine

Kit Fine appeals to Aristotelian notions of matter and form in developing his account of material composition. In "Things and Their Parts," Fine sets up his account of composition, as with van Inwagen, against Universalism. Fine appeals to an example of a ham sandwich to illustrate his position. If we understand composition to be merely "aggregative," as Universalism does, a material object exists whenever the right parts exist in the world. Then, e.g., a ham sandwich will exist anytime there is an appropriate sum of ham and bread in the world. Yet, obviously, two slices of bread on opposite sides of the universe and some ham floating elsewhere in space do not constitute a ham sandwich; instead, "if the sandwich is to exist, it is not sufficient for the ingredients merely to be around. They must be appropriately assembled."[22]

Fine holds that what it is for some ham and bread to be a ham sandwich involves those parts existing in the right relation to each other. In addition, whatever the right relation is between the ham and bread that relation should not itself be counted among the ingredients of the ham sandwich; "it is hard to believe that [the arrangement] is a part in the same way as the standard ingredients."[23] Fine therefore suggests that composition should be understood to involve a species of relation between parts. He proposes two different varieties of composition relations, which involve different kinds of parts: those parts that are relative to a time ("time-relative" parts), or time-variable, such that all parts specific to that embodiment are only parts of that embodiment relative to a time t, and those that are not ("timeless" parts). Fine's example of a rigid embodiment is the ham sandwich, such that whenever or wherever the ham and bread are in appropriate spatial relations, a ham sandwich is constituted. His example of a variable embodiment is "the water in a river," where that water is variable, being the water flowing through a review at some particular time, and so the function describing the water relative to the river (the principle of embodiment) will pick out different parts (the water) relative to a time t.

The idea of variable embodiments is then that some objects change parts while remaining numerically the same object and we need a distinct composition relation to explain how these parts come to be parts of the object over time. For example, a flowing river does not always have the same particular constituent water parts, but there is some function by which we can specify what water at some given time is a part of that river's water. Or, in the example of the car and carburetor, there is some function F according to which we can determine, over the time when my car exists, whether this carburetor is part of my car or not.[24]

Fine calls both sets of relations "principles of embodiments" because these relations, like Aristotelian forms, become "embodied" in the parts of the new object and lead us to count those parts as composing a whole. The parts are the "fixed matter" of the embodiment.[25] These principles of embodiments are relations in virtue of which the parts of an object compose that object. Fine conceives of these principles as themselves constituting or composing *the objects* that are their embodiments, and not merely constituting states of affairs or facts about that object: "the relation R preserves its predicative role and somehow serves to modify or qualify the components .... The result of the modification is not a fact or state. It is a whole, whose components are linked by the relations, rather than the fact or state of the components being so linked."[26]

Fine had argued that an "aggregative" view of composition could not include the relation among parts as an additional proper part; "it is hard to believe that [the arrangement] is a part in the same way as the standard ingredients."[27] However, Fine considers a variable embodiment designated as "/F/," where "F" is the principle of that embodiment, and Fine explicitly affirms that the principle F is a *part* of /F/.[28] And Fine sometimes claims that the principles of embodiment can be characterized intensional or conceptual "parts" of the identities of material objects:

> there will be an intensional or conceptual element to the identity of many material objects .... These principles [of embodiments], which are intensional or conceptual in nature, are directly implicated in the identity of the embodiments and hence also in the identity of the material things that are explained by their means. Indeed, I believe that it may plausibly be argued that these principles are *parts* of their embodiments and hence parts of the corresponding material things.[29]

These apparently conflicting claims might be understandable in light of Fine's explicit claims that his theory of embodiment is a variety of hylomorphism. Classical hylomorphists made a distinction between "metaphysical" and "integral" parts that seems to correspond to what Fine means here. We could then distinguish the way in which a relation is not an integral or material part of a material object, from the way in which that relation holds among the material parts and characterizes the object as a whole, which allows us to think of a principle of embodiment as something like a "metaphysical" part of those objects. For that reason, I suggest that he holds the view that principles of embodiment have a *sui generis* relation of parthood to the object they constitute, unlike mereological proper parts.[30]

Fine's theory is thus supposed to invoke hylomorphic principles to explain how composite material objects are one. Principles of embodiment are formal principles that account for the conditions under which wholes of a given sort exist, or the conditions of identity for these wholes, whereas the material principles specify the conditions under which the wholes possess either features relevant to space-time location, or those concerning that whole's descriptive character (e.g., color and weight).[31] Yet, compared with Aristotle, Fine's version of hylomorphism is less ontologically robust. Fine criticizes Aristotle for holding that the difference between objects (i.e., substances) and non-objects is a difference in their unity, where what made some object a genuine object was a distinct "operation of composition," or the way in which its material parts "come together":

> However reasonable it may have been for Aristotle to hold this view, it is not reasonable for us. For with the advance of science, we know that there is no special force or principle which binds together the different parts of the body and yet is not operative in the universe as a whole; and in the absence of any such force or principle, it is rather hard to see what ontological basis there could be for distinguishing between the constituency of substances and of mere heaps. Thus the idea that there is a distinctive notion of constitution, terminating in the concrete substances, is one that should be given up. However, this is not necessarily to give up the idea that there is something distinctive about the concrete substances themselves. For one can grant that something is genuinely one, without thereby granting that what makes it genuinely one is some distinctive way in which its constituents come together.[32]

Yet, while Fine rejects the Aristotelian notion that there are privileged or unique operations of composition that constitute genuine wholes, i.e., substances, Fine does not reject the language of "substance." Instead, as he says, giving up the Aristotelian idea that there is a distinctive operation of composition "is not necessarily to give up the idea that there is something distinctive about the concrete substances themselves."[33] Fine's embodiments either can be called or are supposed to be relevantly equivalent to Aristotelian substances, even if he denies that there are ontologically privileged "operations of composition." This is to say that, for Fine, something is a "substance," an object, if that thing is characterized by a principle of embodiment.

In later papers, Fine even reappropriates the term "genuine whole" for any whole that results from an operation of composition, according to some "principle" that will come to thereby characterize the parts. Each operation of composition requires material and formal principles that specify how and when the operation of composition occurs, and so these "principles of composition operations" are equivalent to "principles of embodiments." A "genuine whole" is thus defined in "Towards a Theory of Part" as follows: "a genuine whole of a given kind k may be taken to be an object that has an explanation of its identity in terms of the associated operator Σ_k."[34] In other words, any object that is the embodiment relative to some principle of embodiment is a genuine whole. What principles of embodiments *do* is give some set of material things an "explanation of their identity" in terms of a composition operation.

What Fine seems to deny is that there is any extra-mental difference between objects characterized by principles of embodiments and "mere" heaps. The problem is that this view seems overly permissive, because Fine imposes no apparent restrictions on what kinds of principles of embodiments there could be. Recall Fine himself argued against Universalism on the grounds that an "aggregative" account of composition does not specify the right relation existing between the parts of material objects; all one has is a sum of things, not parts of a whole. Thus, Fine also alleges that certain sums do not plausibly count as "parts": "Consider the sum of the ham and Cleopatra or, more dramatically, the sum of the ham and all objects that existed only before or after the sandwich existed .... it is ludicrous to suppose that this monstrous object—of which Cleopatra and all merely past and future galaxies are parts—is itself a part of the ham sandwich."[35] But, as Koslicki points out, Fine's own view seems to countenance just such "monsters." If we specify a principle of rigid embodiment where the relevant R relation is nothing more than summation of four material things, two slices of bread, a piece of ham, and Cleopatra, Fine *would* be committed to saying precisely that Cleopatra is a part of the ham sandwich.

Koslicki has suggested that, therefore, Fine's view would countenance even more material objects than Universalism. Whether or not a material object exists depends on how we specify its principle of embodiment. Depending on how we specify a set of possible principles, not only could can any sum of two or more material things constitute an object, like Universalism, but also "each occupied region of space-time is inhabited by numerous rigid embodiments which share their objectual components and only differ in how their intensional component is specified."[36] Koslicki therefore claims Fine's restrictions on composition, his principles of embodiment, "amount to no restriction at all."[37] In fact, Fine explicitly accepts this proliferation of objects as an implication of his view.[38] He also concedes his theory admits monsters like Cleopatra-ham sandwiches, but holds "there can be no theory that is internally satisfactory in providing a precise and principled basis for determining what exists and yet also externally satisfactory in being consonant with what we ordinarily take to exist."[39]

Koslicki asks: "But what are these principles and how is it that each object has such a principle associated with it? Some of Fine's remarks... suggest that the answer to this question might ultimately refer back to us, if the intensional components of embodiments are thought of as being of a conceptual nature and commitment to them is not 'ultimate.'"[40] While she discounts the interpretation that Fine holds that the existence of material objects is mind-dependent, or something similar, Koslicki finally proposes that Fine's view seems to entail an "ontological relativism," because his method of postulating objects "is a means of extending one's ontology... [Through] an interpretative act, by which existing quantifiers are interpreted as ranging over new objects."[41]

Clearly, Fine does not intend to hold that human beings can create new objects at will.[42] Something is missing from Koslicki's reading of Fine. Fine seems to suggest that whatever exists can be grouped into various objects or parts according to the way we human beings divide the world or "count" the things that exist. We might think that the principles of embodiments are mind-dependent, so that the way we select among possible principles to count objects or parts is a matter of our interests or explanatory aims. Fine seems to embrace this conclusion: "what there is will be relative to what has been introduced. There is no absolute sense in which there is what there is since what there is always capable of being extended through the introduction of new objects."[43] Yet Fine offers some clarifications on how we "introduce" new objects, such that his view is not are radical as it appears to Koslicki.

Fine appears to confirm Koslicki's interpretation by saying that he accepts that "within certain domains of objects, what exists is inevitably an arbitrary matter."[44] Notice, however, that Fine claims that what exists is arbitrary only in *certain* domains. He does not countenance arbitrary objects in every domain.

Whereas mathematical objects (Fine claims) are a plausible example of such domains where we can introduce objects arbitrarily, "surely material things—elementary particles or people or the like—are given, not introduced; and so there is no reason to think that they will suffer from the same kind of arbitrariness in their existence."[45] He notes that his view would be compatible with the view that some, but not all, of the material objects that exist are introduced. These objects would be introduced on the basis of some "given" objects, so that the given objects are ontologically prior to the introduced objects:

> it is not altogether unnatural to suppose that some material objects—perhaps elementary particles and the like—are God-given while the others are the 'work of man'. There would then be no special difficulty in supposing that the boundaries to the domain of material things were arbitrary as long as they were arbitrary in the right way, i.e. with respect to the objects that were introduced.[46]

He gives some examples of how we might extend our counting of material objects. A first example is that of "a future religious sect holds the view that cars are endowed with souls who migrate to a neighboring bouquet of flowers after a gestation period of nine months (stranger religious views have been held). The putative bodies of these souls are called 'car-bouquets.'"[47] In this future situation, Fine believes, a new object has been introduced by a kind of stipulation or postulation of the religious sect that comes to be part of the general community's usage of our quantifiers, such that the community comes to quantify over "car-bouquets." Thus, "everyone is willing to recognize the existence of car-bouquets, [although] there is considerable disagreement over whether they have souls."[48] A second example is that every culture has a notion of star-groupings, "constellations," and yet different cultures admit different constellations into their ontology. He claims: "surely each culture is correct in recognizing the constellations that it does."[49] The point of these examples is that, given some starting set of objects, we can construct further objects through operations of composition.[50]

Fine nevertheless is non-committal as to whether there are any "given" objects at all. None of these ways to divide reality by reference to any principle of embodiment is more natural or ontologically privileged than any other: "I would wish to maintain that the objects we ordinarily recognize—chairs and tables and the like—are not ontologically privileged. Whatever kind of ontological commitment we have to them we should also have to the more bizarre forms of rigid and variable embodiment."[51] Fine then countenances the possibility that there could be no "given" objects and that *every* material object could be "introduced" in this way: "What goes for material objects in general will go for the rigid and variable embodiments of my theory in particular. Thus it might be supposed that some (*perhaps all*) of them are introduced while the others (*perhaps none*) are given [my emphasis]."[52]

Obviously, for Fine, substances come cheap—we can extend our quantifiers and come to count new objects as genuine wholes. For example, we can understand some set of stars as parts of one material object (e.g., a constellation) as long as they satisfy relevant criteria provided by a suitable principle relating those stars to each other. Satisfying the relevant criteria, a possible principle of embodiment, is then that in virtue of which that object exists. And Fine seems to think such principles involve an "explanation of the identity" of an object in terms of how it came to be composed. I will return to Fine's ontology in the final chapter, arguing that something important is missing in this account, but Fine's view is not precisely the same as holding that our acts of counting make the world to be a certain way (as Koslicki held him to believe).

It should be clear, however, that Fine accepts the possibility that substances can compose other substances as proper parts. Fine's account clearly implies that, ordinarily, substances are composed of other substances as proper parts. On one hand, Fine requires treating the constituent matter of any rigid embodiment as specifiable independently of that embodiment's principle.[53] That matter is independently specifiable due to some other embodiment principle proper to that matter. Consequently, the material parts of rigid embodiments are themselves objects. If all parts are specifiable by their own embodiments, does this lead to a regress, where these parts are only definable in terms of their parts, ad infinitum? One way to stop the regress, which Fine suggests elsewhere, involves an atomism where all composite objects are built from simples, non-mereological objects.[54] On the other hand, while the matter of variable embodiments are specified by their characteristics or properties rather than "rigidly" pointing out some particular object (e.g., rivers are composed of water, but do not require some particular water), these material parts are generally objects with their own embodiment principles (e.g., the variable embodiment "car"). This seems to entail that the matter of variable embodiments, too, is embodiments of some sort, and thus is characterized by their own principles of embodiment.[55] Whether variable or rigid embodiments are at issue, then, it is clearly not only possible but generally the case for Fine that principles of embodiments take other "genuine whole" objects as their matter.

Given that substances come cheap, and principles of embodiment only account for the unity of a set of material parts in terms of their "identity" (as an *intensional* relation among the parts), then there seems to be no principled reason one substance cannot be a proper part of another. Composite material objects, structured by principles of embodiments, can serve as the matter of other principles of embodiment because any embodiment can be specified by their own relation at the same time that they are matter for other embodiments.

Kathrin Koslicki

Kathrin Koslicki follows Fine in arguing that Universalism, if it were the correct account of the nature of material composition, would require our conception of material objects and their parts to be radically revised. We would have to admit into our ontology all of the "monstrous" material objects that result from those theories (e.g., trout-turkeys). By contrast, Koslicki "assigns to the mereological proper a more limited set of responsibilities directed at the characterization of those mereologically complex entities whose existence is already confirmed by independent evidence to which the mereologist must hold himself accountable."[56] Put more simply, she takes it that a good answer to the SCQ should respect the independently given (in her view, scientific), non-mereological data for what materially composite entities there are in the world. In short, Koslicki holds there is no good *mereologically independent* reason to believe trout-turkeys, or most of the entities that would result from an unrestricted view of material composition, exist.

For this reason, she proposes a moderate solution to van Inwagen's SCQ, on which material composition is restricted, and offers a Neo-Aristotelian account of parthood and material composition.[57] Koslicki proposes that objects are structured wholes, composed of material and formal components.[58] Koslicki's formal principles of material objects are, unlike Fine's intensional principles, extra-mental "structures" of those material objects.[59] Structures, the formal components of material objects, are compared to "recipes." Structures specify an "ingredient list" of parts and the conditions under which those parts come to compose an object.[60] Koslicki characterizes her position with three formal principles. The first two are:

1. Restricted Composition Principle (RCP): Some objects, $m_1, \ldots, m_n$, compose an object O, of kind, K, just in case $m_1, \ldots, m_n$, satisfy the constraints dictated by some formal components *simpliciter*, $f_1, \ldots, f_n$, associated with objects of kind, K.[61]

2. Mereological Analysis of Constitution (MAC): Some objects, $m_1, ..., m_n$, *constitute* an object O just in case $m_1, ..., m_n$ are O's *material components*, i.e., $m_1, ..., m_n$ are those among O's *proper parts* which satisfy the constraints dictated by O's *formal components*, $f_1, ..., f_n$.[62,63]

This ontology is "restricted" because material composition occurs only under some definite conditions: an object is composed of parts when some other material objects satisfy formal conditions associated with a natural kind.[64] In both RCP and MAC the "material" components of an object (its content/matter) are the proper parts of that object. These proper parts are themselves objects.[65] *Prime facie*, it might seem that "matter" is necessarily a structured object with its own matter and structure. But Koslicki does admit the possibility that material parts could be mereologically simple entities. While she argues her theory does not require that there is some "first level" of composition where the matter or content is mereologically simple (not composed of anything), she argues her theory does not advert to simples because it would not need to account for their material composition. By definition, naturally, simples are not mereologically complex and hence are not structured wholes with matter and structure.[66]

RCP refers to "kinds" of objects, which Koslicki understands to be "natural kinds." This is where the extra-mereological set of considerations that are intended to motivate acceptance of her (restricted) hylomorphic mereology enters the picture.[67] Koslicki broadly appeals to an account of natural kinds, inspired by Richard Boyd, where there are certain natural similarities among the structures of material objects, indicated by clusters of appropriately similar properties. Instances of H_2O, for example, exemplify similar properties. Koslicki proposes that the reason for the occurrence of similar properties in these cases is that those instances share the same structure (and so form a natural kind).[68] While she offers arguments for the existence of natural kinds in further detail, these are not central to my mereological concerns (as they motivate her view rather than constitute it).

Finally, in laying out her views, Koslicki endorses a controversial thesis that structures are parts in exactly the same way that any other integral proper part is a part of a whole.[69]

- Neo-Aristotelian Thesis (NAT): The material and formal components of a mereologically complex object are *proper parts* of the whole they compose.[70]

Koslicki's argument that structures are proper parts of objects has as its basis four considerations: (1) a whole is numerically distinct from its material components, (2) the material components of an object are its proper parts, (3) it is possible to have a mereologically complex object with one material proper part, and (4) that a special decomposition principle, "Weak Supplementation," is "partially constitutive of the meaning of 'is a proper part of'."[71] WS is the principle that "an object that has a proper part must have at least another proper part disjoint from the first," or, even more simply, that any composite object has at least two proper parts.[72] Koslicki also holds that "it never happens that two numerically distinct wholes have exactly the same parts."[73] She thus rules out the cases where objects possess all the same proper parts, or "coincident" objects.

Let's paraphrase these considerations as a continuous argument. Assume it is both the case that WS is true and that objects can be constituted of only one material proper part. WS dictates that any object with proper parts has at least *two* proper parts. And the whole object is numerically distinct from its single material part. Consequently, WS dictates there needs to be some other part in virtue of which the whole object differs from its one material part. Koslicki therefore concludes that such objects with one material part, if they exist and are composite objects, will require some other proper part. That part, she argues, is a non-material or formal proper part: the object's structure. The structure will then be a literal proper part of the object, and it is in virtue of being composed of both its material proper part *and* the structure that the whole is numerically distinct from its material proper part. To illustrate, Koslicki takes the case of Goliath-Lumpl as one involving an object (Goliath, the statue) composed from one material part (Lumpl, the clay). We assume that, if two objects share all the same properties, then they are identical.[74] Yet the statue, Goliath, has differing persistence conditions from Lumpl: if we crush Goliath, Goliath ceases to exist but Lumpl remains. So then it seems Goliath cannot be strictly identical with Lumpl because it does not share all of Lumpl's properties.

Koslicki argues that, if Goliath is qualitatively distinct from Lumpl (i.e., having some properties not shared by Lumpl), then "the following explanation of their numerical distinctness is actually *dictated* by our endorsement of the Weak Supplementation Principle ... we know that the *something extra* which distinguishes the statue from the lump of clay that constitutes it must in fact be an additional *part*."[75] Since the clay, Lumpl, is the single material proper part of the statue Goliath, "we arrive at the conclusion that the formal components of a whole ... must be counted among its proper parts."[76] Thus, Goliath has an additional proper part that distinguishes Goliath from its single material proper part Lumpl: namely, Goliath's structure or form.[77]

It might not seem that adding another proper part to an object accounts for why those parts constitute an object, any more than the original parts themselves explain why they constitute that object. Koslicki responds to this kind of objection by claiming the problem only occurs when the parts are of the same ontological kind: "according to the present conception, the additional parts which help to explain the nature of the relation between a whole and its remaining proper parts belong to a *different kind*; viz. they are formal components eligible to compose a whole of that particular kind."[78] So, naturally, adding another material proper part does nothing to explain why the parts are parts. But Koslicki argues that a *formal* part, by reason of being a structure, is precisely what explains why those material parts constitute an object.

Of course, such a view of parthood might seem problematic. But, first, we need to achieve more clarity as to how Koslicki understands what it is to *be* a structure and, consequently, a "formal" part. In fact, though, Koslicki does not provide a single definition of structure, but appeals to various examples in chemistry, logic, music, and linguistics to illustrate structure. The notion of "structure" relies on a distinction between "what is taken as variable and what is taken as invariable relative to a set of transformations that count as admissible in a particular context."[79] Yet, beyond this general characterization, Koslicki leaves explicitly undecided the nature of and ontological category to which structures belong. If we establish that structural components are required for a "satisfactory account of the mereological characteristics of ordinary material objects," and that there are good reasons (viz., WS, etc.) to require that structures are proper parts of objects, Koslicki claims we do not need to classify structures in any given ontological category. She therefore remains ambivalent whether structures themselves should be counted in the ontological category of objects, properties, or relations.[80]

Regardless, the position that structures could be objects would seem to conflict with her response to the aforementioned objection that an additional proper part of an object does not explain the composition of that object. Koslicki had replied that a "formal" proper part is of a different ontological kind than the other material parts. If structures are objects, then one might wonder whether structures would be of the same ontological kind as the other material parts—namely, objects of some kind. In response, Koslicki might be assuming that abstract objects, such as formal objects, and concrete objects, like the material parts of some whole, could constitute distinct ontological categories. Then, structures can both be and compose objects if the proper parts of that object are objects of a different ontological kind from the structure.

Yet this appeal to different ontological kinds is not apparently helpful. When she does offer examples of structures functioning as objects, Koslicki gives examples in mathematics or linguistics of groups composed of other groups, or functions ranging over functions. In these examples, a whole would be composed of the same kind of thing as itself, so that structure can be both part and structured object.[81] It remains unclear how a structure belonging to a kind of distinct ontological kind would help explain the unity of the whole it constitutes as a proper part. And it seems to me that the claims about structures being structured objects in their own right only complicate the problem. I will nevertheless give Koslicki the benefit of the doubt on this point, as it ultimately does not affect the criticisms I will make of her position in the next chapter. There is, I will argue, a *more fundamental* problem. For my purposes, I will assume that structures are not (and could not be) objects; this would conflict with the thesis that structures must belong to a different ontological category from the matter of whatever they compose. The far easier theoretic movie is to reject that structures are objects and hold that their special nature as formal parts is enough to explain why a structure being a part of an object explains or accounts for its unity. (We can imagine, given her other claims, that structures are either properties or relations, but nothing hangs on this.) Consequently, I will proceed with the assumption merely that Koslicki's structures are *formal parts,* a special kind of proper part distinct from material constituents.

Even though Koslicki moves beyond Fine in her more realistic account of structures as literal proper parts of objects, Koslicki shares with Fine skepticism that Aristotle imposed far too strict a notion of how forms unify objects. This is because "the conceptual connection Aristotle sets up between the notions of unity and indivisibility" are such that, for Aristotle, "something's being *one* according to some measure [...] is taken to amount to its being not further divisible into parts according to the measure in question; in fact, the lack of divisibility seems to be identified by Aristotle as the reason for the object's status as a unified thing with respect to the measure at hand."[82] So

> it is not difficult to think of cases in which it is perfectly natural to call something *a* or *one* something-or-other, even when the object in question is further divisible into objects of the same kind: for example, a building may be composed of proper parts which are themselves buildings .... In each case, the fact that an object is further divisible into proper parts which satisfy the same concept is no obstacle to its counting as one something-or-other, relative to the measure in question.[83]

In short, for Koslicki as for Fine, structures or forms make something unified, but there is no need for an object to be unified in anything more than a relative sense, where that object has unity of parts appropriate to a given *kind*. One material object might be characterized by one form that unifies its parts as composing a "cat," for example, while having multiple other forms unifying the other material parts as "paws," "whiskers," and so forth. On this way of considering unity, then, there is no reason that one material substance cannot have substances as proper parts, each with their own respective structures.

In her recent book *Form, Matter, and Substance,* Koslicki does not notably modify this earlier account of hylomorphic compounds, but she does present a clear account of substance that significantly adds to her account. In particular, she qualifies her view to disclaim that she can offer any absolute criteria of substancehood. That is, Koslicki does not give an account of what it is for something to be a substance *simpliciter*. Instead, she holds that we can only give comparative or relative criteria for what is more-or-less a substance compared to other entities.[84] This complicates Koslicki's arguments against Aristotle because she no longer strictly holds that one substance can compose another as a proper part, because neither a whole nor its proper parts will be substances absolutely speaking.

While I will discuss in detail the ramifications of Koslicki's position on the nature of substance in the next chapter, Koslicki nevertheless still intends her term "genuine wholes" to be equivalent to Aristotelian substances—something can be genuinely unified without being indivisible in the way Aristotle holds of substances informed by only one form.[85] And, a genuine whole (i.e., a structured object) can have other genuine wholes as proper parts. If a whole has all of the proper parts specified by the structure, so that the whole counts as a genuine instance of whatever kind of object is specified by that structure, then the whole is a genuine unity, regardless of whether those parts are objects. "Nothing more *needs* to be said or *could* be said" in regard to the unity of such wholes.[86] In light of the new qualifications, it will still be true to say that all Koslicki's hylomorphic composites (or at least instances of, e.g., natural kinds) are relevantly *substance-like*, even if we cannot give necessary and sufficient criteria for substancehood. Yet, even if no particular composite whole counts as a substance *simpliciter*, it is possible that composite wholes have proper parts that are themselves unified composites. Any such object that is comparatively more a substance will in most cases be composed of other substance-like objects. This is because (as we saw) the matter of any composite whole is ordinarily some set of things that are themselves hylomorphic composites.[87]

In addition, Koslicki's misgivings about the possibility of giving absolute criteria of substancehood do not mean she does not identify some *exemplar* cases of substancehood. As she notes, the Aristotelian should want to hold that instances of natural kinds, especially organisms, hold an ontologically privileged place as at least more unified and so deserving of being called "substances" than, e.g., heaps.[88] And she argues that identifying natural kinds of objects, the natural kinds that are the exemplar substances, is independently motivated by non-mereological considerations.[89] The hylomorphic composites that are instances of natural kinds are also exemplar instances of the *unity* Koslicki will take as the criteria relevant to substancehood; this concept of what it is for a thing to be "unified" will be explored in the next chapter. Nevertheless, these exemplar wholes, hylomorphic compound objects that are members of natural kinds (e.g., organisms), all have parts that are themselves compounds of form and matter. Further, it is explicitly allowed that these parts may also be instances of natural kinds.[90] Thus, even if Koslicki is reticent to identify some hylomorphic compounds as substances *simpliciter*, her exemplar substance-like hylomorphic compounds admit of having proper parts that are themselves also relevantly substance-like compounds. That is to say, Koslicki accepts the possibility of substances compose other substances, given appropriate qualifications, because her mereological, structural version of hylomorphism construes "matter" so as to require the possibility of substance-parthood.

Even in light of these qualifications, Koslicki continues to hold that substances can have other substances as parts. A significant motivation for this position is that she believes Aristotle's view that forms constitute objects with something more than qualified unity presents a serious problem for understanding changes among material objects and their parts. She presents Aristotle's "Homonymy Principle" as this claim: "no object that is *not* already part of a whole that is unified under a single form can survive *becoming* part of such a whole; and no object that *is* already part of such a whole can survive *ceasing* to be part of it."[91] This is because "any such transformation would essentially involve a change in *kind membership*."[92] Aristotle holds that a hand, for example, separated from a body is no longer a "hand" except in name alone. The hand is only a "potential part" while part of the organism (not an "actual" proper part) so that the hand becomes a different thing when separated from the whole. Koslicki rejects such a view of the kind of unity characteristic of substances, arguing that a requirement that these genuine whole substances can have only "potential parts" is unnecessarily strong.

Notice, however, that there is more room for nuance than Koslicki admits. For something to be a "potential part" (in the sense required by the stronger

Aristotelian view) merely implies that such a material part that is *not itself a substance*. One could imagine an Aristotelian holding that substances can have proper *integral* parts of various kinds, such as spatial parts—a right or left half—or functional parts—hands and hearts. Thus, a human hand can be a proper part of a human being, and has its own structural components that are derivative from those of the whole substance of which it is a part, and yet we can count the hand among the proper parts of the human without counting the hand as a substance in its own right. This is to say a substance can have "materially composite" integral parts, even if these parts might be metaphysically potential in some other sense; e.g., that these parts are potentially, not actually, substances.

In light of this qualification, Koslicki's view then requires that, when some part ceases to compose a whole or becomes a proper part of another whole, this thing in question undergoes no change in kind. This the stronger Aristotelian approach will not admit. Koslicki's argument for the possibility of substance-parts is then, like that of Fine, that we do not need to say anything stronger about what it is to be a substance than that to be a substance is to be a thing belonging to some natural kind. Koslicki and Fine, despite their differences on the ontological robustness of structured objects, concur in holding that all structures need to do is to make something unified according to some measure. On this way of thinking about substances and their structures, there is no good reason why one object cannot be unified in many different respects—that is, no reason why one substance cannot have other substances (and their structures) as proper parts.

William Jaworski

In keeping with Koslicki's extra-mereological motivation for a moderate or restricted view of material composition, Jaworski holds that "determining which parts and wholes exist is not a matter of stipulation but of discovery, and our concepts can succeed to greater or lesser degrees in corresponding to what parts and wholes there are."[93] In fact, structured individuals are emergent, in the sense that there can be certain empirical conditions to bring about a new individual with irreducibly unique powers where no such powers or individual having these powers previously existed.[94] Jaworski individuates what counts as individuals by appeal to their emergent properties. He gives some criteria to pick out these emergent properties: they are first-order properties, not epiphenomenal but having a distinct causal or explanatory role, and possessed by an individual because of its structure.[95] As with Koslicki, nevertheless, the details of how to pick out the substances are less central to my concerns than *how* structures are supposed to account for them.

On Jaworski's hylomorphic account, structure is an irreducible ontological principle that accounts at least in part for what things essentially are and for their powers, thereby explaining the synchronic and diachronic unity of things.[96] To be a material object, a substance, is to be a structured whole. Jaworski is explicit in using his hylomorphic account of material objects to answer the SCQ: "composition occurs when and only when an individual configures materials: there is a *y* such that the *x*s compose *y* if and only if *y* is an individual that configures the *x*s."[97] He distinguishes "individual-making" structures from "activity-making" structures, where the former structures constitute individuals and the latter activities. Individual-making structures are those structures that explain the synchronic and diachronic identity of individuals as well as why they possess powers that are distinct from that of their parts.[98] In fact, structures "confer whatever powers they do necessarily. It is metaphysically impossible for my structure not to confer on me the power to grow lungs, skin, and bones."[99]

Jaworski goes beyond both Fine and Koslicki, however, in proposing a unique hylomorphic account of structured individuals where structures are causal powers. Specifically, structures are "powers... to configure (or organize, order, or arrange) materials."[100] Jaworski is more globally committed to a substance-attribute ontology, where substances and properties are the "fundamental" entities that exist. While Jaworski admits that there are, for example, "events" or "states of affairs," these "are not fundamental entities since they depend on entities of the other sorts; they consist of individuals having properties or standing in relations."[101] Given the earlier characterization of composition as occurring "if and only if *y* is an individual that configures the *x*s," Jaworski is careful to say that the structure is only a power *of* its substance. It is the substance, then, which configures its own parts by means of the special structural power that it possesses.

> hylomorphic forms on this account are not things such as individuals. Accordingly, forms are not agents. Strictly speaking it is incorrect to say that my form is responsible for unifying the diverse materials that compose me. It would be more correct to say that I myself am responsible for unifying those materials, and that I accomplish that unification on account of my ongoing forming activity.[102]

The way that Jaworski conceives of structures is then as a species of particularized property-power, directed toward characteristic manifestations—

namely, those activities that constitute some parts as a material object.[103] While that activity (and the power to engage in it) is not identical to the substance, the structure is neither an individual, an agent, nor a proper part of the substance—the structure of a substance is instead a special kind of *trope*. Jaworski uses the term "trope" to characterize the way properties exist, given that he holds each property exists as a particular rather than a universal—"each [property] is a *way* an individual can be."[104] Given that Jaworski accepts what he calls a "sparse" theory of properties, which is to say that only those properties exist which play distinct causal roles. Tropes are therefore causal enablers, confer powers, ground similarities and dissimilarities between individuals, and ground the objective features of objects.[105]

Unlike other tropes, however, it is essential to a given substance that it be engaging in that activity following upon its structure, precisely because something exists as a substance only when its parts are being so engaged in the activity of an individual-making structural power.[106] Some work is necessary to see the way in which there could be *one* power that constitutes a material whole as an individual even though that individual might be engaging a whole series of different essential activities. A human being, for example, configures material parts not only in one way but several; e.g., digestion, growth, respiration. In light of the fact that most composite objects are going to have more than one such activity that is essential to them, Jaworski's view that what unifies them is a single power will be more plausible if all of these activities can be manifestations of one structural power.

Jaworski appeals to the "powerful quality" view of properties held by John Heil and C.B. Martin, who held that all properties are both qualitative and causally powerful (although Jaworski modifies their terminology by referring to "properties" rather than "qualities").[107] There is some debate on how to construe the Heil/Martin view, but this is unnecessary for our discussion—Jaworski straightforwardly endorses an identity theory of properties and powers. For Jaworski, all properties are *identical* with causal powers. A consequence of this identity thesis of properties and powers is that the "causal basis" of a power is identical with that power. Jaworski endorses a definition of "causal basis" where "the causal basis of a power P is a property (or complex of properties) that under the right antecedent conditions is sufficient to cause the manifestation of P."[108] In contrast with Heil/Martin's view that powers generally come in sets of "manifestation partners," which act together to produce some manifestation of the power, Jaworski's property-power is conceived of as "a single power with different manifestations that vary as a function of external circumstances."[109]

On Jaworski's identity theory of property-powers, to talk of a (i.e., one) property conferring many different powers is "to speak implicitly of the variety of ways that one property can manifest itself in conjunction with different disposition partners."[110] These claims are supposed to give the desired result that one power can account for all the essential activities or properties of an individual, because (for example) my structure can confer on me the powers to engage in respiration and other essential activities, and nevertheless constitute *one* power that, in turn, constitute me as *one* individual.

Given that structures are powers for causing material parts to engage in activities, there is again no obvious reason that substances cannot compose other substances as proper parts. In addition to holding that there is no good reason to deny substance-parts, Jaworski also attempts to make a positive argument that one and the same thing can be *numerically identical* across all of these changes of composition. He rejects the "Thomist" view of parts, which holds that whatever comes to compose a new object ceases to exist (in its own right) and acquires a new dependence on the whole of which it is a part. He illustrates such a view with the following: "If I inhale an oxygen atom, that atom does not survive being incorporated into me. It is instead replaced by something else—something that perhaps has many of the same characteristics as the original atom, but that is nevertheless numerically different from it."[111] Yet, contrary to this Thomist position, we see no such replacements happening when substances come to acquire new parts, e.g., the oxygen atom does not appear to be replaced by a "token" oxygen look-alike. And, if the causal powers of these numerically different things (the oxygen atom and the "token" part of me that looks like an oxygen atom) are identical, then the Thomist posits a difference without a difference.[112]

Further, Jaworski claims that, if a substance has no parts that are numerically identical with those of the former substance that comes to compose it, we seem to deny something required for change: an existing substratum that remains numerically identical in a process of (substantial) change.[113] Take the case of the generation of an H_2O molecule, and assume that H_2O and the atoms that compose it are individually substances. The hydrogen and oxygen atoms that preexist the molecule cease to exist when they come to compose H_2O. Instead, a new thing—a molecule—comes into existence. And all the properties and parts of the individual hydrogen and oxygen atoms also cease to exist when that new H_2O molecule is generated. While the new H_2O is not generated *ex nihilo*, because it is generated from the atoms that compose it, nothing of those atoms seems to persist over the change (none of their parts, properties, etc.). Thus, the Thomist apparently has to deny substrata in substantial changes or posit some other notion of a substrate that is *sui generis*, namely, what Thomists call "prime matter." Yet Jaworski thinks a notion of prime matter is seriously obscure and unnecessary. By contrast, his theory needs no commitment to prime matter and therefore (he argues) should be preferred to the Thomist theory.[114]

Liberated from the Thomist view, Jaworski can hold that some properties of individuals are due to their structures, and some properties "due to their materials alone, independent of the ways they are structured."[115] These other properties will be due to a separate structure that constitutes those materials as individual substances in their own right. Because structure is a property, an electron that comes to serve as my matter will come to acquire a new property insofar as it is part of me and so configured by my structure, but the electron will retain all of its independently specifiable properties *qua* electron.[116] There are similarly two kinds of parts: parts that can exist independently of the wholes they compose (i.e., because those parts are substances) and others that cannot.[117] Changes in parts then can occur in which one and the same thing, like the oxygen atom in the earlier case, remain *numerically the same* whether they compose something else as a proper part or not.

In fact, Jaworski holds that it is ordinarily the case that there can be two individual-making structures in the same individual, where one structure S "unifies the fundamental physical materials in such a way that they compose x at t," and yet also another structure "S*, which unifies a different quantity of physical materials in such a way that they compose a part of x at t."[118] As Jaworski accepts that one individual can have another structured individual as one of its proper parts, and individuals (constituted by individual-making structures) are supposed to be nothing other than traditional, property-bearing substances, it immediately follows that one substance can have another as a part.[119] Jaworski therefore holds that an individual-making structure is a kind of property/power that explains the unity of a material object, but that this does not exclude an individual or substance having other individuals or substances as parts.

At this point, I have laid out three kinds of structural hylomorphism that are "on offer" in contemporary metaphysics. Even though the views are generally agreed that we can explain the composition of material objects by appeal to structure, each holds a different account of what it is to be structured and what structures *do* to account for the unity of material objects. I can summarize the positions on offer:

> Some set of *x*s compose a *y* (where a *y* is a material object or substance or individual) if and only if those *x*s:
> 1. satisfy a kind of intensional relation (Fine),
> 2. or come to include the right kind of formal proper part (Koslicki),
> 3. or come to be modified by a special kind of property (Jaworski).

These variations of hylomorphism are important for my objections and for the overarching argument that there is an interesting connection between hylomorphism and restricted composition. As was illustrated, each of these three accounts of hylomorphism holds that it is possible for substances to compose other substances as proper parts. As I will argue in the next chapter, however, such a possibility undermines the coherence of these contemporary hylomorphic solutions to the problems of material composition. Even if there is something appealing about hylomorphism, there are then good reasons not to accept the versions of hylomorphism that I have outlined here. Yet reflecting closely on why these versions of hylomorphism are not satisfactory solutions to the problems of material composition will reveal an interesting result: if we reject the possibility that substances can compose others as proper parts, hylomorphism will, in fact, follow from certain plausible general assumptions about how we should offer a "restricted" response to van Inwagen's SCQ.

2

Structural Deterioration

We have seen that Kit Fine, Kathrin Koslicki, and William Jaworski accept that structures account for the fact that parts compose wholes, so that the genuine material objects exist when their material parts are informed by some structure. In this chapter, I will propose that there are problems for these structural versions of hylomorphism, stemming from accepting the possibility that one substance can compose another as a proper part, which is to say, the possibility that substances can have "substance-parts." After clarifying the thesis that it is possible for one substance to compose another as a proper part, I will attempt to give a general characterization of the problems that result from its acceptance. All of the assumptions made by structural hylomorphists about the conditions under which composition occurs are in deep tension with the possibility of substance-parts. And I will show that these problems do not affect merely hylomorphic theories of composition, but follow from the general conditions of specifying appropriately a theory of composition that answers problems of material composition in a restricted way.

The possibility that substances can have substance-parts results in incoherence on all those theories of material composition which hold that it is true both that there are material objects with parts and that any two material things do not necessarily compose a whole. These two conditions are supposed to describe a certain class of theories of material composition that fall between the logical extremes of the Nihilist view that composition never occurs and the Universalist view that any two or more (nonoverlapping) things necessarily form a material object (i.e., that composition is unrestricted).[1] Thus, these theories assume it is true that there are material objects with parts, but that it is false that any two or more things necessarily compose a whole. Consequently, on the set of theories of material composition in which I am interested, the xs compose a y only under some restricted set of circumstances or conditions. For simplicity's sake, I will refer to these theories of material composition as "restricted" theories.

Assuming that there are some restrictions on composition, and that there are objects with parts, there is some limited class of the things that satisfy those conditions under which composition occurs. This class of things is obviously the class of material objects with parts. I will at times refer to the objects that satisfy the restricted set of conditions, on a given theory of what those conditions are, as the "genuine material objects" proposed by that theory. This is to distinguish those objects satisfying the restricted conditions of composition, proposed by a given account of composition that holds that composition is restricted, from the objects that would exist according to a theory of composition that would hold that anything could be a part of anything.

While I will return to this notion of a "genuine material object," in this chapter I will stipulate that any genuine material object, which results from the occurrence of composition (on some theory of composition where composition is restricted), is also a "substance": that is, a substance is a y such that the xs compose y.[2] The merit of this simplification is that my stipulative definition makes substancehood directly dependent on the conditions of composition posited by a theory of material composition, where substances are precisely whatever what counts as an instance of a composite material whole on that theory. On an account of composition like that of Peter van Inwagen, only living organisms will count as substances because these are the only instances of things with parts. By contrast, if someone held that having a set of things in close spatial proximity was a condition under which some things composed a whole, then a box of matches could count as a substance. Or perhaps the parts need to undergo a more significant change in order to compose a substance, as we will see in Aquinas, where substances are strictly those things that belong to natural kinds.

As we saw in the first chapter, Fine, Koslicki, and Jaworski all aim at offering accounts of material composition on which composition occurs only when some given set of things are *structured*. Structure is thus supposed to account for the existence of these objects in this way: the restricted conditions under which the xs compose a y are if and only if the xs are structured.[3] For this reason, the stipulative definition of substance matches the way that these three authors hold that substances (or their equivalent) are nothing more than the material objects that result from the cases under which composition occurs.[4] Thus, conversely, there is no material object that has parts and is lacking in structure.

The point of this stipulative characterization is that it helps us understand what is generally the problem with the possibility that a substance composes another as a part, for any theory on which composition is restricted, abstracting from any specific account of "substance." What I will show is that a problem arises even without specifying the way that composition is restricted—as long as composition *is* restricted, then the possibility of multiple substances composing one another as parts will lead to incoherence. I will begin by showing why such problems result generally for restricted theories of composition that admit the possibility of substance-parts. Then, I will examine two of the accounts of composition that were reviewed in the first chapter, Jaworski's and Koslicki's, and show that each theory suffers from different versions of a similar problem. To this end, I will examine how each thinker accounts for the specific way that structure is supposed to be that in virtue of which some parts compose a whole. The particular ways that each author thinks structure restricts composition will lead to specific versions of the problem for each theory. The conclusion will connect these criticisms to the overall goals of the book and situate my arguments against Kit Fine's version of structural hylomorphism.

The Substance-Part Principle in Detail

To begin with, we need to get clear on what is meant in saying that it is possible for one substance can compose another as a proper part or, similarly, for a substance to have other substances as substance-parts. Since I refer to this possibility multiple times, in what follows, call the thesis that there is such a possibility the "Substance-Part Principle," or SPP. We need some clarifications as to what the SSP is and is not. Given my stipulative definition that a substance is whatever material object results from the composition of some parts, the SSP could appear equivalent to the claim that it is possible x and y are both substances at the same time x composes y. (More completely, that there can be an x such that x composes a y as a proper part at some time t, and, at that time t, x and y are substances, and $x \neq y$.)

This way of stating the SSP requires further nuance. Recall that, in my stipulative characterization, to be a substance is to be nothing more than to be a material object composed of parts. We could expand my characterization of SPP as follows: there can be an x such that x composes y as a proper part, at some time t, and, at that time t, it is possible that z composes x as a proper part, and $x \neq y \neq z$. While this characterization of SPP is more accurate, it still remains unsatisfying. If SPP requires only the view that something composing another thing as a proper part can itself have proper parts, everyone (except Nihilists of course!) could accept such a view. My fingers compose my hand, and my hand composes my whole body as a part. As long as my fingers and hand are not substances—but I am—the claim that these things compose each other does not entail SPP. Instead, SPP is controversial in being the claim that two things can count as *both* "genuine material objects" and "substances," *even when* one composes the other as a part. What would be controversial, to continue the example, would be to say that my fingers are substances *in addition to* the body that they compose.

Before clarifying the view further, it is helpful to lay out a different case, as we already saw that SPP is usually motivated in the context of stories about changes of parts. Consider first the simple case of hydrogen and oxygen atoms changing into an H_2O molecule by a reaction that takes place over time. Let us presume that hydrogen and oxygen atoms and H_2O molecules are all individually substances. At time t_1, there are two hydrogen atoms and an oxygen atom in the ambient atmosphere. At time t_2, we initiate a reaction and the oxygen atom bonds with the hydrogen to form an H_2O molecule. At time t_3, there is now a fully formed H_2O molecule, whose proper parts are the atoms bonded together. Presume too that SPP is true—and that it is true in this particular case that the atoms do not cease to be substances when they compose H_2O. SPP then entails that, at time t_1, there were three substances, namely, the two hydrogen atoms and an oxygen atom. Yet, at time t_2, there were four substances: the three atoms and the molecule that they compose. Thus, there is nothing to distinguish each in respect to being an instance of a genuine material object or substance, even though one might result from composition of a different kind. Even though atoms are composed of quarks, whereas molecules are composed of atoms, the atoms and molecules are substances "in the same sense." More importantly, the atoms remained the same substances they were even after they composed the molecule as proper parts. The atoms were "just as much" substances when they existed individually at t_1 and when they composed the H_2O molecule at t_3.

The example helps us see how SPP entails in this example that the atoms are supposed to be "the same substances" or substances "in the same sense" both at t_1 and at t_3. The case presumes not only that the atoms remain substances in general, as if SPP would be true if the atoms had become another substance when they composed the molecule, but instead that the atoms remain the same substances they were at t_1. What this brings out is that, on SPP, it is possible for a substance to be "the same substance" or a substance "in the same sense" *whether or not* they compose anything else as a proper part. This is ultimately the core commitment of SPP.

But what is it to be "the same substance" or a substance "in the same sense"? The stipulative characterization of substances sets us up to assume no particular view about the nature of substances or the conditions under which some parts compose a material object. Instead, substancehood is merely to be an instance of material composition, on some account of restricted composition. Yet I will propose ways to supplement the account of substancehood. There are, as I see it, only two fundamental ways that accounts of material composition could specify how a thing is either "the same substance" or a substance "in the same sense," whether or not that thing composes another as a part. The central difference between these options is the sense in which the parts retain identity throughout the process of composition/decomposition.

The first option is to say that a substance is the same substance when that substance is identical with itself, whether or not it composes another as a proper part. Thus, the relation of being the same substance is merely identity, i.e., $x = x$. As material objects are particular things, rather than, e.g., operators or predicates, we might expand this option as holding that a substance is the same substance if that substance is the same particular thing.[5] Further, since this option needs to be incompatible with the other, this interpretation will hold that it is both necessary and sufficient for a substance to be the same substance that the substance remains the same particular thing when it composes another.[6] Thus, for example, a difference in kind membership will not result in a substance being a different particular thing. Socrates would not cease to be the same particular thing—Socrates—whether or not he was a human or a planet. All that is necessary for something to be the same substance is for that substance to be self-identical. And the natural way to understand this claim is in terms of *numerical* identity.

However, this first option needs to be nuanced. If we read the first option as claiming that composition just is identity, such that for the *xs* to compose a *y* is for those *xs* to be identical with *y*, it is generally acknowledged that this view entails that there are *no* restrictions on composition.[7] That would then be incompatible with the assumption that composition is restricted, the assumption that makes SPP a meaningful and controversial thesis. So, we must construe the first interpretation as the view that a substance is the same substance if it is self-identical, whether or not it composes anything, but not that it is identical with the whole it might compose; i.e., $x = x$ but $x \neq y$, even when *x* composes *y*.

The other way to understand what it is for something to be a substance "in the same sense" goes beyond merely (numerical) identity by invoking class membership in a *kind*. We already saw that, for Koslicki, SPP entails that a substance retains its membership in the particular kind to which it belongs, whether or not that substance composes anything else.[8] Thus, if SPP were false, every time the *xs* came to compose the *y*, those *xs* would have to undergo a change in kind membership.[9] Koslicki draws a distinction between two different ways a thing can belong to a kind. One type of kind membership is such that anything is necessarily a member of that kind in virtue of satisfying certain criteria implicit in the kind itself, rather than in every member of that kind having some common feature. By contrast, another type of kind membership could be such that all members necessarily satisfy some given criteria of membership, and they do so in virtue of having some features common to every member that makes those things members of the kind. Koslicki sees the latter as holding that things are grouped into kind membership on the basis of common features that make something a member of the kind, which constitute those things "essence."[10] Call the aforementioned, then, an "non-essentialist" and "essentialist" approach to kinds, respectively.

Even though Koslicki takes pains to distinguish these, I take it then that we do not need to read too much into the notion of a "kind" to understand how the general way that kind membership works for SPP. For example, Fine's embodiments apparently come in kinds even though they are not *natural* kinds (as, e.g., Koslicki or Jaworski envision), where one kind of embodiment can have other kinds of embodiments as parts. Here, my stipulative characterization of substance makes it that we can consider fulfilling a set of restrictions on composition as producing a distinct sub-class of "genuine material objects" or substances on that theory, whatever those restrictions are. For example, if bringing some set of things into close spatial proximity could produce a composite object, then matchboxes (composed of the box and matches as parts) could be in the kind "spatial-proximity-substances," whereas, if being caught up in a life were another condition under which parts composed a whole, then there would be a distinct kind of substance "living things." One could then apply SPP and hold that it would be possible for something to be a living thing substance, composed of bundles of spatial-proximity substances (e.g., bundles of particles) as proper parts.

Applying these options, we get two different interpretations of SPP. Recall my way of stating as SPP as the view: there can be an x such that x composes y as a proper part, at some time t, and, at that time t, it is possible that z composes x as a proper part, and $x \neq y \neq z$. The first interpretation of SPP is that what it means for the same conditions under which composition occurs to be satisfied, at the same time, by both x when it composes y and z when it composes x, is for all of the *xs* and the *ys* and the *zs* to be numerically the same particular material objects whether they compose any other things as proper parts or not. In our example, the atoms that compose the H_2O molecule would be the same particular atoms whether or not they compose that molecule.

The second interpretation is that all of the *xs* and the *ys* and the *zs* satisfy the criteria for membership in their respective kinds of material objects whether they compose any other things as proper parts or not. In the context of the example, the atoms that compose the H_2O molecule would be such that they necessarily satisfy criteria of membership in the kind "atom," and, at the same time they those atoms compose the molecule, the molecule is such that it necessarily satisfies criteria for membership in the kind "molecule." We can point out that the "essentialist" reading of natural kinds would go further and say that the molecules and atoms cannot continue to exist as the same thing without changing kind membership, but the critical point of agreement is that it would be possible for something to remain a member of its kind *even while composing something else as a proper part*.

The ways in which Fine, Koslicki, and Jaworski endorse versions of SPP broadly correspond to the second of these interpretations of the SSP.[11] Koslicki is the clearest in holding that substances can compose other substances without a change in kind membership, so appealing to membership in a kind as that which accounts for the way in which something can be "the same substance" whether or not it composes anything else as a proper part. Fine seems to pursue a variant of this same approach, where these principles are understood to be something like a relation or function that can be multiply instantiated by different embodiments, each relation having distinct essences. A thing can, for example, be characterized by a principle of embodiment that is timeless or rigid, and then become a part of another variable embodiment, belonging to two "kinds" at once. Jaworski, too, will endorse the appeal to kinds, holding that one object can be characterized in different respects by two distinct powers, respectively constituting that same thing as a member of two distinct kinds. Consequently, all three of the thinkers surveyed here appeal, in different ways, to something like a *kind* to explain how it is possible for a substance to compose another as a proper part.

A Grounding Problem for SPP

To set up the argument that SPP makes hylomorphic accounts of composition incoherent, we need to consider the role that structure is supposed to play in accounting for or explaining the composition of material objects. A hylomorphic account of composition holds, broadly, that the *xs* compose *y* if and only if those *xs* are structured in such a way as to compose *y*. Structures are thus supposed to be that "in virtue of which" or "explain" or "account for" the composition of parts in genuine material wholes. I will try to cash out, in my particular criticisms of Fine, Jaworski, and Koslicki, the specific sense they intend to give to the way in which structures account for material wholes. But it is nevertheless helpful to have some general term to illustrate the general problem for *any* account that embraces both SPP and a restricted view of material composition.

The contemporary *lingua franca* in metaphysics is to interpret such locutions as referring to "grounding" relations, where one would say that structures "ground" the composition of material composites. I too will say that structures ground, or are that in virtue of which, the xs compose y, and pose the problem for SPP as a grounding problem for structural hylomorphism—and, indeed, for any account of restricted composition. But, in spite of making use of the term "grounding" (around which a serious literature has developed), I do not take myself to commit myself to anything more than a heuristic term for classifying and grouping together the various ways that structures are supposed to function in each account of material composition.[12]

To say there is a "grounding problem" for these hylomorphic accounts that embrace SPP is to say, ultimately, nothing more than that there is a problem with the way that structures are supposed to explain material composition. Specifically, when we hold it possible for there to be substance-parts, the way that structures are supposed to explain occurrences of material composition (i.e., answer the Special Composition Question) conflicts, I argue, with the overall motivations we have to restrict composition in the first place. I will begin by showing, first, why a grounding problem occurs for all restricted theories of composition that embrace the possibility that a substance can have another as a proper part. Then, second, I will show that the two hylomorphic accounts of material composition addressed below, that of Jaworski and Koslicki, both involve incoherence that arises from accepting SPP, such that the account is viciously circular.

Accounts of restricted composition are motivated by an intuition that there is a significant or meaningful difference between cases where some parts compose a material object and the cases where they do not. We saw Koslicki and Jaworski explicitly invoke this intuition to differentiate their views from Kit Fine, arguing that we have extra-mereological reasons to believe there are certain objectively "unified" wholes. Peter van Inwagen's own approach in posing the Special Composition Question was motivated similarly, as it seemed implausible or otherwise false to him that there were no material composite objects or that any two arbitrary things would necessarily compose an object. In particular, restricted accounts of composition stand opposed to the latter view—viz., Universalism—on which there might exist many objects that are merely arbitrary sums of other things (e.g., a trout-turkey). We might say restricted theories are predicated on a distinction between a class of "pseudo-objects" such as trout-turkeys and that class of whatever the theory posits as instances resulting from the true composition restrictions. (The latter are what I have been calling "substances" or genuine material objects, relative to a given theory of material composition.)

Accounts of restricted composition thus aim that their restrictions on composition meaningfully distinguish pseudo-objects from substances, as the account is motivated by thinking that there *is* a difference between them. We might then say that such accounts posit restrictions—some conditions under which the xs compose ys—that identify, in a broad sense, *that in virtue of which* some things compose a whole. These restrictions account, at the same time, for the way in which any material object is a member of the "genuine material objects" that exist on that theory. For example, Peter van Inwagen appeals to "life" as a principle according to which some parts compose a whole, and this explains why living organisms are the genuine material objects (and nothing else except simples) on his theory. Thus, on van Inwagen's account of composition, trout-turkeys are pseudo-objects, not substances, but cats such as Tibbles (whose material parts compose a whole in virtue of being caught up in the life of Tibbles) are substances or genuine instances of material objects.

This fact about whether some material parts compose a whole is critically a *contingent* matter for views of restricted composition, because the view on which any two or more material things compose a composite necessarily is just Universalism (entailing the existence of trout-turkeys). Nevertheless, the advocate of a restricted account of composition also needs to give some sense in which those material things, the parts, compose the wholes that they do in a distinct sense that, necessarily, if the conditions that the theory specifies as those under which xs compose y are satisfied, then the xs compose y. If the parts composing wholes did so in a way that, even when the conditions that the theory specifies under which the xs compose y were fulfilled, it could be false that the xs compose y, then it would clearly be impossible to characterize the restrictions under which composition occurs in any meaningful way. What one has to do is distinguish that (1) for a thing merely to be "material" does not necessarily entail that it composes anything (because that would be Universalism), and (2) that material things necessarily do not compose anything (that would be Nihilism), but nevertheless have it be such that (3) the theory of composition will impose meaningful restrictions encompassing the "material things" in some broader sense.

This sets up a problem for those who hold that there is a possibility of substances composing others as proper parts. As Thomas Aquinas will exemplify in the next chapter, other kinds of hylomorphists that reject SPP have no problem with holding that there are multiple kinds of composition in one substance. For example, I can have hands as parts, and my hands can have fingers as parts, and so on. Even if these parts can belong to kinds of parts, all the view requires is that those kinds cannot be kinds of *substances*. There is then a difference between whatever makes something a member of the kind *substance* and the other kinds of parts that a substance could have. On the views that reject the possibility of substance-parts, the material parthood relation is transitive, because all instances of something being a part composing a whole involve the same relation of material parthood, the same sense of "whole" (and it is analytical that one cannot be both a part and whole). Aquinas holds that any composite material object and its parts can therefore only be characterized by exactly *one* form that constitutes it as a genuine material object or substance, even if we can distinguish other kinds of forms or structure within that substance, for just this reason. By contrast, SPP needs to hold that the parts of one substance or genuinely unified material object can be, in turn, substances or genuinely unified material objects *in just the same sense* as the whole composed of them. This is to say that some wholes can also be parts of other things without ceasing to be wholes, and this entails that there are multiple species of a material parthood relation, with no transitivity between parts of one kind of whole and those of another.

The problem with the first interpretation of the SPP, on which being "the same substance" is to be "numerically self-identical," is that it cannot be made coherent once we recognize this implication. This account seems to make being a "whole" correlate with being numerically identical with itself (recall, too, that we rejected the view that "composition is identity"). On this view, being a part is not exclusive with being a whole, as something could be *numerically identical* with a whole at the same time it is numerically identical with a part. But, without appeal to any other explanation or indexing of what it is to be a "whole" apart from identity, the account's use of the term "whole" now just seems to border on incoherence. If the account is presupposing some stipulative sense of "whole," it would not make much sense to stipulate the meaning of "whole" in this way, because the term "whole" already has content that goes against the way it is being used by the theory.[13] It is for this reason, to evade the obviousness of this kind of incoherence that the second interpretation of SPP appeals to distinct kinds of "whole."

Endorsing SPP requires that what it is for a *y* to be a "whole" can possibly be unrelated to whether that *y* composes anything else. The sensible advocate of the position holds that, within the given kind of whole, there is a parthood relation that resembles other kinds of parthood in being transitive, reflexive, etc. This is not enough, by itself, to mean that each of these relations counts as "material" parthood (many other relations can be transitive, reflexive, etc.). What one has to do is make "material thing" a kind to which all of the other more specific kinds belong, making "material thing" like a genus, where the other senses of "whole" are all its species. Consequently, in virtue of belonging to one of the lower-level kinds, one is thereby a material object. Yet facts about composition need to be contingent, rather than necessary, as an account of restricted composition is premised on the assumption that two or more material things do not necessarily compose anything. This requires that being a "material thing" does not necessarily entail being a "y such that the xs compose it." These requirements, however, set up a dilemma. SPP is only plausible in light of a subtle equivocation on the sense in which the material parts *necessarily* compose the whole they do.

A structure is a particular, not a universal, and the fact that something has a structure is supposed to account for why an object's material parts compose a whole of some kind. In addition, hylomorphists need to have a structure be of a separate ontological kind from the parts, such that a structure is not a material object or a material thing at all. If a structure were an additional material part of an object, then one would plainly be involved in an infinite regress in explaining material composition by appeal to the presence of such a part. One would explain why the xs compose y in terms of the fact that a further material part, z, composes x and y. Naturally, one can ask what it is in virtue of which z composes those other things, and the infinite regress ensues. It is the fact that z is of the same sort of thing that it only contingently composes x and y that the infinite regress ensues, because we have assumed (as holders of a theory of restricted composition) that the xs do not necessarily compose y. The plain fact, consequently, is that for the appeal to structures to be meaningful as an explanation for the occurrence of any material composition whatsoever, structures need to be such that they essentially are not "material things."

The fact that structures are not essentially material objects does not, of course, entail whether "structured thing," that class of things which have a structure, is or is not identical/co-extensive with the genus "material thing." If these were not co-extensive, then the presence of a structure in a thing would not by itself explain why that thing is a material object because it would not be essential to "having a structure" that one is a "material thing." We would need to appeal to a further thing, that in virtue of which some structures were essentially those of material things and others were not. The sensible defenders of this position will appeal to the *essences* of each particular structure to do this; i.e., structures come in two different kinds, some are essentially the structures of material wholes and other structures essentially of other kinds of wholes. Kinds of structures are a disjoint class from kinds of material whole, because only those structures that essentially constitute things as a material whole are essential to the members of the kinds of "material thing." But this seems to entail that it is *not necessary* that everything having a structure *and* belonging to the kind "material thing" would be a "*y* such that the *x*s compose it," unless these two kinds were co-extensive.

On one fork, if it is the case that possessing a particular structure does not *necessarily* constitute a set of material things as a whole, this would set up an infinite regress, for the same reason that appealing to another material part is unexplanatory. We would not have said what it is in virtue of which some *x*s compose *y*; neither having a structure nor belonging to a kind of material thing makes it necessary that one is a composite whole such that the *x*s compose it. Even though the fact that an object is characterized by a structural particular is supposed to be a contingent fact, the appeal to the essence of structures disguises the next step in the regress. If it were the case that it is not essential to *this* particular set of material things that they are characterized by *that* particular structure (even though things of this kind are necessarily structured), the essence of a particular structure only answers to the fact that this kind of structure essentially constitutes material wholes *in general*. But material composition questions concern whether some *particular material things* compose a whole. So, we would need some other thing to explain why *this* structure is such that, when it characterizes *these* material things, those things compose a whole (since neither the structure nor the things nor both together necessarily compose anything). The account is consequently involved in an infinite regress, which an appeal to structures, or any other similar particular that is not essentially such that it constitutes a material whole (a *y* such that the *x*s compose it), does not resolve.

On the other fork, if "material thing" were to have as its members entirely and only those objects that are wholes, *y*s such that the *x*s compose them, the result is going to be unhelpful for maintaining a restricted account of composition. Intuitively, the position is too strong; a mereologically simple object by definition cannot be a "*y* such that the *x*s compose it," and no member of the class "material thing" is mereologically simple, and so the position would entail that it is *necessarily* the case that there are no mereologically simple material things. More seriously, on the assumption that anything that is a "material thing" is a "whole," i.e., everything that is a "material thing" is such that it is a "*y* such that the *x*s compose it," then it is necessarily the case that anything which is a material thing is composite. This would seem to imply that if anything is a material thing, then it *necessarily* composes a whole—which would be to say that the *x*s will necessarily compose *y*, contradicting the assumption that composition is restricted.

In order to maintain the assumption that composition among any two or more particular material things is not necessary, we could appeal to the fact that whether some particular thing(s) are characterized by a particular structure will be a contingent matter. This would trade on the fact that not all structures are of the material-thing-constituting sort. But it is not contingent that a particular material thing is constituted by a structure, since to be a "material thing" is identical or at least co-extensive with the class of composite wholes, "*y*s such that the *x*s compose," *and* all such "*y*s such that the *x*s compose" are structured things. Nor is it a contingent matter whether a structure constitutes a material whole of a specific kind, because it needs to be essential to a *particular* structure that it constitute something of just the kind it does.

So, the fact that a material thing is contingently characterized by a structure can only be in virtue of the fact that it is not essential to a particular structure to constitute a *particular* material thing. But then we get another problem as to what makes it the case that the structure does constitute a particular material thing, since it is not essential to the structure that it constitute the particular material thing, *nor is it essential to the material thing that any particular structure compose it*. And, clearly, this would generate an infinite regress, of such a sort that the only way to stop it is to provide a further factor, which is essentially such that, in virtue of characterizing the structure and material thing, they form one "particular thing." But here there is a contradiction: in order to answer the problem of material composition in the way that someone like a hylomorphist wants, whatever factor does this would seem to have to be *particular*, as it is the particular *x*s and their particular structure that form a "particular."[14] So, this fork ends more dismally than the first, in a dead end of incoherence.

One might think that the way to avoid these dismal alternatives is to deny the assumption, which makes it the case that to be a "material thing" is necessarily to be a "structured thing." This is precisely what van Inwagen does: if one admits that there are mereologically simple material things (e.g., fundamental particles), these are material things that have no material parts, by definition. Then it is not true, on his account, that any material thing is a *y* such that the *x*s compose it—because it could be a simple. Further, even though van Inwagen admits that living organisms can be composed of other living parts (e.g., Tibbles is composed of cells), he rejects that this is the case of one whole organism composing another. What does the structuring—on van Inwagen's account, "lives"—are "jealous": Tibbles only has one life and her cells are not living things *in addition to* Tibbles.¹⁵ Thus, there is at most *one* life per material composite, and van Inwagen denies the possibility of substances (in the stipulative sense of "material composite" that I outlined at the beginning of this chapter) composing another substance as a proper part. Hence, accounts like that of van Inwagen do not run into any of the incoherence that I sketched above.

The whole reason all of the complications are introduced by the sensible defender of SPP—a hierarchical relation among kinds and so forth—is to avoid the apparent absurdity in claiming that *one* material object is numerically identical with the *many* material objects that are (presumably) spatially co-located with it and which are its proper substance-parts. That is, there is something undesirable with saying that one material composite can be at the same time numerically identical with many material objects. Introducing kinds avoids direct contradiction or incoherence but moves that incoherence into the relation between kinds and the restrictions on composition, which move only appears plausible because of a subtle modal equivocation. The grounding problem shows us that accounts of composition with embrace the possibility of substance-parts either contradict the assumption that there is a *restricted* answer as to what it is in virtue of which some parts compose a material whole, or they are involved in some incoherence or unresolved infinite regress. Varieties of this general problem affect both William Jaworski's and Kathrin Koslicki's species of hylomorphism, as I will now argue.

Structures as Property-Powers

William Jaworski gives a central role to structure in answering questions about substances, but only one of the two kinds of structures of his account are supposed to answer the question of why some set of parts compose a genuine material object or substance. For this reason, I will only concern myself here with the "individual-making structures" that account for substances. Jaworski uses such structures to construct a restricted theory of material composition; in which "there is a y such that the xs compose y if and only if y is an individual [i.e., substance] that configures the xs."¹⁶ Jaworski draws a parallel between his account and that of van Inwagen. For van Inwagen, some xs compose a whole y only when "the activity of the xs constitutes a life (or there is only one of the xs)."¹⁷ Thus, on van Inwagen's account, lives are a kind of event, and the activity of the xs constitutes that event.[18] Jaworski's account of composition imitates in important ways the account of van Inwagen. van Inwagen's "life" is an event, an activity in which some parts are "caught up" and in virtue of which they then compose a whole; Jaworski's structure is understood as a power or property that causally configures the parts that compose a whole, causing those parts to be "caught up" in the whole. However, rather than seeing the parts as individually engaged in an activity, Jaworski holds that the whole substance is acting, by means of a structural power, on its own parts in order to configure them into that selfsame substance they constitute.[19]

Structures therefore account "at least in part, for what objects essentially are ... for what things can do, the powers they have ... [and] the unity of composite things."[20] More specifically, structures are *powers* possessed by substances in virtue of which the parts of that substance compose a whole, but also in virtue of which that substance has other kinds of properties and powers.[21] For example, the structures of a living substance involve being able to engage in the activity of living, as well as any other activities associated with that kind of organism. Consequently, for Jaworski, to be a substance is to be a thing having a certain structure or power for configuring the xs. To be more specific, then, Jaworski's account of restricted composition claims the following: there is a y such that the xs compose y if and only if y is a substance that has *a power for configuring the xs*.

It could seem that there is already an obvious confusion in the account. If structures account for the fact that some xs compose a y, then it would seem straightforwardly circular to say that the xs compose a y when there exists a y composed of the xs! Jaworski often expresses his account in what might appear to be a circular fashion. For example, he says "the *configuring activities in which individuals engage* are like lives in van Inwagen's sense ... the [structures] that are like van Inwagen's lives are *structures that make individuals what they are*; they are individual-making structures [emphasis mine]."[22] It is hard to make sense of the idea that an individual engaging in an activity is what makes an individual to exist, because it would seem something has to exist *logically prior* to being able to engage in an activity. The account of composition would be viciously circular if one needed to be y prior to engaging in the activity that make one to be a y.

van Inwagen takes it that a composite organism exists when some xs are engaging in the appropriate activity (a life). But, for van Inwagen, it is the xs that are engaging in the life and that there are metaphysical "simples" or part-less substances that come to compose living organisms. The *parts* are engaging in activities by which they compose an individual. We might want to read Jaworski as merely expressing van Inwagen's position in a less perspicuous way. If some xs compose a y when those xs have a power that constitutes them as a y, then it is only the *parts* of an individual that preexist and come to acquire a power. This, it is in virtue of each part acquiring a power (to engage in the individual-making activities) that each part composes the whole individual. But, while he takes no definite stand on whether the proper parts of a substance are always themselves composites (at a lower level) or metaphysical simples,[23] Jaworski seems to claim in different contexts that the *individual* is causing the parts to engage in a certain activity: "composition happens exactly when there is an individual that configures materials."[24] Unlike van Inwagen, then, Jaworski explicitly accepts that individuals have powers to configure their own parts, such as a power for Tibbles to cause her own cells to compose her as a material whole—it is just such powers, i.e., individual-making structures, that account for the existence of substances.

One way to make sense of these claims would be, perhaps, if substances are reducible to power of some kind: i.e., a substance being nothing more than a special kind of power-property trope. Travis Dumsday illustrates such a position, proposing that a substance is nothing more than "a simple, single-track passive power to receive/ground/bear/possess one or more fundamental intrinsic properties upon receiving an appropriate causal stimulus... Such a power would enable the possession (and hence linkage) of a range of diverse, inherently separable fundamental properties."[25] To be a substance is not, then, to be *bearer* of powers, but a *power*. Yet, as Dumsday notes, this would require that "the category 'power' cross-cuts the more basic ontological categories of 'substance' and 'property' [so that] a substratum can be a power even while also falling under the category of 'substance.'"[26] If Jaworski were to adopt this perspective, it is true that one would no longer defining substances in terms of powers because substances and their (individual-making) powers are identical. To say that an individual "configures its own parts by means of its powers" would be a misleading circumlocution for saying that the individual is nothing over-and-above a power to configure some parts.[27]

Jaworski holds instead that to be a power is to be a power *of* something, characterizing the distinction between a "substance" and a "power" as follows: substances are agents and powers are those capacities that enable agents to act.[28] More simply, powers are those things borne by bearers (substances), whereas substances are what bear powers.[29] Since for Jaworski powers are tropes, the reduction of substances to powers would entail a version of trope bundle theory rather than hylomorphism.[30] Similarly, if "bearing powers" were an activity or manifestation of the individual-making power, an individual already needs to be engaging a power in order to bear powers at all, and an infinite regress ensues. Some metaphysicians have therefore expressed a worry about invoking "downward" causation of wholes over their own parts. John Heil, for example, notes that "there is something distinctly off-putting in the thought of a whole that includes a part causally influencing that part: parts would causally influence themselves."[31]

Jaworski attempts to avoid the bootstrapping worry by appeal to different kinds of causal influence. A whole having causal influence over its parts *in some respect* is supposed to be unproblematic. Consider that I, as a whole individual, engage in lots of activities that, to common sense, appear to configure my parts and maintain my existence over time: breathing, eating, going for a jog, and so forth. In these respects, it is quite true that I am acting upon my parts causally, but in a perfectly innocent sense. Moving my arm up and down is for me, the substance, to act upon that part of me that is my arm. What makes these non-mysterious is that in all of these cases I am only acting upon myself *in some respect*. I move my own arm in virtue of moving other parts that then act upon the moved parts. Raising my arm involves muscles receiving nerve impulses, and then working in concert, contracting to elevate the other material parts in my arm. While one part of my arm can affect another part, or one side of my hand interact with the other, what seems impossible to make sense of is the idea that a part could be affecting itself by means of just that same part, as (e.g.) my hand touching itself. A similar case is, of course, exactly what makes the image of someone trying to pull themselves up by their bootstraps amusing. A whole, just like a part, cannot be affected by its own action in that kind of way.

In order to avoid the straightforward absurdity, Jaworski makes two distinctions. First, he draws a distinction between parts and the substances they compose, appealing to a hierarchical account of composition. A single substance can have various "levels" of proper parts that are substances, and those parts can have parts that are substances, and so on.[32] This is to invoke the SSP. The second distinction corresponds closely to what I suggested is the typical move required by sensible adherence to the possibility that substances compose other substances as parts: he draws a distinction between distinct kinds of causal influence in virtue of the different kinds to which a whole can belong.[33] Given the distinction between kinds of wholes at different levels of the compositional hierarchy, each kind of whole is essentially such that it can exercise and or would be affected by different kinds of causal influence (but not others). The idea is then that parts need not be *wholly* affected by the causal influence that the whole which they compose exerts upon them, even though they compose the whole as parts. This is because a part can itself be a substance in its own right.

A substance-part can be affected by the whole it composes *insofar as it is a part* (but not insofar as it is a substance*)*, whereas its own causal influence is exercised *insofar as it is a substance* (but not insofar as it is a part).

To illustrate, we can assume that electrons are substances, and have their own structures, because electrons are characterized by powers that are not reducible or dependent upon the powers of their component parts (e.g., quarks). Similarly, Tibbles, a cat compose of electrons, is also a substance having her own structure, in virtue of having her own powers as an organism, where her properties/powers as this organism are not reducible to those of the electrons composing her. Tibbles is able to "harness the power of those [electrons] in ways that contribute to [her] own biological ends."[34] She is the cause of the electrons to engaging in certain activities, such as moving through space as she walks around the house, even though the electrons are material parts of her. Further, the electrons are causes in their own respect when they engage in activities that are independent of their parthood in Tibbles—for example, an electron composing Tibbles might be involved in causing some lint to cling to Tibbles' fur, and Tibbles herself was not exercising any causal influence over her electron to cause it to do so.

Jaworski regards as illegitimate the demand for a further account as to what it is in virtue of which Tibbles has a power to configure her parts. When one asks what it is in virtue of which an individual substance is characterized by the power to configure its component parts, this is to ask why it is that a substance of that kind has such a power essentially. We can give the history of how some such structure came to inform some *xs* and compose a *y*, but we cannot give a general account of why there is such a structure as that which constitutes *ys*, where *y* is a natural kind of substance. This would be to give an explanation why it is essential to a power to constitute a certain kind of substance. Structure is, in this context, "primitive."[35] In other words, Jaworski thinks the hylomorphist should hold that there are no answers to what it is in virtue of which a substance bears its (essential) power to configure its parts, aside from pointing out the fact that it is *essential* to that substance that it do.

Jaworski is saying that there is nothing, aside from its essence, that accounts for why a substance bears the structural power that it does. In one respect, this is a well-known response to these kinds of problems. This move is theoretically similar to holding that "bearing powers" is not itself a power, just as in bare substratum theories one might say that the ability to bear properties is not a property, but rather that it is essential to a substratum to do so. In another respect, though, the move is theoretically unsatisfying by reason of the context of Jaworski's wider commitments. Appeal to a claim that something can have a power by reason of its essence does not apparently respond to this problem of how it is that something appears to both bear and be affected by the same power, in the same respect.

What we need to clarify then is *what* an individual-making structural power is supposed to be doing and how that relates to constituting a substance. A structure is that "in virtue of which" some material parts constitute a whole individual, being a power in virtue of which the whole configures its parts to constitute that same individual. Recall that substances are supposed to be power-bearers, as it is in virtue of bearing a power that one can act by means of it. And there is a distinction between *bearing* a structure and being *acted upon* by one. Distinguishing different respects in which things can *act upon* other things does not help in giving a coherent and non-circular characterization of precisely how it can be that a substance can exercise a power without that substance already being able *to bear* that power. But this seems precisely what we might imagine an individual-making structure to do: to constitute some material parts in such a way that those parts constitute a substance, that is, a bearer of powers. The claim that a material whole exercises a power *upon* its parts, configuring them, already requires that the whole *exist* in order to have the power to do that. And it looks like it is precisely its acting upon the parts that constitute the whole as having its very ability to bear the power it has.

What is doing the bearing of this power to configure the materials, if not the material parts so configured? Jaworski agrees with this as, on his view, "all of the powers of structured individuals [are] essentially embodied,"[36] so that the powers that constitute some xs as an instance of a material whole (a y) are essentially such that they must be powers of some xs. This is to say that the powers of a structured individual are borne by its material parts. And the account further holds that a substance having parts of a certain sort is necessary and sufficient for that substance to have certain powers.[37] Yet Jaworski denies that the powers of substances are reducible to those of their component parts. Instead, the power by which the parts compose a whole substance can never be reducible to the powers of the parts.[38] This imposes the condition that structures are not caused by or produced by the parts of the individual produced by the structure—"structures in general are not generated or produced by the things they structure"[39]—even though all structures are necessarily "seated" in some given set of material parts as powers *of* those parts. And Jaworski holds that the structure of the whole is not merely an aggregate of the powers or properties of those parts, as might be the case for a physical arrangement or heap of things.[40] What it is to be a structured substance is to be a thing having irreducible, unique powers not possessed by their parts; "even if *x* is exhaustively decomposable into the *y*s, *x* will still have some properties that the *y*s lack, namely the properties due to its structure."[41]

His illustrative example is the difference between Godehard and what results after we, placing Godehard in a "very strong bag," crush him to bits.[42] Jaworski is appealing intuitively to our extra-mereological reasons to believe there is a difference between Godehard, a genuine material object, and the bits that result, even though the material parts are all the same (as no material escaped from the bag in the process of crushing). We are supposed to recognize, in the example, that Godehard has powers irreducible to his material parts, and which then (Jaworski argues) are attributable to the structure in virtue of which those parts constitute Godehard. Structures are *casual enablers*; they "make a difference" to whether the material parts compose Godehard or not. We should then be motivated to attribute such structures to whatever we have extra-mereological reason to believe is a thing having a power that is irreducible to the powers of its material parts.

But it is difficult to see what it is to be an "irreducible power" when we introduce the levels of causality. Godehard can act upon his parts by virtue of the powers seated uniquely in him. And the material parts that compose Godehard might act upon him in various ways, as when Godehard's foot causes him pain. But now assume that Godehard does not have a subsistent soul, so that he is nothing more than the material parts appropriately structured (this follows from Jaworski's claims about "exhaustive decomposability"). If so, that power borne by Godehard to act upon his parts seems like it should be *borne* by his parts. But that leads to an obvious situation: Godehard bears the power to configure his parts in virtue of his parts bearing that same power, but he does not bear the powers that his parts have to configure *their* materials. Clearly, since Jaworski rejects the "Thomist" view that whenever one thing composes anything else it *ipso facto* ceases to bear its own powers at all—or, similarly, that a part only bears powers derivatively insofar as the whole bears them—the parts are property bearers. So Godehard's material parts apparently bear the property to configure themselves.

In keeping with the prior claim in regard to levels of causality, we could try to expand Jaworski's answer by importing the idea of things only bearing powers *in some respect*. The material parts of Godehard, *qua* being Godehard's parts, bear the power to configure (i.e., act upon) those same things in a distinct respect, namely, *qua* not-Godehard's parts. The serious incoherence that results is that Jaworski would then be unable to straightforwardly claim that the powers unique to Godehard are irreducible to the power of his parts.

What these commitments entail instead is that the powers supposedly essential to Godehard, and irreducible to the power of his parts, *are* powers of his parts, but in a mereologically inflected sense: the powers that are unique to Godehard are powers of Godehard's parts *insofar as those parts compose Godehard*. So now the kinds that are relevant to dissolving the bootstrapping problem are being defined in terms of what things compose what. That is, when we look at the parts to determine what powers are unique to the parts, we would already have to be able to differentiate whether these parts compose a whole or not to distinguish those respects in which the parts can bear powers.

Others have claimed that Jaworski is illegitimately engaging in "bootstrapping." The bootstrapping lies not in his account of causality as such. It instead results from accepting the possibility of substance-parts. Since the class of material kinds is conceived in such a way that anything belonging to the kind is a material whole, a *y* such that the *x*s compose it, and it needs to be necessary or essential to any structural power to constitute a whole of a specific kind, the contingency of composition (i.e., that not every thing necessarily composes every other) needs to be found in the fact that an individual-making power does not constitute *any particular* material thing. But conversely, as it is not essential to the material thing that any structure compose it, that structure is modifying or characterizing that one material thing in two different respects—as part and as whole. And therein lies an infinite regress, because we still have to answer what it is in virtue of which these two respects constitute one material particular. The fact this results in incoherence on Jaworski's account is clear because it involves causal activity; it does not look possible to give a further factor that would essentially unify these two respects in the context of causal powers, because it would involve an explanation how it is that a material object can both bear a power and act on itself by means of the same property. I can't be exercising a causal power to configure my material parts if those same materials need to be configured so that I have the power in the first place![43]

Structures as Proper Parts/Relations

One might have disagreed with the foregoing analysis that the problems for Jaworski's account came not from his admission of the possibility of substances as parts, but rather only in his assumption that a substance *causally acts* on its parts and thereby pulls itself up by its bootstraps into existence. Koslicki does not however presume that structures are that by means of which substances *act* to configure their own parts. Structures, on her account, are supposed to be that in virtue of which some material parts compose a whole material object, and this use of "in virtue of which" is, unlike Jaworski, not to claim a formal part, or the substance which it informs, causally influences itself. The claim Koslicki makes is that *having* such a part, being informed by a structure, is necessary and sufficient for being a material composite.[44] The grounding worry for Koslicki's account of composition therefore involves a subtler form of such "bootstrapping," bringing out more clearly the general problem alleged to follow from admitting substance-parts into an account of restrict composition. What is problematic in the account arises not in the relation between a power and its bearer, but the relation between composition and kind membership, such that Koslicki's account involves vicious circularity.

On Koliscki's hylomorphism, recall that material parts compose a whole in virtue of having another part—a *formal* part, but a proper part in just the same sense as that object's material parts. This raises the specter of an infinite regress. If a formal proper part is a part of a whole, and that same formal part is that in virtue of which anything composes the whole, then the formal proper part is that in virtue of which *itself* composes that whole. Why don't we need to posit another proper part to account for why that structural part composes the whole? Koslicki argues that, because structures belong to a distinct ontological kind of part, namely, *formal* proper parts rather than material proper parts, there is no infinite regress.

To unpack this claim, it is helpful to recall that Koslicki's structures are not powers, but are (as I argued in the first chapter) better thought of as relations. When we say that a formal part "composes" a material object as a proper part, what she seems to mean is that a given relation *holds* between a set of material parts. The fact that such a relation holds between a set of material parts, i.e., that a formal structural part structures them, is "that in virtue of which" those material parts constitute a material whole. But why call this kind of relation a "proper part"? It should be obvious that not just *any* possible relation among a set of objects makes those objects to count as parts of a material whole. An object could be the relata of the relation "being to the left of the Pope," but being the relata of that relation does not obviously constitute that object as a proper material part of anything. Not all kinds of relation plausibly correspond to restrictions on material composition, in the way "being to the left of the Pope" does not correspond to any way that the xs could compose a y.[45] We need to determine the *right* class of relations that, by being formal proper parts of material objects, constitute them as genuine wholes.

A distinction is often drawn between two kinds of relations. An internal relation is one that exists whenever the relata all exist. These are typically understood to be relations that result from some features of the relata. For example, whenever four interior right angles of the same square exist, there will be a relation holding between these angles such that they add up to 360 degrees. Those angles are the relata of that relation, and this relation of adding up to 360 degrees holds merely in virtue of the angles existing. By contrast, "loving" is not such an internal relation, because, e.g., it is not true merely in virtue of Romeo and Juliet existing that they love each other. Relations like "loving" are referred to as external relations. One popular view is that external relations hold between two or more thing in virtue of some feature of one of the relata, where that feature is not itself a relation.[46] Then, when Romeo loves Juliet, the relation "Romeo's loving Juliet" could not exist without those two relata (Romeo and Juliet), nor could it fail to relate those two, but the external relation of "Romeo loving Juliet" holds only in virtue of Romeo (because he loves Juliet).

It is widely held that ungrounded external relations, relations that hold between things in virtue of no features of anything, are problematic.[47] In the context of material objects and their parts, it is easy to see that relations of material composition holding in virtue of *nothing* would not be adequate for a restricted account of material composition (more to come on this point in the final chapter). Relations by which some object is a material part or a whole should be, by contrast, relations that hold in virtue of features of objects themselves. This is to say that structures have to be *internal relations* among some objects if structures are going to account for why some material parts compose a whole. And Koslicki conceives of her structural parts as internal relations in just this way, and therefore conceives of those relations that constitute some parts as a material composite as a proper part of the material whole. This claim that structures are "proper parts" of a material object is supposed to indicate that such a structural relation is grounded by or exists in virtue of the material parts themselves, rather than being merely a mind-dependent way of carving up the universe.

As Koslicki says, a structure that constitutes a genuine material whole is "that explanatory principle within a matter-form compound which accounts for the compound's structure, identity and unity."[48] Formal parts are those parts of objects that account for the identity of a given object at a time, over time, and across possible worlds ("cross-world identity").[49] Further, structures are *really distinct* from what they compose; "facts about the numerical identity of [structures] are distinct from facts about the numerical identity of hylomorphic compounds whose cross-world identity and distinctness are supposed to be explained by appeal to their individual [structures]."[50] Since Koslicki holds a structural relation is a particular that functions like a proper part, not a universal, having a structure is then a feature of the object itself, not (for example) a feature of my ways of counting the material objects.

Koslicki's strategy to avoid an infinite regress can be sensibly interpreted in light of these clarifications about structures as relations. As internal relations (necessarily) hold *among* material objects, such that they are not objects themselves, there is a way to make sense of the claim that structures belong to a distinct ontological kind from the things that they structure. In appealing, then, to structural proper parts as that in virtue of which some material parts compose a whole, one is not appealing to something akin to yet another material part. Rather, one is appealing to something better akin to a property possessed by or a relation holding among those parts. It is much harder to see what the regress worry could be in this case. In fact, as I will argue in the next chapter, classical hylomorphists have thought about forms as parts in a way similar to Koslicki and clearly understood the problems that might arise from failing to distinguish the way that a form is a part (a "metaphysical" part) from the way that a material part (an "integral" part) composes a whole. As we saw with van Inwagen, too, his "lives" that constitute organisms as material objects serve as a similar principle, distinct from the material parts, but nevertheless affecting or being "in" all of those parts. As a life is not an additional material part of an organism, it does not raise the specter of regress.

And this seems inevitable for any account on which composition is restricted, for good reasons. Conceiving structures as internal relations follows from Koslicki's and van Inwagen's overall goals of aiming to give a restricted account of material composition. Such accounts are premised on those extra-mereological motivations we have already discussed, such that Koslicki and others do not see there to be good reasons (apart from already being committed to the mereological principle of unrestricted composition) to believe in the existence of things like trout-turkeys. As long as we have such extra-mereological motivations to believe there are genuine material wholes, one will need to provide some explanatory factor in virtue of which the material parts compose a whole, without making this factor into an extra material part, but while also explaining how such a factor is *mind-independent* in the right way. That is, composition will need to "make a difference" in the world. Traditional claims that a form *inheres* in, *informs*, or is otherwise "in" the substances they constitute mirror Koslicki's claims that structures should be conceived of as parts of substances. There is more that needs to be said here, as well as an important needle that needs to be threaded regarding the way in which composition facts are mind-independent. These concerns I will leave to later chapters to develop.

So far so good. In the aforementioned respects, Koslicki's hylomorphism is—in my estimation—more coherent overall than Jaworski's by avoiding commitments to things resembling downward causation. Koslicki's shared commitment to what I have called the SSP, however, requires her to qualify her claim that having a structure is necessary and sufficient for some parts to constitute a material object. Clearly, if a substance has other substances as parts, each of these subsidiary substances have their own structures, all of which appear to be, in turn, parts of the whole substance—in addition to the structure of that whole! Thus, Tibbles' cells can be wholes in virtue of each having their own structures, as well as being structured (by Tibble's cat soul) as material parts of Tibbles. Yet not all of these structures make Tibbles to be a member of all these kinds at once. Since Koslicki's formal parts are supposed to be just like other material parts in a composite, what we have to do is to deny something relevant to the transitivity of parts. One therefore has to introduce a new condition that a structure has to characterize material parts *in the right way* for the structure to be *sufficient* for those parts to compose a whole.

Koslicki appeals to essences in this context because an appeal to an essence allows us to specify how different hylomorphic compounds can compose one another and retain membership in their distinct kinds.[51] This method of utilizing essence was clear in her response to a dilemma Alan Sidelle had posed with the case of two spatiotemporally coincident objects, Lumpl and Goliath. These are supposed to have different modal properties: Goliath, the statue composed of Lumpl, cannot survive being crushed, but Lumpl, the clay which composes Goliath, can survive crushing. Koslicki holds that the properties of Lumpl and Goliath can be attributed to the distinct structures of each, even when they compose each other.[52] It is a basic or primitive fact for certain things that they are essentially structured in certain ways: "Certain facts about the essences of concrete particular objects are taken as basic and other facts concerning their modal profile (viz., facts about what is necessary but non-essential to these objects) are regarded as, at least in part, derivable from these primitive facts about essences."[53]

As we've already said, because one part can be structured multiple ways, having a structural part is not sufficient for something to compose a material object. Instead, it has to be the case that one and the same thing can have structural parts in different respects. When one material composite has other material composites as parts, the structures of each composite are not inherited by higher-level composites. What blocks the transitivity among the hierarchical levels for Koslicki is the appeal to kinds and their essences. In regard to the case of Goliath and Lumpl:

> we should not infer from the fact that Lumpl's form, f*, is a proper part of Goliath that Lumpl's form, f*, is therefore also Goliath's form or that it must therefore also figure in Goliath's essence. Rather, I take it to be a basic fact about Goliath that f, and not f*, is Goliath's form and that f, and not f*, figures in Goliath's essence; and correspondingly for Lumpl and its relations to f and f*, respectively.[54]

Consequently, one thing could count as a part and a whole according to kind membership at different levels, even as a material object can only have one structure at each level of the hierarchy—these are limitations built into the account of natural kinds Koslicki endorses. For example, it is my kind membership in "human being" that prevents me from being structured into an atom despite having atomic parts that compose my body, each with their own atomic structures that otherwise would compose me.[55]

Sidelle argues that Koslicki's apparent appeal to a brute distinction between these objects, that they have distinct essences, fails to be explanatory in the right way: "to merely point to the brute fact that there are such differences without explaining how these differences arise... [is not so much a solution] as 'a denial that the basic differences between the objects need to be grounded.'"[56] As we saw with Jaworski, Koslicki also holds that the hylomorphist should reject "the very idea that a reductive analysis of a compound's relation to its form can be given or needs to be given."[57] Why different objects have their structures essentially is a fact about their kinds, and so these questions as to why that kind essentially involves that kind of structure "cannot be expected to receive an answer in more basic terms, since non-modal facts about the essences of matter-form compounds are assumed to be explanatorily basic according to the approach at issue."[58]

Unlike Jaworski's problematic claim that a material part is conferring a power on itself by configuring itself, one and the same thing can be characterized by any number of relations without seeming to engage in "downward causation." The same thing belonging to two distinct kinds is not apparently mysterious or counterintuitive. The problems for Koslicki's account lie in showing how it is that her account does not impose circular or trivial requirements on composition. That is, even if structures do not make a causal difference, they still need to make a *real* one, so that structures are that in virtue of which some parts compose a whole in just the extra-mental sense that Koslicki's claims about formal parthood were supposed to safeguard. I will show, however, that the commitment to substance-parts makes this incoherent.

Membership in a natural kind, in virtue of having two distinct essences, is what Koslicki appeals to in order to explain how two things can be parts of each other while simultaneously remaining members of their kind.[59] The account then requires that every member of a natural kind is *essentially* a whole (relative to that kind). The sense in which a member of a given kind is "essentially a whole" needs disambiguation. Clearly, it is a contingent matter whether *these* set of *x*s compose a *y* of the relevant kind, not a necessary one; for example, that the atoms in Homer's donut compose him is not necessary to those atoms, even though they can come to compose his atomic parts after he consumes the donut and metabolizes them. In order to get the particulars to fall under the relevant kind, they need to be structured. If the structure were (let us imagine) existing somewhere in space, apart from the material parts, it would not constitute anything as a material composite. The structure is a particular, alongside the particular material objects. The structure is also then merely contingently composing *these* material parts. Homer's soul does not necessarily compose *those* atoms that come to be part of it after metabolizing the donut.

One sense of the claim that a composite is "necessarily a whole" is then one where a member of the kind is "necessarily a whole," *de dicto*: necessarily, whenever something is a member of the kind, it is a whole. This kind of reading, however, does not entail that something can be a whole whether or not it composes another as a proper part, because it only requires that, *if* something is a member of the kind, then it is a whole. But, on this reading, if something is not a whole, then it is not a member of the kind. The defender of the possibility of substances having other substances as parts therefore needs the stronger *de re* reading: whenever something is the member of the kind, it is necessarily a whole. The *de re* reading would then seem to imply that, if something is the member of the kind, then it is *essentially* a whole.

Since it is kind membership that determines whether something is a whole, structures are merely necessary, but insufficient conditions for whether some parts belong to a kind. In fact, they are theoretically otiose in the account of composition, because the criteria for kind membership Koslicki appeals to involve the *essence* of the members. What it is to be a cat is not merely to have the structure of a cat, but to be the whole composed of all its parts in an appropriately feline manner. Yet then the *essence* is what "unifies" the parts, because it is that in virtue of which all those parts, including the formal part, count as being a member of the kind "cat."[60] The point then of having a formal part is lost.

But, exactly as we saw with the general problem, the account collapses into incoherence insofar as natural kind membership, and the essences appropriate to those kinds, are universal. Tibbles, the actual thing whose parts are structured as a cat, is a particular. If essences are universal, and every cat shares the essence "cat," then it turns out essences are not plausibly "that in virtue of which" the *x*s compose a particular cat. While appeal to essences as that in virtue of which something is a member of a kind tells us *what it is* to be a member of the kind, the essence of 'cat' will not be that in virtue of which some particular material parts compose the particular cat Tibbles. Appealing to a universal alone does not explain why Tibbles, a particular, is characterized by an essence such that accounts for why her parts compose her. If all those parts of the appropriate kind of material object "cat" composed a whole necessarily, in the sense that they compose a whole whenever they exist, the view would likewise entail that all of those things composing any structured whole compose them necessarily. But that is mereological Universalism, not a restricted account of composition.

Further, though, the claim that one and the same material thing can be characterized by distinct kinds requires that one and the same thing be characterized by distinct essences. This entails it is either *not essential to* the *x*s that they are characterized by the essence that they have when, for instance, the *x*s compose Tibbles, or that those *x*s are characterized by different essences *in different respects*. Those respects in which things can have an essence resemble part-whole relations—i.e., having an essence *qua* part or *qua* whole—precisely because what we are aiming to account for is the way in which *one* material object is composed of its essence, structure, and material parts. But then, as we saw with Jaworski's account, you would need a further thing in virtue of which those respects of Tibbles' essence form one thing with their corresponding structure and material parts. Nevertheless, this ends in incoherence, because whatever can unify these things, stopping a potential infinite regress that would ensue, needs itself to be a *particular* of some kind, or characterize the particulars in a particular way, such that it can be contingent that some material things are characterized/composed by all these things (essence, structure, parts) at the same time. For we are not offering a restricted account of composition if it were the case that any two or more objects compose a whole by reason of their essence.

Conclusion: Rejecting SPP

I conclude not only that there are serious grounding problems with the hylomorphic accounts of material composition given by Koslicki and Jaworski, but that this grounding problem is inevitable for any restricted theory of material composition which accepts that substances can have other substances as parts. The possibility of substances having other substances as parts necessarily requires appeal to kinds of material wholes to be sensible. Moreover, accounts of composition on which not any two or more material objects necessarily compose a whole need to give non-trivial circumstances under which some material parts compose a whole, alongside criteria according to which something is a member of a kind.

Given the commitment to substance-parts, all such accounts require that being a material whole is always to be a whole relative to some kind or other. Nevertheless, the coherence of the appeal to kinds gets undermined because there is an irresolvable explanatory circularity. Since the members of at least some kinds of material object might be essentially wholes, such that they are essentially ys that the xs compose, and the explanatory factor that accounts for why some set of material parts compose a whole (the structure) belongs to the kinds of wholes it constitutes essentially, the account requires the introduction of some way that the explanatory factor differs from the particular material parts and does not characterize them necessarily. This preserves the fact that composition among all the particular material objects does not occur necessarily in light of the fact that everything that is a composite whole is one in which the explanatory factor, the structure, is also necessarily present. The accounts, of course, would not explain that in virtue of which composition occurs if it were possible for the particular material objects that compose a whole to do so *sans* explanatory factor.

Yet the explanatory factor is supposed to be a particular—a formal part and causal power trope, respectively—on both Koslicki and Jaworski's accounts of composition, but one which does not belong to the same kind of thing as a material particular. This results in a serious incoherence, because (necessarily) neither the particular structure nor the particular material object essentially composes one another. One would need to invoke yet another, higher-level explanatory factor that would unite these. But the fact is that it does not look promising that we can find any good candidate that would fulfill the desiderata of providing an account of composition as restricted, because any such candidate higher-level factor would not itself be particular in the right way.

Recall that kinds were invoked, not only by Koslicki or Jaworski but also by van Inwagen, in order to motivate the restrictions on composition. As there are no good extra-mereological reasons to believe in trout-turkeys or other pseudo-objects, conversely, an account of why some parts compose a genuine material object appears to be motivated by the fact that we have *extra-mereological reason* to believe there are xs that compose ys (but not trout-turkeys). To appropriate Jaworski's motto: composition needs to *make a difference*. This is reason, then, that both Koslicki and Jaworski (and, indeed, van Inwagen) posit an extra-mental particular as that explanatory factor in virtue of which composition occurs among some material parts: they hold it is a particular fact about the objects, not relative to our conceptual schemes or concepts, when those objects compose a whole.

One might notice that I have, so far, not discussed Kit Fine's account of composition. There is good reason for that. The criticisms I have made in regard to restricted theories of composition and the possibility of substances having other substances as parts relies on an important assumption. Fine's view of embodiments resembles in many ways the hylomorphism of Koslicki. But Koslicki (and Jaworski) disagreed with Fine precisely because they believed his account seemed to deny that there are extra-mereological motivations for restrictions on composition. If Fine does deny this assumption, which I will argue that he very plausibly does, then my grounding objection does not apply straightforwardly to his account.

In order to show what goes wrong with Fine's account, I need to show both that restrictions on composition *do* need to make a difference and then clarify the difference that needs to be made. In the fifth chapter, I will argue that, without such extra-mereological reasons to think that material composition occurs in some cases and not in others, it is hard to see what would set apart an account of "restricted" composition from the other extreme views of Nihilism or Universalism. However, before I can defend this kind of position, I need to lay some significant groundwork to help us see a way in which hylomorphism can be coherent without substance-parts as well as the way in which hylomorphism is premised in important respects on the assumption that composition makes a difference. These goals will be accomplished in the next and subsequent chapter. From these two points, an argument that Fine's account of composition fails to be a theory of *restricted* composition will set us up immediately to see why any successful, coherent account of restricted composition is functionally a version of hylomorphism.

3

From Structure to Substantial Forms

In the last chapter, I argued that accounts of material composition which accept that composition only occurs under some limited set of circumstances, rather than necessarily between any two or more things—i.e., a "restricted" theory of composition—should reject the possibility that substances can have other substances as parts. What I pointed out in the last chapter was that accepting the possibility of substances as parts requires multiple kinds of "whole" in the context of material composition. This is, because, to make the claim sensible that those wholes can become proper parts of other wholes while, at the same time, remaining wholes, the defender of the possibility of substance-parts needs to hold that at least some things are such material wholes necessarily. However, the claim that composition is always relative to a measure leads to a conflict with the desiderata that inspire restricting composition in the first place, and it undermines the aim of providing a coherent, non-trivial, and non-circular account of the circumstances under which material composition occurs.

As noted, rejecting the possibility of substance-parts does not require rejecting that a structured whole can have parts that are themselves structured. Nobody need reject the obvious fact that my hand, despite being a part of me, has its fingers as parts. Rejecting the possibility of substances composing other substances as parts only entails that, in the context of material composition, we are referring to one kind of composition and so one kind of whole. Being a composite material "whole" and composing another thing as a material "part" are always mutually exclusive. It might be, too, that there *are* other kinds of wholes aside from material wholes, but the rejection of the possibility of substance-parts only requires rejecting that there are multiple kinds of composition among the *material* wholes. As a result of holding that being a material whole is not relative to some measure, that something is a "whole" is merely for there to be (1) a y such that the xs compose y as proper parts and (2) where that y does not compose anything else as a proper part. We can therefore much more simply define what it is to be a "material substance" as co-extensive with whatever things count as wholes, given the restrictions a theory might impose on when material composition occurs. Examining the restrictions on composition posited by a theory of composition will reveal the substances, the genuine material objects, that result from that theory's restrictions on composition.

While accounts that do not make being a material "whole" relative to some measure will not suffer from the grounding problems that I alleged beset those of accounts of composition admitting the possibility of substance-parts (such as Koslicki's or Jaworski's), it is nevertheless true that there remain two prominent difficulties. The first results from the fact that the parts of substances are not substances. But, since material wholes sometimes undergo a change of parts over time, these accounts apparently require that whenever a substance becomes a part of some other substance, the substance that becomes a part ceases to exist. If we imagine an oxygen atom and two hydrogen atoms coming to compose an H_2O molecule, this theory of composition is committed to the seemingly absurd result that the atoms cease to exist when they come to compose H_2O. The second problem is that the reasons we rejected the possibility of substances composing other substances as parts appear to require rejecting hylomorphic accounts of composition. One might worry that, as a matter of course, the hylomorphic account of composition appears to introduce different kinds of "wholes" in the context of material composition, introducing non-material or *metaphysical parts* (form, structure) to account for when some material parts compose a whole.

Consequently, the hylomorphist (such as myself) needs to show that the rejection of the possibility that substances can have other substances as parts, even though the problems with this possibility were illustrated in the context of criticizing two hylomorphic theories of composition, does not entail we should reject hylomorphism. One of the aims of this chapter is to give an account of the role of form in composition that is general enough to characterize many different theories of composition and which avoids the grounding problem alleged to beset those accounts embracing substance-parts. In the subsequent chapters, I will argue that all coherent accounts of restricted composition will appeal to entities functionally equivalent to Aquinas' "forms" in order to account for material composition. The other aim is to show that there is at least one coherent and plausible account of material composition that can respond to the worries about changes of parts in a sensible manner.

For this reason, in this third chapter, I turn to the account of material composition held by Thomas Aquinas. Aquinas is a well-known historical proponent of a hylomorphic theory that appeals to "form" as that in virtue of which composition occurs, and he explicitly rejects the possibility of substance-parts. Why appeal to Aquinas in particular? A man is said to have been asked by his pastor whether he believed in infant baptism. The parishioner is said to have responded, "Believe in it? Hell, I've seen it done!"[1] I appeal to Aquinas, in other words, because his answers to the two aforementioned difficulties appear to me to be coherent and plausible. Nevertheless, even though I appeal to Aquinas in this way, it is important to recall that the overall argument of this book is *conditional*. In what follows, I will present certain of Aquinas' responses to puzzles about material composition. I am not arguing that the Thomistic account of material composition is *the* true theory of composition, nor that even that there are objects with parts. I am only presenting Aquinas' answer to these puzzles as plausible and coherent—the kind of response an account of material composition that rejects the possibility of substance-parts should make.

For this reason, the success of this chapter in supporting my overall argument will primarily depend on my account of structure, not on my defense of Aquinas' solution to puzzles. The chapter will be successful if it makes clear what a structure is and what it does in such a way that any theory of material composition could appeal to these structures. Doing so will enable me to classify theories of composition according to whether they appeal to structure or not in order to account for composition. I will conclude, therefore, by giving a statement of the role that substantial forms play in material composition, by appeal to which we can identify a hylomorphic theory.

Part I: Substantial Forms in Aquinas

The term "structure" is being used by Neo-Aristotelians such as Fine, Koslicki, and Jaworski as a functional term to denote whatever accounts for the composition of substances, as distinct from the substance or its (material) parts. Aquinas' metaphysics is in this same family of theories of material composition: "hylomorphic" theories of composition that posit two corresponding principles, matter (*hyle* in Greek) and form (*morphe*), to account for the composition of substances. I see no *a priori* reason not to use the term "structure" or "configuration" to characterize what Aquinas refers to as "forms" (*forma*), and some use these terms inter-changeably,[2] yet I will hereafter use the term "form" in order to distinguish the Thomistic metaphysics of material composition from the other theories. Aquinas' substantial forms are simply those forms that account for the existence of *substances*.

While Aquinas does not propose a formal definition for "substance,"[3] he states that a substance is: "a thing to whose nature it belongs not to exist in another."[4] My characterization of substances as "those material objects that do not compose any other as a proper part" is intended to mirror Aquinas' own characterization, although mine simplifies in important respects.[5] For instance, I specifically qualify that the account presented here is intended to cover only *material* substances and material composition.[6] For my purposes, too, I will leave open questions that might arise about artifacts, like chairs or tables, by characterizing substances in terms of the "genuine material objects."[7] What I am doing by bracketing these issues in this way is to frame the discussion squarely on the ontological role that substantial forms play in constituting a substance, rather than considering what things might be substances. On my simplified characterization of substance as a material object not part of another, it is definitional that anything that composes another object is *ipso facto* not a substance and, by implication, that substantial forms cannot structure substances as their matter.

In what follows, then, I focus on characterizing what forms are and what they do in substances. Aquinas' account of form requires us, first, to draw distinctions between two importantly different senses of "matter" that both play a role in his metaphysics of material composition. Substantial form constitutes matter to compose a material whole, yet Aquinas' theory is distinctive in that forms do so in such a way that they account not only for the composition but (additionally) the determinate existence and nature of all that substance's parts. Second, I offer an explanation of Aquinas' theory of the ontological role of substantial forms in accomplishing that feat that focuses on the way in which substantial forms are closely related to causal powers. In short, a substantial form is a principle by which a set of material parts are actual as instances of a kind of substance, in a similar manner to the way in which a causal power's being activated by some manifestation conditions is the principle by which that power manifests. This uniquely Thomistic character of substantial forms needs to be shown to avoid entailing either triviality or an infinite regress within the account of material composition. Lastly, I will clarify the sense in which such substantial forms can be considered to be "metaphysical parts" of the substances they constitute and thereby delineate generally what it is for a theory of material composition to be hylomorphic.

A Primary Approach to "Prime Matter"

Structural hylomorphists, like Koslicki and Fine, seem to follow out the natural grammatical tendency to hold that structures structure *something*, and that such a "something" must be a composite substance or set of substances, which comes to be structured in some way. If structure is only comprehensible in terms of structuring something independent of structure, it follows from this way of conceiving of structure that, if there were a lowest level of material part, it would be something like a part-less atom or simple. Substances would consequently only be the result of configurations of those simples. Indeed, this is a natural consequence—I argued—of adherence to the possibility of substance-parts. But this highlights a significant difference between contemporary hylomorphism and that of Aquinas: Aquinas' account does not envision or presume a particulate or atomistic concept of whatever kind of matter might exist at the lowest level.[8] Quite the opposite.

Aquinas begins with the view that a substantial form is precisely that structure or form, which accounts for the existence of material substances in general, including those that might be part-less simples, the substantial form accounts for the existence of their matter. For this reason, Aquinas draws a distinction between two senses a material composite can have matter. One is the familiar sense in which a material substance has its *integral* parts, such as my hands or fingers or toes, which are the material parts composing me. These are the "proximate matter" of a material substance. Another sense is much less familiar. This is the way of considering matter in a general sense as a part of any material composite substance. And Aquinas indeed is known for characterizing this sense of matter as a *potentiality*. This potentiality is what Aquinas calls "prime matter" (*materia prima*):

> Prime matter is ... matter without any form at all, "materiality" (as it were) apart from configuration. When it is a component in a matter-form composite, prime matter is the component of the configured composite which makes it the case that the configured thing can be extended in three dimensions and can occupy a particular place at a particular time. But by itself, apart from form, prime matter exists just potentially; it exists in actuality only as an ingredient in something configured. So we can remove form from prime matter only in thought; everything which exists in reality is configured in some way. For this reason, Aquinas sometimes says that form is the actuality of anything. Configuration or organization is necessary for the existence of anything at all; without form, nothing is actual.[9]

Aquinas is not therefore claiming that there is one obscure material stuff which is a part of every object, an ultimate material substrate of which everything else is a modification.[10] Aquinas is strongly against such a theory, in fact, as he argues that prime matter must not be a special kind of matter, in the sense in which my flesh or calcium are kinds of matter, but needs be devoid of all form because, if all material objects had one substratum with its own form, and this substratum was part of every material object, that substratum would be the only true substance and every other object would be a modification of it.[11] It would be an inverse of an atomistic universe, with everything forming one "blobject."

Prime matter is thus not an integral part, but the potential to be a material object, considered apart from any particular actual way something could be a material object by being a member of a determinate kind of thing. The characterization of prime matter as the potentiality for a thing to have location in space-time and extension in three dimensions follows from the fact that Aquinas holds these features as proper to all material objects in general, of any kind. These features of matter in general are not merely a relation, or a feature of our concepts or definitions of matter, but are essential to matter in general; i.e., "the potentiality of matter is nothing other than its essence."[12] Aquinas' claims about prime matter are therefore claims that what is essential in being a "material object" is that something has dimensions and spatiotemporal configuration, but not that one has those features in any determinate way. For something to be "material" is only to have indefinite dimensions and space-time location. Prime matter has a further role aside from being the principle in virtue of which things have dimensions because, as we will see, prime matter plays a theoretical role in how we should understand certain kinds of material changes. Prime matter is the matter *from* which some set of integral material parts are constituted.[13]

Inasmuch as prime matter is only the potential to be a material substance, Aquinas holds that prime matter could not exist without having a substantial form to give it particular properties and to determine what *actual* dimensions or location would have. Moreover, Aquinas argues that prime matter alone *necessarily* cannot constitute any particular kind of object, as it is strictly *contradictory* to claim that prime matter to exist without being informed by any substantial form. For prime matter to exist by itself, without the actuality of any form, would be to say that something purely potential could be actually existent yet without being actual in any way. That would be nonsense.[14] All this is to say, in short, that prime matter is a *metaphysical part* of material composites, having a similar kind of relation to a substance as that which a substantial form does: as Aquinas puts it, prime matter is "*incomplete* being without the substantial form."[15] In the next section, I will begin to clarify what it is for substantial form and prime matter to be metaphysical parts of a material substance by first describing the way that a substantial form is the correlative actuality to the potentiality of prime matter.

Actual Substances

Actuality and potency are of central importance to Aquinas' metaphysics and to his account of substantial form. As noted, prime matter is merely the potential to have a material spatiotemporal structure, but it does not involve *actually* having one; instead, "the act to which prime matter is in potentiality is a substantial form."[16] Aquinas understands a substantial form as that by which a material substance is one such actual configuration of matter (rather than any of infinitely many potential others), so that a substantial form is that in virtue of which a substance is actual.

Aquinas thus defines forms in terms of their role, forms being that in virtue of which something has actual existence in some way: "all that from which something has existence [*esse*], whether that existence is substantial or accidental, is able to be called a 'form' … and because form makes [something] to be in actuality, therefore form is said to be an actuality [*actus*]."[17] As prime matter lacks any actuality and is essentially a potentiality for being configured by a form, the substantial form of a given substance accounts for everything in terms of which that material thing is a determinate member of its kind, e.g., having essential properties or powers.[18] According to Aquinas' way of thinking, "there is no such thing as existence beyond the specific ways of functioning manifested by specific kinds of things."[19] This is why Aquinas claims that a "substantial form gives being [*esse*] to matter *simpliciter*."[20]

Yet, corresponding to the way in which there are two senses as to what the "matter" is in a material substance, Aquinas distinguishes two senses of what potentiality in a substance that the substantial form actualizes. Even though the matter *from which* every material composite is constituted is prime matter, and "no other substantial form intervenes between [a substantial form such as] the soul and prime matter,"[21] no object is merely actualized prime matter. Instead, the matter *of which* some material substance is composed is its proximate matter, e.g., its integral parts. Hence, the immediate potentiality which the human soul makes actual is a living human body (and all its parts); "the human body is the matter proportionate to the human soul; and it is related to the soul as potency to actuality."[22] Aquinas considers such proximate matter brought into existence by the substantial form as a *particular way* in which the potentiality of prime matter is actualized. Since no one substantial form actualizes all of the potential of prime matter, this is only some specific potentiality of matter that corresponds to the specific actuality that a substantial form brings about: whatever matter, under whatever determinate conditions, that is essential to the kind of substance the form constitutes.

Obviously, on this way of understanding forms as being that in virtue of which not only some parts are configured into a composite material substance, but that all of that substance's matter *exists*, it is not easy to see what pluralism about substantial forms could mean. If a substance had two substantial forms, this would be for one and the same substance to exist "twice over," and that just seems nonsense. Aquinas therefore treats pluralism about substantial forms as a conceptual confusion: "since every form gives a certain *esse*, and it is impossible for one thing to have two substantial existences (*esse*), it is necessary that if the first substantial form coming to matter gives substantial *esse* to it, a second superadded form must give an accidental existence (*esse*)."[23] Forms either make a substance to exist, simply speaking, or they otherwise configure that substance to exist in some way (e.g., as having a property). And if the substance already exists, any further forms in the substance can only bring about modifications within that already-existing substance, i.e., further forms would not be *substantial* forms.

Aquinas therefore also treats the view that a substance can have other substances as parts as a conceptual confusion. Having other substances as proper parts is just what it is to be an aggregate, not a substance. Substantial forms, on Aquinas' view, account for the existence of a substance precisely because they account for the existence of every part of that substance:

> the soul as the form of the body ... is united directly to the whole body, because it is the form of the body as a whole and of each of its parts. And this must be maintained, for, since the body of a man or that of any other animal is a certain natural whole, it will be said to be one because it has one form whereby it is perfected, and not simply because it is an aggregate or a composition, as occurs in the case of a house and other things of this kind. Hence each part of a man and that of an animal must receive its act of existing and species from the soul as its proper form.[24]

Notice, however, this way of thinking entails that substantial form is *intrinsic* to the substance and all of its parts. An arrangement, for example, is not something intrinsic to the things arranged, and this is what makes an arrangement an accidental rather than a substantial form—it is only a relation among substances. Aquinas uses the illustration that a mass of bronze coming to be a statue only involves an accidental change or alteration because "the bronze, before the advent of the form or figure, has actual existence and its existence does not depend on that figure."[25] If the statute's shape were a substantial form, that shape would not only result in the existence of bronze shaped-as-a-statue, but the existence of its matter as well. "A form must be something *of* that to which it gives existence, for form and matter are intrinsic principles constituting the essence of a [corporeal] thing."[26]

Similarly, a substantial form is not like a causal *agent* internal to some parts, e.g., gathering them together or pushing them through space. To say then that a substantial form is that in virtue of which a substance exists or is actual is not to say that the substantial form creates or generates its own material parts. A chemist who makes a new chemical compound by combining the constituents in the right way is bringing into existence that compound, certainly, but in a different sense. Aquinas thinks of a causal agent as making some matter *to have a form*: "corporeal forms are caused ... by matter being brought from potentiality into act by some composite agent."[27] This account of causal agency, even though utilizing an act-potency distinction, presumes that forms play a distinct role. The forms are that *in* what is actual, whereas the agent remains outside of what she actualizes. Whereas the chemist does not become the chemical compound she mixes up, the substantial form and the matter actualized by it "must have one and the same act of existing (*esse*), something which is not true of an efficient cause and an effect to which it gives *esse*."[28] This, of course, requires us to clarify what it is for a substantial form to be "in" a substance and in what sense a substance is actualized by it.

Substantial Forms as *Essentially* Actuality

Aquinas' most significant claim about substantial forms is that a substantial form *is* an actuality.[29] Aquinas appeals to the nature of substantial forms as essentially actuality in order to explain why it is impossible to find a further principle in virtue of which a substantial form unifies the parts of a material substance:

> a thing is one, according as it is a being. Now the form, through itself, makes a thing to be actual since it is itself *essentially an act* [my emphasis]; nor does it give existence by means of something else. Wherefore the unity of a thing composed of matter and form, is by virtue of the form itself, which by reason of its very nature is united to matter as its act. Nor is there any other cause of union except the agent, which causes matter to be in act."[30]

Aquinas' position is then that a substantial form is essentially nothing other than the *actuality* of the substance it characterizes. As we already saw, Aquinas says that the substantial form and the matter of which it is the actuality have "one and the same act of existing," which is a very tight identification indeed.

Aquinas' notion of actuality is thus cross-categorical, because powers and things other than substances can be actual or potential in various respects. Understanding what it is for something to be an actuality in this sense requires significant clarification since "actuality" is a primitive in Aquinas' metaphysics, and the best we can do is give functional characterizations in terms of analogies and distinctions.[31] Aquinas clearly differentiates a substantial form from a causal agent, or its activity, because the substantial form is intrinsic to what results from the activity of that agent. One other actuality that is in the neighborhood of substantial form, because it seems intrinsic to an agent, is *engaging in an activity*. Yet an activity is an activity *of* some agent or of some objects, and so an object already has to exist in order to exercise an activity—this would not be the right kind of actuality that a substantial form is.[32] So there are very good reasons to think that my existing as a human being is not an activity that I am constantly engaged in:

> If there is a most general activity that a human being (or anything else that engages in activities) engages in—presumably it would be something like "living" or "getting older"—it is simply wrong to call it "being" .... One cannot, of course, engage in this most general activity (supposing there to be such an activity) unless one *is*, but this obvious truth is simply a consequence of the fact that one can't engage in any activity unless one is: if an activity is being engaged in, there has to be something to engage in it.[33]

What should give us a clue in the right direction for understanding the actuality that is a substantial form lies in a traditional puzzle for hylomorphists. Hylomorphists, like other advocates of restricted composition, generally take it that the existence of material objects, and whether they are composed of parts, to be a mind-independent matter, not one merely relative to our conceptual schemes. The hylomorphist takes it that, when material composition occurs, the factor there is in virtue of which the xs compose y is somehow "in" the xs and y. Yet that factor cannot be an additional material part, a z, that we add to the xs, because this would generate an infinite regress. If one admits the need for an explanation as to why some set of material parts compose a whole, then adding another part does not provide anything explanatory—i.e., it is that the xs and z compose y. What one consequently needs is some factor that is both intrinsic to all the material parts and the whole, but not identical with any of them. The hylomorphist solution on this score is the distinction between "metaphysical" and "integral" parts, which, as we saw employed in Koslicki's response to this problem, requires that these are two different *kinds* of parts. Forms belong to a different ontological kind than the material wholes or the material parts whose composition they explain. Whereas the material things, the xs, are not such that they necessarily compose anything (this being a general condition of all such *restricted* theories of composition), the idea is then that metaphysical parts like forms are of such an ontological kind that they are *essentially* unifying.

Aquinas sometimes discusses this aspect of substantial forms, explicitly addressing this problem of providing a sufficient answer to the infinite regress worry in material composition. A form cannot have its own integral parts, because that would defeat the whole purpose of appealing to something that is of a distinct ontological kind to account for the unity of some material things: "If therefore this [form] is a thing having diverse parts, and it is not one in itself, it is necessary on this account to be something unified. But this cannot go on infinitely, but it is necessary to come to something which is one in itself. And the soul is this to the highest degree."[34] A substantial form is therefore not the sort of thing to have integral parts at all.[35] But, by contrast, a form is precisely the kind of thing that *essentially* is such that it unifies the material parts; "we find the composition of matter and form only in things with parts, one of which is related to the other as potency to act."[36]

Since a form is supposed to be that which accounts for the unity among the integral parts of a material substance, this consequently requires that forms belong to a distinct ontological kind from material substances. When Aquinas characterizes a form as nothing more than an actuality of a substance, he is identifying a form as belonging to an ontological category such that the form is neither a material thing nor composed of matter.[37] This is also why Aquinas was at pains to clarify that a form does not act as an agent, configuring its parts. Forms would then be parts that influence themselves, causing themselves to compose a whole, and "there is something ratbaggish in the thought of a whole that includes a part causally influencing that part: parts would causally influence themselves."[38]

In Aquinas' characterization of "substance" as "a thing to whose nature it belongs not to exist in another,"[39] he comes close to contemporary accounts of substances as those things that are "property-bearers." John Heil holds the view similar to Aquinas that to be a substance is to be a property-bearer. Heil has us imagine a complex consisting of a particular arrangement of three simple substances. Pretend that the complex arrangement of these three substances is a tomato and that the tomato is red. "Is the tomato's being red a matter of the complex's possessing a property? ... . Ascribing a property to *it*, to the complex, as opposed to the substances making up the complex, has the aura of a category mistake."[40] This intuition follows, Heil thinks, from the fact that "the sense in which a simple substance bears a property—the substance is some way or other—does not extend univocally to complexes made up of substances standing in particular relations. You could say that a complex is a particular way... but in that case the 'way' is the way these constituents are organized. The tomato's 'being the red way' just *is* a matter of the tomato's constituents being as they are, organized and interrelated as they are."[41] A property is, by definition, not the kind of thing to bear properties, and pointing to further properties does not answer the question of what it is that *bears* those properties.

Aquinas grasps that there is a theoretical similarity between the problem of how something can bear properties and how something can be composed of material parts, and he cashes out this similarity in terms of the trans-categorical act-potency distinction. Note that all of these cases resemble that problem that the hylomorphist has in explaining how whatever unifies some parts into a whole is a member of a distinct ontological kind from those parts, a metaphysical and not an integral part. But the problem of bearers of properties is the inverse, mirror-image of the former. There needs to be a sense in which being a bearer of properties is a potentiality, not an actuality, so that the buck can stop with the "actualized thing"— the bearer being so characterized—without infinitely deferring the question of why it is that these properties characterize it. In Heil's example, bearing a bearer of properties is a *potentiality* that can be actualized in various ways, whereas being characterized by a property is a way that substance is, an *actuality*.

The reason such responses answer the questions is that to be an "actualized thing" is to be an intrinsically unified thing, such that, even though we can ask legitimately (for instance) how the potency was actualized, it does not make sense to ask what "binds" the potency and the actuality of that actualized thing together. For example, when sitting at a stop light, the stop light is potentially green (and actually red) for the period I am stopped, and then actually becomes green at the appropriate moment to indicate I can now drive. It makes sense to ask how the light went from one state of affairs to another, as we can point to the change in electric current, or the timing device in the base of the light pole, etc. But it seems nonsensical to ask a question such as the following: "But what makes the *being green* stay in the light?" Actuality is the kind of thing at which the metaphysical buck naturally stops.[42]

It is just such a characterization that Aquinas intends to give substantial form, such that it is the actuality of a material substance, and where it becomes nonsense to ask for a further actuality in virtue of which substantial forms characterize their substances or make their parts actual. There is no further entity in virtue of which a substance is characterized by its substantial actuality and no need for any such account, because a substance is an "actualized thing" just like the green stoplight. Within the ambit of material composition, a material composite substance is an "actualized thing" of such a sort, the *y* which the material parts compose. In keeping with the same way of thinking we can distinguish potentiality, actualized thing, and actuality: the material parts that which *from which* the substance is composed, the substance that *which* they compose, and the substantial form is the actuality *in virtue of which* the parts compose it. The form and matter composing a human being are explicitly identified as such an "actualized thing," which makes it "unnecessary to ask whether the soul and the body are one, just as it is unnecessary to ask whether the wax and its impression are one. But with respect to its act of existing, the impression cannot be separated in any way from the wax. Consequently, with respect to its act of existing, the soul is not separated from the body."[43]

But there is an important distinction to be drawn between kinds of actualities, corresponding to different kinds of actualized things. A stop light only came to be in a certain state (for the green light to be illuminated), akin to acquiring a certain property. It was actualized in a way that Aquinas refers to a "secondary" actuality. A secondary actuality is an actuality by which a substance has a property or is engaged in some activity, because it depends on a more basic "primary" actuality: the stop light had to exist in the first place for the stop light to be able to acquire or lose properties, let alone have properties at all. A "primary actuality" then is an actuality by which a substance exists, as a determinate instance of its kind. Activities, properties, and so forth all constitute secondary actualities. This is because to be a substance is not an accidental feature of a thing, unlike the way in which a stop light can continue in existence without being green. "Being illuminated green" is not essential to the stoplight, and so that actuality is only a secondary actuality of it. "Being a kind of machine," by contrast, is a primary actuality of the stoplight, because the stoplight would not exist if it were not the kind of machine it is.

The kind of actuality involved in substantial forms is for something to be *a thing* rather than the secondary actuality to be *so-and-such*. These locutions immediately make us think of the relation between a property bearer and its properties, where a substance is the *thing* and the substance is what gets modified *so-and-such*. It is not immediately evident why it is the case that the answer to something like the Special Composition Question requires such a *strong* account of the unity of material objects, such that it would identify the things that are material composite wholes with bearers of properties. One could think it a contingent matter whether these two sets of things are co-extensive. Aquinas rejects such a proposition and shows that there is an important connection between the two issues.

Matter, Material Parts, and Property Bearers

I noted that Aquinas does not hold that matter is fundamentally or essentially particulate, and it is apparent now why he cannot think it is. If matter were fundamentally particulate, it would be essential to those particles that they are mereologically simple, and it would consequently be false that they could ever compose a whole object. Aquinas' claims that matter is not essentially particulate does not merely constitute medieval empirical speculation, lacking knowledge of the existence of fundamental physical particles, but follows directly from the assumption that there are material composites (and that any arbitrary two or more material things do not compose an object)—that is, that material composition occurs only under some restricted circumstances.

An account of material composition would be involved in an infinite regress if it only specifies the conditions under which some things come to compose a whole without explaining what the things are which *get* composed. This would be akin to explaining what it is to be a bearer of properties, a thing defined in terms of being what bears properties, by appeal to a distinct property of that thing.[44] Aquinas' earlier objection to a plurality of substantial forms in one substance is that it involves one in an infinite regress of exactly the same sort; it infinitely defers the question as to what has the potentiality to be composed or it assumes an ultimately atomistic account of reality as a necessary truth (viz. Peter van Inwagen's account of composition).[45] If matter were essentially particulate, then this would seem to mean that *to be a material object* is just to be one of the particles, that is, it *necessary* for the material objects that they be mereologically simple. But this position would involve a confusion between two different senses of what it is to be a material object: being the sort of thing that essentially has integral parts and being the sort of thing that essentially has dimensions, occupying a spatiotemporal location. But it is false that being the sort of thing with dimensions and a spatiotemporal location necessarily entails being the sort of thing that is essentially mereologically simple.

To put it another way, even though prime matter characterizes every material object, it is only a way to describe the potentiality to be a material object and has *no* essential characteristics at all. Prime matter is thus an explanatory principle in virtue of which it is a contingent matter whether *any* material substance exists—i.e., it is not essential to any material thing, merely in virtue of being material, that it be actual. Consequently, whatever constitutes "materiality" cannot be something that has any essential properties (neither a property or a property-bearer), but rather that special sort of potentiality that corresponds to the potential to be a material substance: namely, that no material object exists necessarily, but only contingently. Prime matter has to be "pure potentiality" in this way in order to thread the needle between the views that composition among two or more material things occurs of necessity (Universalism) and that material objects are essentially mereologically simple (Nihilism).

In fact, Aquinas argues that, if there are things having dimensions and spatiotemporal location, they are *by that very fact* composite objects—composites precisely inasmuch as they possess spatial parts: "from the fact that matter has corporeal existence through forms, it immediately follows that there are dimensions in matter whereby it is understood to be divisible into different parts, so that it can receive different forms corresponding to its different parts."[46] Inasmuch as material objects have parts that are spatially distinguished, these are *integral parts*, and we find that distinct integral parts can bear distinct properties or evince different structures (i.e., spatial parts of one object can bear distinct accidental forms). Aquinas' point is that spatial parts of a substance are the right kind of thing themselves to have properties in various ways. We can, for example, characterize one spatial region of the same substance as hot and another as cold, because spatial parts can have distinct properties.

John Heil denies this and argues, to the contrary, that if substances can only have spatial or temporal parts, then that is enough to claim that they are "mereologically simple."[47] The only realistic candidate substances would be particles or fields, whereas macroscopic entities like humans are not.[48] This is because fields or particles would not have parts that bear distinct properties from the whole. The whole field has one set of properties borne directly by the field, and all of its spatial parts (considering the field's extension in space as a way to divide it into spatial parts) have the same properties. Whereas a substance like a field or a particle can have many properties, properties are not parts of those things. Properties are not parts of their substances.[49] The argument is to the effect that, if Aquinas admits that a material object has integral parts, and these parts can bear properties, then those parts must be substances. Aquinas would therefore be contradicting the shared assumption that only substances are property-bearers.

But Aquinas has not assumed that integral parts of a substance, among which are that object's spatial parts, are bearers of properties *in their own right*.

Aquinas just denies this implicit premise of Heil's argument. What is required is a distinction between the fact that some things essentially bear properties and that other things bear properties in a derivative way. That is, there is no contradiction if integral parts bear properties only *accidentally*, i.e., only in virtue of composing something that is *essentially* a property-bearer, a substance. When my hand is white, then *I* am white with respect to my hand. My hand is not a property-bearer in its own right, but bears properties only in virtue of being a part of me. Yet, understanding integral parthood in this way such that integral parts bear properties in an only accidental way, we not only can divide an object according to its spatial dimensions—top half, right half, etc.—but also in terms of the way in which each distinct part can bear distinct properties, or have a power, or be structured.

Further, Aquinas is not claiming that it is necessarily the case that there are material objects, but only that there would be no problem of material composition if there were no material objects. From Aquinas' perspective, if the scientific data shows us that the world is built entirely from fields, and fields are things that entirely lack spatial parts and spatiotemporal location, then it would merely be the case that the existence of spatiotemporally located objects is merely *apparent*. (Of course, one would need to explain how the fields exist and how these fields generate the apparent spatiotemporal world.) The point is that, once we admit that there are objects that have spatial dimensions, we are committed to the fact that there exist material composites and consequently that we can pose questions as to the way in which their composite parts compose one whole. Consequently, if there are material objects with parts in Aquinas' sense, they at least that bear the property of being a y such that the xs compose it, and so these are all *ipso facto* going to be the kind of thing that can bear (one or more) properties by reason of the kind of thing they are.

This only shows that the material substances are all essentially such that they can bear at least one property, not that the class "substance" and "material composite" things are co-extensive. And this result is natural, as Aquinas' broader metaphysics, of course, invokes immaterial substances such as angels. But since, as noted, substances are just those things of the sort that bear properties, Aquinas holds that substances are also the only things that exist, strictly speaking:

> existence (*esse*) is attributed to something in two ways. In one way, as to that which properly and truly has existence or exists, and in this way it is attributed only to a substance that subsists *per se*. Thus *Physics* I [186b4–8] says that a substance is what truly is. All those things, on the other hand, that do not subsist *per se*, but are in another and with another—whether they are accidents or

substantial forms or any sort of parts—do not have existence in such a way that they truly exist, but existence is attributed to them in another way—that is, as that by which something is—just as whiteness is said to be not because it subsists in itself, but because by it something has existence-as-white (*esse album*).[50]

Obviously, if something were not the sort of thing to bear a property either accidentally or essentially, then it would be a thing with no properties. It is hard to make sense of what such a thing could be, let alone whether such a thing could exist. Surprisingly, Aquinas argues that *one* such thing exists: God. God can be something that exists without bearing properties because He is *essentially* His own existence.[51] And, necessarily, there is only one such object, Aquinas argues, because everything other than God is a metaphysical composite of "essence" and "existence." Aquinas' account of the composition of essence and existence is yet another invocation of the trans-categorical notion of act-potency, even though distinct from the kind of composition that exists in any material composite between its matter and form.[52]

It is beyond the scope of this chapter to fully clarify the relation between existence (*esse*) and form, but the way in which the two come apart is illustrated by immaterial substances. Angels are immaterial substances, the sort of things that can bear properties, even though they are composed of no matter; they are "subsistent forms." Yet they are not *necessarily* or essentially existent things; God created them. Hence, there is an act-potency relationship in anything that does not exist necessarily (i.e., is a contingent being). And, as with other instances of these cases, Aquinas' solution is to say that an immaterial substance is thus a species of "actualized thing," which we can distinguish as being characterized by an actuality—*esse*—and a potentiality—the angel's essence.[53] Thus, even a form is characterized as a metaphysical composite at a higher level of composition.

To say, then, that a substantial form is an actuality is not to say that a substantial form necessarily exists in the way that God does. An "actualized thing" is therefore understood to be a peculiar sort of (metaphysical) composite. We *can* distinguish the way in which something goes from being potentially *x* to being actually *x*, like I did with the stop light—so there is a real difference between being actually green and only potentially so. Yet, obviously, to be *potentially green*, as with *actually green*, is a property *of* the stop light. The actualities of an actualized thing are *intrinsic* to what they constitute as metaphysical parts. A property, as an actuality, is intrinsic to what bears that property, much in the same way a substantial form is intrinsic to what it constitutes; to distinguish an actuality from the actualized thing is akin to selectively considering aspects of one and the same thing.[54] This is why Aquinas defines a form as an "imperfect" part. A composite substance is properly the thing which is actual, the "actualized thing," whereas the substantial form is actual or exists only insofar as it is the actuality of that existing substance.[55] By the same token, a substantial form is an "essential part" of an object, insofar as the form is part of the essence of its substance (with that substance's matter as the other corresponding essential part).[56] Pasnau summarizes Aquinas' view: "only the composite whole [viz. a substance] has existence (*esse*), properly speaking. All the other parts of the substance... though things of a certain kind, nevertheless exist only in an improper sense, in virtue of the whole's existence."[57]

Form Is an Actuality *of* Matter

Forms as actualities might look suspiciously thin, on this reading. Aquinas' answer to problems of material composition *would* be trivial if all there is to the claim that a material whole is characterized by a substantial form is that the parts of that object are characterized by "actually composing" the whole. That would be nothing more than saying that the *x*s compose *y* whenever they *actually do*. But this objection misses the way that a form is explanatory only in the context of the potentiality of which it is the actualization. When we are talking about an actualized thing, such as a power that is manifested, the potentiality of that thing is not *mere possibility*.[58] Aquinas provides two such potentialities that are relative to any substantial form of a material composite object: prime matter and proximate matter. Prime matter is, as we will see in the next section, invoked in the context of explaining how material objects can change kinds. The proximate matter of a substance is that potentiality which is made actual by its substantial form.

The proximate matter of a substance is simply whatever material parts are essential to the kind of substance in question. Aristotle's definition of a soul, appropriated by Aquinas, is that a soul is "the primary actuality of a physical, organic body."[59] As the things that have souls are living things and only living things, such a definition expresses that having a physical, organic body is essential to being a member of the kind "living thing." A substantial form is then the actuality of something *insofar as* that thing belongs to some kind, being characterized by whatever properties or powers are essential to members of the kind. Stump therefore puts it that a substantial form is a "configurational state of a material object that makes that object a member of the kind of species to which it belongs and gives it the causal powers characteristic of things of that kind."[60] Substantial forms are thus that in virtue of which a substance's essential material parts compose that thing, as well as being that in virtue of which that whole is the sort of thing that can bear properties.

Aquinas' metaphysics fixes the kinds of proximate matter appropriate to each substantial form according to the determinate kinds of material objects that could exist. This might raise a worry. Essentialism and the existence of natural kinds are topics of significant philosophical controversy, especially in biology.[61] Even though Aquinas himself accepts the existence of natural kinds of biological entities, a specific account of what kinds of substances there might be is not required in order to affirm the kinds of claims Aquinas wants to make about how a substantial form constitutes a substance as a member of a determinate kind. Eleonore Stump helpfully characterizes Aquinas' account of substance as "emergent." Thomistic emergence contrasts with other contemporary views because it is usually taken, as we saw with Koslicki's account of lawful interactional dependence, that some object is emergent when the parts engage in a particular kind of activity or are characterized by a certain kind of property. Stump reminds that "on Aquinas's way of thinking about material objects what can emerge when form is imposed on matter is not just properties but substances."[62] Instead, on a Thomistic way of thinking, "W is an emergent thing if and only if the properties and causal powers of W are not simply the sum of the properties and causal powers of the constituents of W when those constituents are taken singillatim, outside the configuration of W."[63]

Obviously, this characterization as it stands can be misleading. "There are plenty of examples of material objects having—on account of their structure or external relations—emergent properties or functions that the parts individually do not have, without such objects *ipso facto* being substances."[64] Stump's claim should be interpreted instead in terms of what properties are *essential* to a material object. That is, a thing is a substance when it has powers and properties that are essential to it, but are not a sum of the powers and properties essential to those things that could potentially come to compose it. What this characterization highlights are cases of what Aquinas calls "substantial changes," where a substance is generated from some other substances, or, conversely, decomposes into them.

Given that Aquinas holds that the material composites are essentially such that they belong to kinds, then the crux of the account rests on identifying what is essential to what. Substantial changes are one such way to do this, because when a certain object ceases to have an essential property, e.g., the stoplight ceases to be a kind of machine, it thereby ceases to exist. At this point, though, notice that Aquinas' account is not unique among theories of restricted material composition that appeal to extra-mereological considerations to fix what the material whole objects are. Aquinas presumes that our discovery and classification of the kinds of material composites is then not a matter of speculative metaphysics, but natural science.

The ontologically relevant payoff of distinguishing between prime matter and the proximate matter of material parts is that it allows Aquinas to draw a distinction such that he can affirm both that, even though these parts potentially could constitute something else, these parts actually compose a substance's essential parts. On one hand, distinguishing a substantial form as a particular, a metaphysical part of a composite, is to say that the substantial form is not identical with those material parts or the whole they compose.[65] Substantial forms are *particulars* which, in virtue of characterizing some set of material parts, account for why those parts constitute a whole of some kind. It is not a feature of our counting or conceptual schemes that the material xs are such that they compose y, but an extra-mental fact about the xs that they compose y, since they do so by reason of the substantial form that is intrinsic to that material object and all its parts.[66] This is what it is to say that the substantial form is the actuality *of* that substance y and its parts, the xs, is that each of the xs (and the substantial form) are such that they *actually* compose y in virtue of something that is essential to them (the substantial form[67]), even though the substantial form is not identical with the xs or the y.

On the other hand, there remains a sense in which *those* material things, the xs, could have composed z instead of y. Insofar as the xs are adequately characterized by being "material" (i.e., composed of prime matter as a metaphysical part), Aquinas holds that material objects in general are essentially such that they can undergo a change of kind—one material object can serve as matter *from which* we generate the matter of another material object of a different kind because prime matter is just the potentiality of any material object to come to constitute a distinct kind of material object under the relevant conditions.[68] It is not essential to their matter that the xs compose y, and thus z's parts could be composed *from* the xs. I explore the implications of this in the next section, and whether these claims are sufficient to account for continuity across changes of parts among substances, responding to the worries that many have about the Thomistic analysis.

Part II: A Controversial Thomistic Thesis

A substantial form is not merely a relation among already existing things, in virtue of which (for example) the arrangement or configuration of those things would count as a substance. The substantial form is responsible for the identity or nature of the relata that come to exist between the parts of the substance that form constitutes.[69] Substantial forms do not have substance-parts as that which they characterize. Substances are therefore such that if some substances come to compose them, those things that become parts must *ipso facto* cease to be substances. Aquinas' controversial claim can be roughly put as the view that substances are members of their kind in virtue of their substantial form. When a part ceases to compose a substance, it ceases to be the kind of part which would compose the kind of thing that is its parent substance.

As an illustration of the implications of this claim, consider the death of Socrates. Aquinas holds that "the soul … is the form of the whole body and each of its parts …. Thus it is necessary that each part of a man and that of an animal receive its existence and species from the soul as from its proper form."[70] When Socrates dies, all of his parts, his body, and his eyes and his skin, cease to exist as parts of a human being, *ipso facto*, cease to have any essential properties that result from composing Socrates. Since only living things have eyes or hands or skin, after Socrates' dies "neither eye nor flesh nor any part remains except equivocally" in his corpse.[71] To put it simply, Aquinas' claim results in the implication that, every time the *xs* come to compose a *y*, those *xs* have to undergo a change in kind membership.[72] This has been called the "homonymy principle."

Aquinas' acceptance that substantial forms inform prime matter, rather than substance-parts, requires him to believe that a substantial form must account for the determinate actuality of every part of the substance. Yet the homonymy principle has appeared to many to be so counterintuitive as to merit accepting the possibility of substance-parts instead. Koslicki argued that, if the homonymy principle were true, then it would be impossible to explain continuity in change.[73] The aim of this section will be to describe the way in which Aquinas' metaphysics can give a plausible and coherent of changes among integral parts and substances, defusing these worries.

In defending Aquinas' view, recall, I am not defending that it is the *true* theory of parts. Rather, the idea is that Aquinas' theory of substantial forms and of the parts of substances is a clear example of a theory of material composition rejecting the Substance-Part Principle. As I have already pointed out, Aquinas' particular account of *how* substances and their parts are determinate, his account of what natural kinds of things there are, is not itself a direct entailment of rejecting the possibility of substance-parts. Further, a non-Thomistic theory of material composition which also rejects the possibility of substance-parts might give an alternative, more plausible analysis of change. Defending Aquinas' theory is therefore only an illustration of the fact that there is at least one consistent and plausible account of composition rejecting the Substance-Part Principle.

Being a Part of a Thomistic Substance

To flesh out the controversial claim more fully, we have to incorporate Aquinas' view that the composite material wholes are essentially property-bearers but integral parts are not. Aquinas therefore insists that every part of a substance, in virtue of being a part, is something "in potentiality" (*in potentia*) to the substantial form of that substance:

> that parts [of a substance] are in potentiality alone is apparent because none among them is separate, inasmuch as, given that all the parts, insofar as they are parts, are united in a whole. For everything which exists actually ought to be distinct from other things, because one thing is distinguished from another by its own actuality and form.... But those things, which are taken to be parts, are separated from each other when the whole dissolves, then indeed they are beings in actuality, surely not as parts, but as matter existing in privation from the form of the whole. Just as, clearly, in the case of earth, fire, and air, which, when those are parts of a mixed body, are not actually in existence, but only potentially [existing] in a mixture. When they become truly separated, then they are in actual existence and are not parts. For, none of the elements, before they are arranged (that is, before they are altered in the mixture and become one mixed thing [composed] from those elements), is one [element] with another, except in the sense that a heap of stones is one thing *secundum quid* [i.e., in some qualified sense] and not simply.[74]

To say a part is only "actual" inasmuch as it is a part of the substance is to say that the actuality of the parts "is in some sense derived from the actuality of the whole, inasmuch as the whole substance, including all of its parts, shares in just a single existence."[75] What is meant by "actuality" in this context is then not the secondary actuality of *being such and so,* such as having a property, but rather *being a part of a substance*. The consequence is that, if a material part ceases to compose a substance as a part, that thing will become some other substance or a heap of substances. Moreover, because it no longer composes that in virtue of which it bore properties (namely, the substance), that part both ceases to be even a "derivative" property-bearer and loses all of the properties or powers that are associated with being a part of that substance.

Aquinas is not going to countenance material parts or wholes "surviving" substantial changes of these sorts. As Koslicki notes of Aquinas' views, "no object that is *not* already part of a whole that is unified under a single form can survive *becoming* part of such a whole; and no object that *is* already part of such a whole can survive *ceasing* to be part of it."[76] So it would be strictly false, on Aquinas' view, that one and the same thing could be characterized at one time as a part and at another as a substance. Potential parts of substances are not the same things as the actual substances they can become.

Aquinas' controversial claim can then be stated more completely as follows: the substantial form not only accounts for the existence of the substance and the composition of other material parts in a whole substance, but for *all* the things we could attribute to the parts, whether existence or actuality or powers or properties. Naturally, this claim also entails that a substance ceases to exist when it begins to compose a part of something else. Then, given that the substance no longer exists when it becomes a part, all of its properties or powers also cease to exist. Further, composing a whole with certain properties, like being human, entails that the parts also necessarily have certain properties in virtue of being parts. Thus, my hand is a human hand merely in virtue of composing me, but ceases to be a human hand when it ceases to compose me. These claims are nevertheless apparently highly counterintuitive: for example, why does the thing formerly known as my hand weigh the same after I cut it off, if nothing of the hand survives ceasing to be a part of me?

The Puzzle of Parts

Now a puzzle looms. These claims about my hand ceasing to be a hand when I die, or my body ceasing to be a body, both seem empirically false. Consider a case presented by William Jaworski as a counter-example to Aquinas' theory of composition:

> OXYGEN: in a process of respiration, oxygen atoms, as molecular oxygen (O_2), enter a human bloodstream. Those atoms oxidize red blood cells, becoming parts of those cells and, by extension, a human being. After circulating in human blood, those same oxygen atoms are eventually expelled, albeit in a different molecular configuration (CO_2).[77]

If we assume that oxygen atoms, molecules, and human beings are all substances, Aquinas is apparently committed to saying that these oxygen atoms were not the same atoms at every point in this process. When those atoms begin to compose a human being, those atoms *ipso facto* cease to be substances, property-bearers in their own right, and to have any properties essentially associated with the kind "oxygen atom." In fact, Aquinas seems to need to say that those atoms *never* existed because they always composed some other substance at every step of the case.

And this appears straightforwardly empirically false. We could have used radioactive isotopes to tag the atoms within the molecular oxygen and then identify the same two atoms at every point in the process. If these atoms ceased to exist or never existed, how could we track each particular atom, their properties, and their causal powers? Oxygen atoms do not disappear when they compose other molecules, nor do their properties or powers just cease to exist. Cases like OXYGEN are not exceptional or infrequent. When we break up a composite substance, the ingredient substances can come back into full existence, with entirely the same properties they had before they composed anything. Oxygen atoms do not just "pop" into existence when we break up H_2O molecules with hydrolysis; the atoms were parts of the molecular structure of the water molecule already!

This puzzle should not be as puzzling as it might seem. Aquinas holds that substances cannot be parts of other substances, and if an atom becomes a part of a molecule, *ipso facto* that atom ceases to be a substance. Nevertheless, Aquinas does not hold merely that the atom no longer exists. Rather, his claim is simply that the thing that was an atom substance *became* an atomic part of a molecule. For Aquinas, if the oxygen atom was a substance and remained a substance over the event described in OXYGEN, the atom would not compose that molecule but only become, at best, spatially co-located with the molecule. More accurately, as molecules are not separable things from the atoms that compose them, it would be that molecules are nothing more than spatial arrangements of atoms; i.e., molecules are not genuine material objects, but pseudo-objects.

Further, every substance exists in a determinate way, that is, as a member of a kind. If *oxygen atom* and *hemoglobin protein* each are a distinct kind, it is easy to see that the implicit assumption is likely empirically false. When incorporated into an oxyhemoglobin molecule, an oxygen atom is configured differently from when it is not incorporated into a protein. When, in respiration, oxygen atoms are incorporated into the hemoglobin in red blood cells, those atoms bond with the hemoglobin and their structure changes. A free-floating oxygen atom undergoes a series of changes when it bonded with hemoglobin, such that it comes to have different properties and structural relations to other things (e.g., the hemoglobin).[78] In becoming a part of a protein, then, the Thomistic account holds that the oxygen atom ceases to be a substance when it becomes a structural component of the substance that is the protein. It is no part of the account, *pace*

Jaworski's objection, that the oxygen atom is replaced with a completely identical look-alike when it bonds with hemoglobin; instead, the oxygen atom becomes quite different structurally and in its other properties at the moment it becomes a structural component of a protein.

Consider for a moment the simpler case of H_2O molecules. H_2O and O_2 are distinct molecules with distinct properties and powers. These two molecules have distinct properties and powers because they are distinct structurally. Further, their oxygen parts are distinct structurally as well: the oxygen in H_2O has two distinct covalent bonds with hydrogen, and dioxygen's atom parts have a double covalent bond. These kinds of bonds modify the distinct properties of the whole in a way that the whole has properties and powers distinct from other possible configurations, but it is also true that the oxygen atoms being so bonded are distinct in powers and properties from a single free-floating oxygen atom. Thus, an individual atom might react under certain conditions (hydrogen gas will react with O_2 in combustion), whereas in the molecule it does not so react (H_2O does not combust, even as a gas). If each constitutes a distinct kind of substance, it is not clear how molecular oxygen coming to compose a thing of a distinct kind has *not* ceased to be an instance of "molecular oxygen."

The only way in which the case of OXYGEN could be a counter-example to Aquinas' theory of composition is if it described a case where something came to compose another without any change of essential properties. First, the case does not plausibly show this, since it is an empirical matter whether there *is* such a natural kind as an "oxygen atom,"[79] and the atom in the case underwent a great deal of changes that contrast with the way that we ordinarily take an atom to be determinate when it is *not* part of those compounds. Second, it is not clear how such a case *could* disprove Aquinas' views without assuming what it intends to refute. Aquinas' views are that something only counts as an instance of material composition when the parts depend on the whole in a certain way. If the case was taken to describe merely extrinsic changes of spatial location among the atoms, Aquinas would just flatly deny that the atoms composed anything throughout the process. Instead, Aquinas' claim only entails that the atom, when it composes a molecular substance, is at best a derivative property-bearer in virtue of that substance (if it is the right integral part of the molecule to do so), and that any properties it has that result from being a part of a molecule would cease when it ceases to compose that molecule.

In fact, the puzzle of parts is actually not a puzzle about material composition, but a puzzle about what persists over substantial change, or the change of one substance into another substance (there would be *no* puzzle if there were no changes of parts). And Aquinas' perspective, bluntly, is that the wrong place to look for continuity in change is in what it is to be a substance. The right place to account for continuity in substantial change is in the relation among the substances that go into or come out of existence, while carefully distinguishing the material parts involved in the changes. The reason that H_2O can be split into oxygen and hydrogen by electrolysis is not that there was both molecular oxygen and a water molecule spatially co-located at the beginning of the process. Rather, the reason one can split out these two components is because water molecules are such that they can be decomposed into hydrogen and oxygen atoms.

What we should appeal to in order to account for continuity in substantial changes is the actuality or potentiality corresponding to the substance, and its integral parts', ability to undergo the relevant changes. Hydrogen and oxygen atoms are "potential parts" of water molecules because they are the proximate matter essential to being a thing of the kind "water molecule." H_2O does not exist without them. But it is not essential to hydrogen or oxygen atoms to constitute H_2O. Further, we can assume H_2O molecules have distinguishable integral parts such that we can identify the hydrogen and oxygen atomic parts, that is, the parts can have their own properties that they bear in virtue of being parts of that substance (the parts bear properties derivatively). Then we can say that, when the water molecule is decomposed in hydrolysis, there are two senses in which *the same* integral parts are what became one hydrogen and two oxygen atom substances.

On one hand, the matter *from which* they were constituted is just the same matter that came from the molecule because their coming into existence consists in an actualization of that potential—prime matter—that was formerly "in" the water molecule. They did not "pop" into existence from nowhere. On the other, the material integral parts of the water molecule were characterized as (derivative) property bearers that had their own internal structures and properties, in virtue of being essential parts of the water molecule. When the water molecule decomposes into the atoms, the new substances only need to lose those properties that were essential to the whole they composed. We can imagine, for example, the hydrogen atomic part being tagged with an isotope is a property that is accidental to both the molecule and the hydrogen. If the atomic parts bore any properties, which were unique to themselves as the parts, these would be accidental to the water molecule, and could come to characterize the new substances as well. There is nothing preventing the hydrogen atom substance, resulting from the decomposition of the molecule, from likewise being characterized by the isotope tagging.

It might be alleged that, in these cases, "scientists do not claim to be tracing powers, but things that bear the powers."[80] But Aquinas' view does not require thinking that all we track are only powers of oxyhemoglobin. Instead, some parts can bear properties insofar as a substance can have a property *in,* or in virtue of, one of its parts,[81] where the whole will be the subject even of accidental properties of the parts; as when, for example, I have the property of "being wounded" in virtue of my foot being wounded. And one of these integral parts can be such that it can become a numerically distinct substance, bearing that property in its own right, when it ceases to compose the whole. Atomic parts are just like this. There does not seem to be any empirical reason to think that, in tracking an oxygen atom through my body with a radioactive isotope, we need more than Aquinas' account can give: a certain isotope was introduced into my body, and, in virtue of a chemical change, came to characterize one of my atomic parts; that atomic integral part of me was tracked, in virtue of the radioactive properties now associated with that atomic part, and then the isotope part or the atomic part ceased to compose me, eventually.[82]

Conversely, Pasnau alleges there is the *inverse* problem: how to explain the fact that *exactly similar* properties persisting over substantial changes. His example is that the skin color of Socrates can be identical with the skin color of Socrates's corpse a moment after death, and "it seems nothing short of miraculous that, without that form, the corpse retains so many exactly similar accidents."[83] Here again it is important to note that, while it is true that Socrates' substantial form is that in virtue of which Socrates and his parts are characterized by essentially human properties, Aquinas' claim is *not* that no qualitatively similar kind of property or part, even an *exactly* similar property, could ever characterize anything else.[84] There is no reason that Socrates and Socrates' corpse could not be qualitatively identical in regard to skin color (and Aquinas explicitly affirms that they could be).[85] Aquinas' view only requires holding that Socrates' corpse is not the same substance as Socrates' body and that no essentially human properties "survive" Socrates' demise.

Some kinds of substances, given their proximate matter, have the potential to become other substances, whereas others have integral parts such that those parts can become substances in various ways. For that reason, organ transplants are not a metaphysical mystery. A heart, when detached and "on ice," is no longer a part of any particular human, although it is suited to become the heart of another person because of its physical characteristics; the heart can retain those properties, while detached, that did not derive solely from composing a human being. For example, muscular cells are still capable of moving under electric shocks and the whole heart is capable, when reattached, of pumping blood.[86] Nothing about Aquinas' position requires that the heart, when it is *in via* during a transplant, will not be a thing "suited to beat and pump blood."[87] All that is required, on Aquinas' metaphysics, is that my heart has undergone some intrinsic, essential change when it ceased to compose my body, such that it is a distinct thing when it is a part of me and when it is not. What we want to know is why, if it is a distinct thing, that the heart outside of my body has apparently very similar properties. On Aquinas' view, the answer is that my heart was just the kind of part that could become such a substance—acquire *that* kind of substantial form—when it was detached from my body, given the proximate matter of which human being from which it was taken was composed essentially included a heart.

In OXYGEN, the relation among the substance kinds to which the oxygen, the hemoglobin, and oxyhemoglobin belong explained the potentiality of the oxygen atom to become a part of oxyhemoglobin. Other things could not compose hemoglobin unless they both underwent some suitable external stimulus *and* were suitable to have potentialities to compose oxyhemoglobin. However, in fact, all of these conditions were met in OXYGEN. Thus, when actualized by some stimulus conditions, the proximity of the oxygen atom to the hemoglobin initiated a chemical reaction of oxidization of that protein, and oxyhemoglobin was composed from those other substances. Similarly, after it comes to compose oxyhemoglobin, that oxygen atom substance becomes an atomic part, typical to oxyhemoglobin and having a certain set of chemical bonds with the protein. Not every oxygen part of any molecule is of such a type as *this* oxygen part of oxyhemoglobin: not every oxygen part bonds with the particular geometry involved in an oxygen part's bond to the rest of the oxyhemoglobin molecule (i.e., an "end-on bent" configuration in bonding with the Fe_2 parts of that molecule).[88] Yet some other kinds of molecules could have oxygen in the same type of configuration as the oxygen parts of oxyhemoglobin.

An objector might point out that the homonymy principle entailed, for Socrates, that Socrates' eye is no longer an eye after he dies. The objector could then argue that we should not think that "atom" is being used homonymously of the atom substance and the atomic part of oxyhemoglobin: "These are 'atoms' in just the same sense, whether or not they compose anything! Whereas it might be plausible that 'eye' is a functional term for a certain kind of part, and we can imagine it ceases to apply to an eye when it is separated from its functional system, surely atoms are not a functional part of that sort."

In response, first, it seems likely to me that Aquinas and Aristotle treat the aforementioned "transplant" cases as the organ ceasing to have any biological properties merely because organ transplants were not then medically possible, and they did not know that an organ's cells do not immediately cease to be alive on detachment. Yet, even if we *were* committed to the homonymy principle for all parts, this can be plausible when we specify the nature of the kinds in question. If we assume that kinds are kinds *of substances*, and substances are those objects composing no other, then a kind such as "oxygen atom" cannot apply to the oxygen in oxyhemoglobin. An oxygen atom as a substance is, by stipulation, something that does not compose anything else, and the oxygen in hemoglobin clearly composes it. As an integral part that essentially characterizes molecules of the kind, the atomic part now belongs to the kind "oxyhemoglobin" in virtue of composing the whole.

The only thing further the objector might be looking for, as we saw with Jaworski, is *numerical identity* of the thing having the property, at every time it has the property (whether as a part or a whole). But numerical identity strikes me as something we cannot just *see*, because we characterize the substances (even for Jaworski) in terms of what is essential to them. For something to be numerically identical is to say that it underwent no change in what it is essentially. To say that the atom is "numerically identical" whether it composes the molecule or not entails both that the oxygen differs in *no* way when it composes oxyhemoglobin, and that oxyhemoglobin is not a kind of molecule. Both seem empirically false. The atoms in oxyhemoglobin have distinct shapes, properties, and powers from the oxygen atoms composing O_2. If oxyhemoglobin were not a kind of molecule, in addition, then the example could not undermine Aquinas' overall thesis, as the atom only gets spatially located very close to the other. Similarly, if the objector were to insist that numerically identical *properties* characterize the oxyhemoglobin and the oxygen atom that results from its decomposition, even though it is conceded that they are exactly similar, such a response would appear to beg the question against Aquinas that only substances (e.g., atoms and molecules) bear properties. The properties, to be "numerically identical," would have to be substances, in Aquinas' sense. If they were substances, however, they could not compose a material object without, necessarily, ceasing to be substances. Thus, it is not clear how to make sense of either attempt to cash out "numerical identity" in a way that does not beg the question against Aquinas' position.

Conclusion: Forms as Metaphysical Parts

The objections that Aquinas' hylomorphism cannot account for substantial change, consequently, are not compelling once we clarify clearly Aquinas' commitments and the assumptions implicit in the alleged counter-examples.

There is then no reason to think that denying the possibility of substances composing other substances as parts commits one to rank absurdities, as Aquinas' view of substantial change appears plausible and coherent.

Nevertheless, one further worry remains: despite avoiding the Charybdis of triviality in saying that substantial forms are actualities of substances, one might suspect that the account falls prey to the Scylla of "reifying" substantial forms and succumbing to an infinite regress problem. Indeed, in some contexts, Aquinas even countenances calling the human soul, a substantial form, a "particular thing" (*hoc aliquid*).[89] Yet, in the same way as we saw with properties, Aquinas need not think only substances are particulars—other parts of those composite wholes can be distinguished as particulars in a derivative sense, and so there is no contradiction in referring to substantial forms, or even some kinds of integral parts like human hands, as "particular things" as well. Substantial forms are of a distinct ontological kind from what they constitute, being actualities that answer to the kinds of potentialities involved in explaining what the xs constitute y.

As actualities *of* a composite of a determinate kind, it is essential to a substantial form that it compose the material whole it does, even in the (exceptional) case where the persistence conditions of a substantial form *could* be distinct from that of the material parts it characterizes, as in the case of the human soul persisting after the death of the human body.[90] Whether my soul could survive the demise of my material body, again, depends on what we think about the natural kind to which human beings belong, but Aquinas is clear that human souls essentially compose their compounds, as this is why he rejects transmigration of souls as metaphysically impossible.[91] As a living human being constituted by my soul, my soul is the actuality *of my physical, organic body*, not a separate particular thing in anything but a qualified sense, because distinguishing my soul from me, the "actualized thing," is only a sort of selective attention to one way in which I am actual.

With these qualifications, however, a "metaphysical part" is not supposed to involve a merely stipulative or *sui generis* sense of parthood, having no or a very tenuous similarity to the mereological "parthood" relation. All hylomorphists agree that a composite substance's form informs or characterizes every integral part of that substance, although the substantial form is neither an improper part nor an integral part of the substance.[92] Such a relationship has, as EJ Lowe pointed out, an analogue in the technical mereological notion of overlap. Lowe points out that a substantial form would not be either a proper or improper part of a material object. Instead, a substantial form wholly overlaps with every part of the material objects it informs.

An improper part is identical with the object it composes, but substantial forms are not identical with what they compose (in a material composite). Nor is the substantial form a proper part, "for there is no part of the [object] which it fails to overlap."[93] For y and z to "overlap" is if there exists an x such that x composes y and x composes z and $x \neq y \neq z$ (and x would be the "overlapping part" of y and z).[94] To say that a substantial form overlaps every other proper part of any substance, then, is to say that a substantial form is a part of every other part, as a "common part," of every (integral) proper part of the substance it informs. As the word "overlap" could perhaps lead to confusion, because of its ordinary English connotations, I will refer to substantial forms as "common parts" of substances. This unique mereological relation to the substance it informs allows a useful characterization of what it is to be a hylomorphist.

It is possible, in light of a notion of "overlap," to propose a model of the mereological role that substantial forms play in an account of material composition. "Overlap" can be understood to correspond to the way in which a form is a metaphysical, not an integral part; consequently, forms are parts of substances in a way that involves a distinct parthood relation from material parthood. Forms have a distinct kind of parthood relation to the material composites than those integral parts, but they are distinct from their composites and their relation to those composites is a reflexive, asymmetric, transitive relation.[95] A substantial form is nevertheless a special kind of part, since, given the way in which it is an actuality of a substance, it is intrinsic to every part of a substance and is characterized by a distinct kind of parthood from material parthood.[96] This is intended only to be a sketch,[97] where what follows should be taken as a model that represents the relation of substantial forms to their material composites:

> A "substantial form" is: [1] that part of a material whole which overlaps every other material part, [2] in virtue of whose overlap a material part necessarily composes that whole, and [3] identical neither with the whole nor any other proper part of it.

To illustrate, if Suzie the parrot is a whole, then Suzie's substantial form accounts for why her beautiful plumage and her beak and her atoms all compose her; these parts compose Suzie because her substantial form is a common part of each of her parts. If the substantial form did not overlap with a particular proper part, or if one of Suzie's parts ceases to be overlapped by her form, that part would not compose Suzie. Similarly, if Suzie has a part, such as her feather, that is part of another part, her wing, Suzie's substantial form is a common part of all of these.

Representing forms as common parts can be illuminating even where, as on Aquinas' metaphysics, the relation between forms and proper integral parts is stronger than the ordinary connotations of "overlap." For Aquinas, a given integral part x of y *does not exist* unless informed by y's substantial form. But the language of the model is still intelligible: for Aquinas, a form will account not only for why a part composes a substance, but also for the existence of that part, by composing or characterizing it. If there were a thing, a z, not being characterized (viz. "overlapped") by y's substantial form, that thing z would not be a part of the substance y at all. For example, my hand composes me because it is a thing informed by my substantial form, and if my form did not inform my hand, my hand would cease *both* to be a part of me and to be a functional hand part.

The model is incomplete in modeling Aquinas' commitments, but this incompleteness is intentional. Characterizing the model in this way makes it compatible with stronger or weaker relations between forms and substances, while nevertheless identifying commonalities among hylomorphic metaphysical theories. For example, not every hylomorphism holds that there can be only one substantial form in an object,[98] nor does every version posit prime matter as pure potentiality,[99] nor does every version hold that substantial forms account for the existence of all of the parts of substances they compose. And the model should be characterized such that it does not specify exactly the way in which the parts of an object come together "necessarily." On a restricted account of material composition, there are some conditions under which some things compose a material object. When those parts compose the whole, they do so, in one sense, *necessarily*: necessarily, whenever a composite whole is composed of parts, the parts compose it. (The further step to a claim that we should think those parts necessarily compose the whole they do involves assumptions that I will defend in the final chapter.) The virtue of this mereological model presented above is that the model can be used to functionally characterize any version of hylomorphism.

As the model allows us to represent commonalities among different hylomorphic theories of material composition, I will propose that to hold a hylomorphic theory of material composition is nothing more than positing something that has the same metaphysical role as substantial form mereologically construed. That is to say that a hylomorphic theory of material composition is a theory in which one thing accounts for the composition of parts in a material object in virtue of characterizing or being "in" every material proper part of that object.[100] In light of this characterization of substantial forms as common parts, the appeal to something that functions like a common part of an object in the context of material composition is not uncommon. For example, there are parallels in McDaniel's account of overlapping parts of possible worlds[101] and structural universals that overlap their instances,[102] Armstrong's account of universals and particulars,[103] and Van Inwagen's own solution to the Special Composition Question.[104] In the subsequent chapters, I will argue that this appeal to something functioning like a common part to account for composition in material objects is not coincidental.

In the next two chapters, I will begin to construct the positive argument that every coherent account of material composition is "restricted" such that there are composite objects, but two or more things do not necessarily compose a composite, and one substance cannot compose another substance as a proper part, is committed to substantial form as what account for instances of composite objects. To get to this conclusion will involve an important detour through medieval China. Not only did at least one Confucian philosopher, I argue, independently arrive at a hylomorphic account of material composition, but his arguments against his contemporaries, namely, Buddhists, are well-suited to position the final chapter. The position required to defuse my argument will be akin to a Buddhist view of the facts about material composition, and the reasons that a Confucian would want to accept hylomorphism instead of the Buddhist view of material objects are very similar to those that I will invoke to conclude that nothing other than substantial forms present a coherent picture of the way in which composition can be "restricted."

4

Zhu Xi's Metaphysics of Material Objects

In the past three chapters, I have argued for two theses. First, that accounts of composition which accept that a composite material whole might be composed of other material wholes are incoherent. Such accounts ultimately conflict with the assumption that, even though there are material composites, any two or more material things do not necessarily compose one. That is to say, that composition is "restricted." Second, that a substantial form is a wholly overlapping part of a material composite, in virtue of which that composite's material parts compose the whole necessarily, but identical with none of the other proper parts or with the whole. And a theory of material composition can be classified as "hylomorphic" if that theory posits things that correspond to this characterization.

Yet the claim that a material object's parts compose that material object *necessarily* needs clarification and, more importantly, defense. Particularly, I aim to show that there is a particular way in which any account of material composition that aims to be a "restricted" theory needs to affirm that the facts about what things compose what is going to be "necessary." For that position to be plausible, I need to set up a certain way of contrasting theories of material composition in terms of whether the facts about composition are "grounded" by the material objects themselves or something else. To this end, I will explore whether the medieval Chinese Confucian philosopher, Zhu Xi (朱熹) holds a hylomorphic theory of material composition that meets the criteria I have laid out for counting as "hylomorphic." Demonstrating that Zhu Xi holds such a theory requires exploring the ways in which he contrasts his own theory of material objects with that of his contemporaries, particularly Buddhists. This contrast will make clear, as I will subsequently argue in the final chapter, that every coherent restricted theory of material composition would need to affirm a similar contrast between the genuine material wholes and the "pseudo-objects" that would result from mereological Universalism.

The Metaphysical Landscape Painted by Zhu Xi

Zhu Xi was a prominent twelfth-century Confucian philosopher, famous for his systematization and development of the Confucian tradition in the area of metaphysics. I will largely bracket his wider philosophical commitments in order to focus on the way in which Zhu Xi's theory of material objects appeals to two basic principles: *li* 理, meaning literally "pattern" or "structure," and *qi* 气, playing the role of whatever gets so patterned or structured. I will leave these terms untranslated, only giving them a functional characterization, for two reasons: to avoid prejudicing the discussion with any particular reading and because the terms are technical terms of Zhu Xi's metaphysics.[1]

Zhu Xi explains the role of *li* in ways such as follows: "the 'nature' (*xing* 性) [of something] is only this *li*… the *li* which is naturally produced is 'nature'"[2] and "*li* is that norm which is every affair and things' norm."[3] Zhu Xi explicitly rejects that anything could lack a nature: "Nothing under heaven is such that there exists an object without a nature. In every case, if there is this object, then there is this nature. Without this object, then there is no such nature" and "it is because in everything there is this *li*, that among the things under heaven it is said there is nothing lacking nature."[4] Clearly, if nothing lacks a nature, and only whatever is characterized by *li* has a nature, then nothing (that exists) is uncharacterized by *li*. This entails that everything that exists is necessarily characterized by *li*. By contrast, *qi* is "by which something has complete visible shape, and *li* is that with which it is endowed."[5] And it is *qi* that receives and allows the expression of all the characteristic activities of each kind of object:

> That by which people are all produced is the union of *li* with *qi*. [While] *li* is surely vast and not able to be fathomed, if there were no *qi*, then although there were *li* it would have no place to anchor itself …. That people are able to speak and act, deliberate and form plans, this is all due to *qi* with *li* being in it.[6]

Qi thus seems to be what constitutes anything as *material*, having shape, and gets structured by *li*.

While in some passages, "affairs" (*shi* 事) are also said to be characterized by *li*, most often Zhu Xi only speaks of "things" (*wu* 物) and I will focus on things because Zhu Xi makes a clear modal claim about how things relate to *li*: "If there is this *li*, then there is this heaven and earth; if this *li* does not exist, then neither would heaven and earth, no people or objects…. Under heaven there is no *li* without *qi* or no *qi* without *li*."[7] The term "heaven and earth" refers to everything in the universe; when he qualifies over all the "objects" within the universe, he is emphatically qualifying over every *material* thing. Again, as there is no material thing *not* so characterized by *li-qi*, Zhu Xi therefore holds that every material object is *necessarily* characterized by both *li-qi*. This makes Zhu Xi's claims about "things" relevant to my aim of discussing his account of material composition in a way that his claims about "affairs" are not.

Finally, although I know of no claim *qi* could exist without *li* in his writings, Zhu Xi sometimes proposes that *li* and *qi* are also "things" (*wu* 物):

> What are called "*li*" and "*qi*"—these are clearly two [separate] things. It is only when we see them in terms of [material] things, the two things [*li* and *qi*] are mixed together, and one cannot separate [them] and [place] each in its place. Yet, there is no harm if one takes each of the two things as a [distinct] thing. If we see them in terms of *li*, there already is the *li* for the existence of a thing even before there is [that particular] thing. Yet, there is only *li*. It is not that there actually is this thing.[8]

In light of the prior modal claims about material objects, these initially puzzling claims can be interpreted clearly. What Zhu Xi is saying is that, while we can describe both *li* and *qi* as "things," this should not mean *material* things, as these principles would not constitute a material thing in their own right. The legitimate reason that we might refer to these principles as "things" is to indicate the way in which we can distinguish them from what they characterize.

The "Priority" of *Li* to *Qi*

A central interpretative question that arises in the scholarship concerns the relation between *the way in which* these principles are supposed to account for the existence of material things. This is because Zhu Xi makes claims about their relationship that appear to conflict. At times, he rules out what seems to be a temporal priority of one to the other by saying that there is no relevant *before* or *after* in characterizing how these constitute a material thing: "fundamentally there is no before or after," he says, as "*li* is without physical form, and *qi* is unrefined and has impurities."[9] Other similar instances are where Zhu Xi qualifies that there was not first *li* of the material things and then afterward the *qi* of the material universe, which indicate the relationship of priority is temporal. Nevertheless, at other times he claims *li* is indeed prior to *qi* in a non-temporal respect. In a representative statement, Zhu Xi appeals to a distinction that involves a technical term "inference" (*tui* 推), claiming that "if it is necessary to speak of inferring [conclusions from] their origins (其所从来), then it is necessary to say that *li* exists first. And *li* is not a thing, but rather, when it exists, is in the midst of *qi*. If there were no *qi*, then *li* would have no place in which to inhere."[10] "Origins," given what Zhu Xi has already indicated, cannot mean the *temporal* origin of things.

The sense in which *li* is that from which one can "infer conclusions from their origins" consequently needs to be specified. As the context of "inference" is reasoning, the initial way to interpret the statement is merely epistemic: *li* is what serves as or which we can appeal to as a basis for inferences or reasoning about things. Krummel gives such an interpretation:

> The priority here is not temporal but logical or conceptual: while involved in *qi*, *li* as an intrinsic pattern emerges in the shape of *qi* for the comprehension of the rational mind. We have to bear in mind however that this priority is not ontological. The logical or conceptual priority of *li* over *qi* as the determinant of the determined, cognized by the rational (*li*-bearing) mind, certainly does not have to be equated with the ontological transcendence of *li* as a distinct *thing* ordering the concrete world of *qi* from afar akin to ... a Platonist *Idea*.[11]

Krummel seems to reason that, as Zhu Xi thinks that *li* is not a separate thing from the things it characterizes, then the *li* of a material thing is not a subsistent Platonic Idea in addition to the material thing it characterizes. This, Krummel concludes, requires that *li* exists only in some mind-dependent sense.

As we have already seen, the first premise of the argument is false. Zhu Xi does not even shrink from calling *li* or *qi* a "thing"—assuming that we make clear that we are *not* using "thing" in the sense of "material thing." And it is not clear that making merely *any* distinction between *li* and *qi* as distinct "things" from the material thing they characterize would imply that one can only refer to *li* as a thing if and only if *li* were a Platonic, subsistent Idea. Further, even if it were true that *li* is not a "thing" in any sense of the word, the argument has an additional false premise that stops the inference altogether. Given Zhu Xi's modal claims that things, and specifically material things, cannot *exist* without *li* characterizing them, the conclusion does not follow unless Zhu Xi were presuming that material things do not really exist in any mind-independent way. Zhu Xi flatly denies that kind of view; he is starkly a realist about the existence of objects in general: "Heaven and Earth are things with existence in their own right; they are not merely products of our minds."[12] Krummel's interpretation does not, therefore, succeed in pushing us in the direction of a "merely epistemic" interpretation of *li*.

Zhu Xi then means to say that the fact that *li* characterizes something is not such that it would be, for example, mind-dependent, because things would not exist without *li*. And Zhu Xi's very use of the word *li*, meaning "pattern" or "structure" (such as the pattern of veins in a leaf), rather than a word indicating our concepts for or talk about such patterns, highlights this extra-mental sense. There are many examples, in fact, where *li* clearly has an extra-mental connotation.[13] That is to say that *li* serves as a basis for inferring or reasoning about objects *because* the things we are reasoning about would not exist, nor have the natures they do, without *li*. Zhu Xi's theory of reasoning and inference therefore relies critically on appeal to *li* as both the origin and aim of our rational inquiry.[14] Zhu Xi's account of what it is to engage in rational inquiry does not say that such investigation aims merely at investigation of language or our concepts about the world, but rather is described as an investigation or study of "things" (*gewu* 格物). Yet he also speaks of investigation of "affairs" as well.[15] In the context of "affairs," one is usually seeking the *li* that would give us knowledge of right moral behavior, and these are facts as to how the natures of human beings relate to right or wrong action (e.g., the fact that humans possess the virtues naturally makes it appropriate for them to act virtuously).[16] Zhu Xi characterizes *li*, when it is the goal or origin of such processes of rational investigation, as the "reason by which things are thus (所以然之故)."[17]

Specifically, Zhu Xi uses *li* as either a synonym for the "nature" of a thing: "nature is just a certain *li* … the *li* [something has] from birth is what is called 'nature.'"[18] For a thing to have a nature is then not such that the nature is imposed on the material thing by our conceptual schemes, but that it characterizes that thing mind-independently, since the material thing would not exist without having such a nature. In addition, *li* is invoked as that in virtue of which an object has characteristic "function." These "functions" are, for example, the ear's ability to hear, or the eye's ability to see; each of these characteristic functions of things result from the nature of those things, namely, *li*.[19] To have a nature, or be characterized by *li*, therefore entails that those things characterized by natures belong to something very similar to a natural kind. This is also to say that anything which is characterized jointly by *li* and *qi*, then *necessarily* constitutes a material thing, since to be a thing that has *qi* and a determinate nature is to be a material thing.

Li is clearly what allows us to classify or separate individual instances of things or affairs, and many interpreters draw from this an implication that has serious implications for what Zhu Xi could mean by attributing "natures" to things. Chen Lai interprets Zhu Xi to mean that we appeal to *li* to explain something as we might appeal to a physical law or moral standard in order to explain an instance.[20] Stephen Angle seems to share this way of reading Zhu

Xi, as he claims that *li* is best understood as "the set of background conditions that make our cosmos possible ... the complete network of interdependencies that makes possible not just our physical world, but also a fully flourishing, harmonious cosmos. It is thus more vast but also weaker than physical law .... Cosmic Pattern limns what can and should happen for all things to fit together."[21] What these interpretations deny is that Zhu Xi's claims that *li* is the "nature" of what it characterizes should be understood in an *essentialist* sense. When he says that the material things could not exist without being characterized by a nature, what he means is that, necessarily, if there are material things, then those things have characteristic functions or identifying characteristics. But these characteristics are not such that the things *essentially* have them. Instead, those characteristics follow from *li* understood as (roughly speaking) the conditions under which physical things could possibly exist, not from facts about what is essential to those physical things themselves. A "nature" is merely a way to describe that way in which material things or affairs can be divided into kinds depending on their relation to the (extra-mental) facts about those background conditions or moral/physical laws.

By contrast, others read Zhu Xi as holding an essentialist account of *li*, where the material things are essentially, or necessarily, characterized by the natures that they have. JeeLoo Liu endorses this kind of interpretation of *li*. She argues that Zhu Xi's *li* is not merely supervenient on some quantity of *qi*: "principle [i.e., *li*] depends on *qi* for its manifestation, yet it is not determined by *qi*... principle determines *qi*'s realization and operation. This determination is also asymmetrical: principle is the determinant while *qi* is the determined."[22] The notion of "determination" that Liu employs is not always clear. She holds that characterization by *li* makes it that things have the properties and powers that they do,[23] that *li* and *qi* account for material composition,[24] and she assimilates Zhu Xi's notion of *li* to the contemporary notion of the "structure" of material objects.[25] The appearance of an essentialist understanding of *li* is confirmed, I think, given the contrast of "determination" with "supervenience," where the latter is a relation between two relata such that a change in one of the relata necessitates a change in the other relata. Supervenience is not an "internal" relation, as the relation is not usually conceived to hold because of the intrinsic features of the relata. If "determination" is supposed to be an internal relation, then Liu is offering an essentialist reading of Zhu Xi. And, further, the reading would allow us to count Zhu Xi as a hylomorphist.

Li: Part/Universal, One/Many?

The interpretations of the way in which *li* characterizes material objects can be broadly characterized as either one on which *li* is essential to an individual material thing (and its parts), as opposed to one in which *li* is not essential to the material things and it is only necessary, in some generic sense, that *li* characterize them. The latter interpretation might be confused, however, for a further controversial claim, prevalent among certain schools of thought, that Chinese philosophy is generally committed to a "process ontology," resembling in this respect the thought of A.N. Whitehead.[26] Personally, I see no good reason to interpret Zhu Xi as holding a process ontology.[27] But making that interpretative case is not relevant to my arguments in this chapter. The claim that all the material things in the world are fundamentally processes or events is not identical with, or entailed by, the claim that the material things in the world do not have their properties essentially.

The latter distinction in fact cuts across the range of possible process ontologies. There is much disagreement among process ontologists, but a division has been proposed between a "particularist" process ontology in which the processes are concrete particulars and a "non-particularist" process ontology in which the processes are akin to "stuff" that permeates spacetime and can be multiply located, concrete but non-particular.[28] Such a division roughly corresponds to positions on whether processes are *essentially* particulars, as both sides agree that processes are "material things" in the sense of being concrete. It is thus unhelpful to approach the issue of interpreting Zhu Xi's metaphysics of *li* and its claims about what way the material things have their natures by answering the question whether those material things are fundamentally identical with events or processes.

The difference to which I will draw attention is not between process and substance, but between "constituent" and "relational" ontologies. The latter ontologies share an agreement that things fall into distinct ontological categories, such as substance and property, or universal and particular, or concrete and abstract. What differentiates the views is that the constituent ontologist maintains that the particulars, or the substances, or the concrete things can have the things of the other category or categories *as parts*, such that the universals or abstract objects or properties can "bear some quasi-mereological relation to" that object or particular.[29] By contrast, the relational ontologist holds that, while universals or properties or abstract objects are *exemplified* by their particulars, it would be a mistake to consider this kind of relation (which I am here calling "exemplification") as something resembling parthood.[30]

Both of these views can agree that properties or universals might be *essential* to what they characterize, but there is an important difference between characterizing something as an essential *part* versus *having a relation to* something essentially. Pretend that I am a concrete particular, having the essential property of being "able to laugh." On the constituent ontology, if some property is essential to a concrete particular, it will be an essential part of that particular. The property of being "risible" is then something similar to a part of me. By contrast, on relational ontologies, for a particular to have a property essentially is for that particular to relate to a universal essentially, not to have that universal as a part. The property of being "risible" would be something to which I am related, but not in such a way that the risibility is a part of me.

The relevant difference lies in the way that each account explains what it is for two particulars to have "the same" property. On the constituent analysis, for two property-bearers to share a property would be for them to share a numerically-identical part. Yet constituent ontologists typically reject this possibility. If another concrete particular person comes by and we share a joke, laughing all the while, what we have (on the constituent analysis) are "exactly similar" properties of risibility, but we would not share that property as a common part of us both. On the relational analysis, both my concrete friend and I are exemplifying exactly the same universal and we share not only a similar property, but the same property. Hylomorphists are constituent ontologists, not relational ones, because it is essential to the substantial form, which is a particular, that it composes the substance it does. For this reason, substantial form has to be particularized in the same way that properties for a constituent ontologist can only belong to particular bearers and (since they make something to be a substance) are necessarily not sharable as a common part among distinct substances.

Radical Monism

The differences between constituent and relational ontology highlight a way in which we can decide among the aforementioned interpretations of Zhu Xi's metaphysics: we can determine whether there is any sense in which it is essential to *li* that it belongs to any particular material object. And this task is easier to do than it might sound, because Zhu Xi is committed to the claim that *li* is "one" in all its instances—"*li* is one, the instances many" (*li yi fen shu* 理一分殊)[31]—which is a dictum he inherits from his philosophical predecessors, the Cheng (程) brothers. Recall I have already shown that Zhu Xi affirms it is necessary for the existence (and nature) of a material thing that it be characterized by *li*, and that both of the interpretations agree that, necessarily, if something is characterized by both *li-qi*, then that thing constitutes a material thing. In order to show that Zhu Xi is a relational ontologist, and not a hylomorphist, one would therefore only need to show that *li* characterizes no *qi* necessarily.

One might think that, since *li* constitutes the natures of things, and there is only one *li*, then Zhu Xi must hold that there is necessarily only *one* material thing. Russell Hatton has argued for just this conclusion, contrasting Zhu Xi's *li* over and against substantial forms:

> the substantial form is to some extent responsible for similarities among different kinds of things, as is *li*. But the specific difference of man's substantial form is unique to men, i.e., rationality. And it is this which ultimately makes a man the kind of thing he is and different from all other kinds of things. *Li*, however, contains nothing that is unique to any species. *Li*… is essentially the same in everything. The *li* of a man contains nothing that is not found in the *li* of a horse, a tree, or a pen …. If [Zhu Xi] can be said to recognize the existence of "kinds" (i.e., species) in the Aristotelian sense, then they must be said to be due to [*qi*].[32]

Hatton then concludes that Zhu Xi must also deny the possibility of substantial change:

> It can in fact, be argued that for [Zhu Xi] all differences are differences in degree among things which are composed of *li*, which is essentially the same in all, and *[qi]*, which is continuously variable in various aspects. Thus it might be said, that the only differences [Zhu Xi] recognizes are accidental differences and that there is no place for substantial differences in the Aristotelian sense within his system. Therefore, there is no place for substantial form. Thus, *li* cannot be substantial form.[33]

That is, if Zhu Xi holds that every change is merely an accidental modification of the one material particular that exists, then Zhu Xi is a radical monist, because the world composes (apparently essentially) one material thing. And many of the objections to a hylomorphic reading of Zhu Xi are implicitly or explicitly accompanied by claims that he believes that there exists only one material object.[34]

Hatton's conclusion, however, is too quick on a number of fronts. The first is that there is a problem with Hatton's inference from a lack of different forms to the denial of substantial change. A hylomorphist has no problem with accommodating the possibility that world, for example, were entirely populated with bunny rabbits and no other material substances. If the rabbits were able to reproduce in this strange world, leaving aside the dark specter of cannibalism, there would be no problem in accounting for a change of the substances when the mother rabbit gives birth to offspring—a new bunny substance would be generated from the mother's material parts. Radical monism only follows on an additional assumption that the "one *li*" is essential to *qi* itself, such that there would be no respect or way in which *qi* could constitute numerically different material things.

Further, there is textual evidence Zhu Xi rejects implications of radical monism. In his *Renshuo* (仁说), a short treatise on the Confucian virtue of *ren* or "humanness," Zhu Xi proposes that *ren* is a kind of "love." An interlocutor asks: "Some say that love is not [*ren*], and regard the unity of all things and the self as the substance of [*ren*].... If what you say is correct, are they all wrong?"[35] The interlocutor seems to be citing the views of a contemporary of Zhu Xi's, the Confucian Yang Shi (杨时), whose views on *ren* seem to involve a version of monism. Yang was, like Zhu Xi, a student of the Cheng brothers, but he interpreted the claim from the Cheng brothers that "*li* is one, instances are many," as the claim that everything composes one entity, the Dao.[36] Zhu Xi criticizes Yang's interpretation of *ren*, arguing that *ren* is only the unity of love among all things, not that all things compose one object: "To talk about [*ren*] in general terms of the unity of things and the self will lead people to be vague, confused, neglectful, and make no effort to be alert. The bad effect—and there has been—may be to consider other things as oneself .... [This] is wrong."[37] His criticism that metaphysical monism will lead to a confused moral doctrine indicates Zhu Xi believes that metaphysical monism is false.

Moreover, if Hatton were right that Zhu Xi is a radical monist, this undermines Hatton's objections to reading Zhu Xi as a hylomorphist. Since the world formed one material particular, it would not be problematic if Zhu Xi thought there was only one substantial form or that there was only one species of thing. That would be exactly what *should* follow for a hylomorphism. That is to say that, the radical monist interpretation assumes that *li* characterizes all of the *qi* necessarily or essentially, and only no *particular* bit of *qi* necessarily—but this is exactly what would differentiate a constituent ontology reading of Zhu Xi from a relational one: if *li* itself belongs essentially to *qi* in some sense, then Zhu Xi is a constituent ontologist. Ironically, then, showing Zhu Xi to be a hylomorphist would be easy if he were a radical monist.

Qi Alone as "Difference Maker" in a Relational Ontology

In order to demonstrate that Zhu Xi is a relational ontologist, and so that *li* is not a part of material things, others focus on the way in which Zhu Xi's *qi* apparently accounts for the distinct kinds of material things. Bryan van Norden calls attention to this fact and infers that not only does *qi* account for the spatiotemporal individuation of material things, but also for their "speciation," i.e., the difference among the kinds of material things there are:

> it is tempting to assimilate the relationship between [li] and *qi* to the relationship between Aristotle's form and matter. However, this comparison is deeply misleading, because there are distinct Aristotelian forms for distinct kind of things.... In contrast, there is only one [li], but it manifests itself differently in different endowments of *qi*. In the technical language of metaphysics, we can say that *qi* is responsible for *speciation* and *individuation*. In other words, [li] is one and the same in everything, so *qi* accounts for the fact that there are different kinds of things, and for the fact that there are numerically distinct individuals.[38]

Lokuang puts the point simply: "The differences of things do not come from principle but from [*qi*]."[39] There are other commentators that repeat these same conclusions.[40]

Zhu Xi gives some analogies of how *li-qi* relate to objects that lend themselves to an interpretation on which it is *qi* that differentiates what kinds of material things result from being characterized by *li*. One such analogy is that *li* is like light shining through translucent material; "[Zhu Xi was asked:] 'is it not the case that wood is itself wood, and fire is itself fire? Then how is it that their *li* is one?' [Zhi Xi replied:] 'It is just like this light: the light is the same whether shining on an ink pot cover or on the ink.'"[41] In another case, citing approvingly a Buddhist saying, Zhu Xi claims that *li* is distinctly present in many particular objects while remaining the same one *li* because "*li* is not cut into pieces, but it is instead as if one moon shines in ten thousand rivers."[42] In both cases, the sense of the analogy is clear: *li* in itself is unaffected by being present in *qi*. Rather, the same *li* can be present in each instance without diminution or change in *li*, even though the same *li* is present in various *qi* constitutes different material things.

Most strikingly, Zhu Xi explicitly claims such that is not essential to *li* that it compose *qi*. On one hand, *li* is neither created nor destroyed when the particular material things it characterizes are created or destroyed: "The nature of man and things is nothing but [*li*] and cannot be spoken of in terms of integration and disintegration. That which integrates to produce life and disintegrates to produce death is only [*qi*]."[43] On the other hand, he claims that *li* would exist even though a particular material object, or all material objects (Heaven and Earth 天地), were to cease to exist.[44] It would not be essential to *li* that it characterizes the material universe if *li* could continue to exist after the material universe ceases to exist.

However, in fact, none of these texts entails as a general result that *li* essentially characterizes nothing, or, only contingently characterize all of the material things that exist. The reasoning is too quick from the analogies to the conclusion that Zhu Xi must be saying that *li*, in some *particular sense* of *li*, is not essential to material objects. For example, it could be that distinct kinds of things have distinct *li*, and that particular kinds of *li* essentially characterize their respective kind of material thing. That is, there is an implicit assumption in all of these cases is that Zhu Xi is a relational ontologist rather than a constituent one, because it does not follow from the fact that *qi* can instantiate *li* in different respects, constituting distinct species of material thing, that the only way this can be accounted for is by something like an exemplification relation with one and the same universal *li*. Instead, what we need to determine is whether *li* is "one" in the sense of being *numerically the same* "universal" that characterizes all of its instances (the material things) or whether *li* could be one in some other sense. Only if the first of these readings of the "oneness" of *li* were true would Zhu Xi turn out to be a relational ontologist.

In comparing Zhu Xi's metaphysics to that of Aristotle, interpreters often make an assumption, explicitly or implicitly, that form always accounts for *differences* among substances. But there is no simple answer as to whether form accounts for what "differentiates" one substance from another, as such a role would depend upon a context where we identify relevant ways one object could be similar to or distinct from other objects. While it is true that a particular substantial form accounts for why some particular substance is a member of a kind, it is also true, within a given species, that form, rather than matter, accounts for what is similar among members of the species. Thus, for example, all humans are humans because they have a species-specific kind of substantial form. Each instance of a substantial form does not require that each form be of a distinct species; Socrates and Plato have distinct souls, but are each an instance of the human species.

It is also often assumed, perhaps as a consequence of the assumed role that form plays in accounting for distinct species of substance, that a hylomorphic theory of material objects *necessarily* entails the existence of more than one essence, species, or natural kind of material object. Nevertheless, such a conception of the functional role of form is inadequate to distinguish hylomorphism from other theories. Form can account for similarities among objects in many different cases. For example, if there were only one material object, then form would not differentiate one object from another (because there would be no others). Alternatively, if there were only one essence, species, or kind of object with many instances, forms would not distinguish one species of object from another. All that is necessary for hylomorphism is that one be committed to material composition occurring in terms of something functionally identical with a substantial form—a common part of a material object, neither identical with the whole or those parts, which necessarily constitutes the parts with which it overlaps as composing that whole.

Even further, on the Thomistic version of hylomorphism, it is quite reasonable to say that *any* similarities among substances are similarities in virtue of form rather than of matter. Substances can be similar not only in sharing a species, but because they are members of the same genus; e.g., humans and horses are similar because both are mammals or animals. Genus-level similarities of these sorts exist in virtue of the form of these distinct substances, not in virtue of their prime matter. Further, it is not precise enough to say that similarities in the matter of material objects are attributable to their prime matter. Similarities in virtue of proximate matter—such as cells—are more properly grounds for similarities among substances—say, humans and other animals—because those are parts and *can have properties or powers* whereas prime matter is not a power but "pure potentiality" (as explained in the prior chapter). Therefore, it is too quick to claim that *li* cannot have an ontological role like Aristotelian form *merely* because *li* accounts for similarities among objects and *qi* their differences.[45]

What needs to be shown is that *li* cannot in any sense be a particular, such that (particular) *li* essentially belongs to *qi*. But there are two ways that this can be the case. The first is that *li* is a unitary universal with "graded" instances or that *"li"* refers to a set of universals. (In Chinese, recall, nouns such as *li* can either refer to individuals or be "mass-count" nouns, like "water" in English.) I will show that these two options do not make as much sense of Zhu Xi's wider metaphysical commitments as a third option: *li* is instead a collective name for particular *li* as well as a general sense in which anything can be characterized by *li*. On this final option, Zhu Xi would be a constituent ontologist and, in virtue of the claims we have already seen him make about material things, a hylomorphist.

Li as Unitary Universal or Collection of Universals

The first of these readings of Zhu Xi's claim that *li* is one because it is a "unitary universal" would be to hold that *li* is one universal, and those things exemplifying the universal share one and the same essence across all instances. The only differences among the instances are such that they exemplify that universal in different respects or degrees, attributable to some fact about their *qi*. At first glance, this is the most natural way to read many of Zhu Xi's analogies with the moon shining on many rivers, or the same light both shining in the ink or on the pot cover.

Further, in keeping with a common way most understand of universals or abstract objects, *li* is not supposed to be casually efficacious because, in many contexts, Zhu Xi claims that *li* itself does not "move" or engage in activity.[46] In a well-known analogy, he illustrates the way that *li* relates to movements and changes of the universe:

> If *qi* is active, then *li* is also active, the two always depend on each other, and in no case can they be separated. [*Li*] is like a person, and movement and rest like a horse, so that the horse is what carries a person, and a person is what steers the horse. The horse goes out and comes in, and the person is also what goes out and comes in.[47]

Then, Zhu Xi applies the metaphor in context to explain how *li* acts in the universe: "Yang is active and yin is tranquil. In these it is not [*Taiji*, or Heavenly *Li*] (太极) that acts or remains tranquil, It is simply that there are the [*li*] of activity and tranquility. [*Li*] is not visible; it becomes visible through yin and yang. [*Li*] attaches itself to yin and yang as a man sits astride a horse. As soon as yin and yang produce the [different types of *qi*, i.e., the 'Five Agents'], they are confined and fixed by [material nature] and are differentiated into individual things each with its nature."[48]

When Zhu Xi wants to indicate the oneness of *li* among all things, Zhu Xi refers to "heavenly *li*" (*tianli* 天理) or *Taiji*/*Wuji* (太极/无极).[49] And he explains that every material object "possesses" (*ju* 具) that one *li* of everything, *Taiji*. Even though individual material things come into existence through various agents or causes, all of their *qi* "receives" (*bingshou* 禀受) the oneness of *li*, which leads to a "material nature" (*qizhizhixing* 气质之性) of that thing that results from this: "the material character of things is a result of [physical forces like *yin-yang*] and the nature [of things] is just the whole state of *Taiji*. When we are speaking of 'material nature', then this whole state [of *Taiji*] descends into the midst of the material character [of things], but there is not another separate nature."[50] The statement that there is no other "nature" is ambiguous, however, since it is taken as a synonym for "*li*," Zhu Xi could mean (1) "there is no other nature for any object to instantiate," which would be to say everything has the same essence, or (2) "there is no other Nature," meaning only that everything, in whatever respect they have a more specific nature, is in possession of *Taiji* itself. We see the ambiguity clearly in a statement like this as well: "to discuss the 'Nature of Heaven and Earth' is to speak merely of *li*; to discuss 'material nature' is to speak merely of *li* and *qi* mixed together."⁵¹ Passages like these passages, then, do not unambiguously imply there is only one nature for everything.

And, to the contrary, Zhu Xi also notes that there are divisions within *li* itself. "There is only this one *li*, but it can be divided into four sections, or again into eight, or again we could keep going and divide it even more finely"⁵²; "There is just one *li* of the Way, but to consider it in division, so as to speak of seasons, and then there is spring, summer, fall and winter… or, to speak of it in terms of the day, there would be dawn, daylight, twilight, and night."⁵³ For example, in the Cheng brothers' dictum, there is an ambiguity: the word *fen* 分, which I translated above as "instance," also has the meaning "part."⁵⁴ We could translate the dictum as "*li* is one but is partaken in many ways." Each of the analogies is also ambiguous, as, while the moon itself could not become part of a river, or a light source become part of a translucent medium, Zhu Xi could hold that the *light* or the *image of the moon* is the analogue of *li*. But then these analogies point to *li* as a particular, because one might think it is the case that one light or one image of the moon becomes a "part" of what is produced in the sense of producing a color or a reflection.

Nevertheless, there is a much more serious problem aside from the textual issues. The problem is that the "unitary universal" reading of the oneness of *li* will again, as with Hatton's radical monism, result in Zhu Xi being a constituent ontologist. A "unitary universal" needs to be one such that, necessarily, when something exemplifies it, that thing exemplifies the universal; also, it needs to be such that each thing exemplifies that identical universal—the universal is "shared" among the instances. But, as we have seen, Zhu Xi is committed to the fact that the *way in which* that universal is exemplified differs among the instances. Van Norden assumed such a characterization implicitly in saying that *qi* accounts for "speciation," but Hatton develops the idea explicitly, arguing that there is one *li* because there is only one set of powers that are, as it were, essential to every object. Differences arise because the *qi* of each object determines ways in which these powers are differently actualized or expressed.⁵⁵

Alongside Hatton and Van Norden, Chen Lai also interprets Zhu Xi to hold that the one *li* is differentiated among many material objects insofar as *qi* accounts for numerically distinct instantiation of *li*, as each object receives that same *li* in a distinct "subject." As he puts it, "the continuous *Taiji* is one, but the individually possessed *Taiji* is many."⁵⁶ Chen Lai then similarly proposes that differences among objects, as for example, between human beings and other things, are on account of receiving this one *li* differently into different "material natures." These natures limit this *li* so that each receives the same *li* but in different qualities of less or more.[57] Unlike Hatton, however, Chen Lai does not apparently assume that exemplifying the universal involves a particular exemplifying a given collection of properties and powers.

The fact that Zhu Xi is committed to there being different exemplifications of the one *li* is expressed in a mantra he repeats in various formulations: "people and things have natures that are fundamentally the same; it is simply that their endowments of *qi* differ."[58] What is problematic about these claims is that, if the "unitary universal" reading of this mantra were correct, it would entail that *li essentially* characterizes *qi*. This is because different degrees of *qi* are taken to contribute to different *degrees* of exemplifying the universal. A certain dog "better exemplifies" canine nature, we might think, because it better exemplifies essential properties of that nature. If being able to breathe is essential to canines, then the fact my dog has asthma is one way in which he does not "fully" exemplify the universal.

In order to say that a universal can be instantiated to degrees requires there needs to be something that unites the degrees (the essence of what it is to exemplify that universal) and something in virtue of which they will be different. Whatever that is, it will need to be such that it has some intrinsic character that *essentially* determines those different degrees of exemplification, so that there is an internal relation between the universal and its degreed instances; it would be problematic for the reading (given Zhu Xi's other commitments) if it would be merely contingent that a thing exemplified *li* to a higher degree. Clearly, on this "unitary universal" reading, what is playing the role of the thing to which *li* essentially belongs is *qi*. Otherwise, the "pure" or "turbid" *qi* of a material thing should not contribute to exemplifying the universal to a higher or a lower degree. Since there is only one *li*, and it is exemplified in higher degrees by more "pure" *qi*, that seems to imply that the thing with *qi* to the highest degree is a "perfect instance" of what it is to be characterized by *li*. This makes *li* similar to the one natural kind.

In addition, the reading will imply a constituent ontology, rather than a relational one, because the "material nature" of those objects differs in degree and the account is therefore admitting some particular sense in which *the way that the qi gets characterized by*, or exemplifies, *li* is not something it shares in common with other material instances. Instead, as each instance is also supposed to be numerically distinct in virtue of the individual *qi* of a material thing, then two such objects of similar *qi* are going to occupy an exactly similar "rank" of exemplification. This is, in fact, how Zhu Xi characterizes what differentiates the nature of humans from various "lower" animals. He claims that *li* is like the light of the sun and moon. In a clear, open field, it is seen in its entirety. Under a mat-shed, however, some of it is hidden.... Man possesses the [*li*] that can penetrate this obstruction, whereas in birds and animals, though they possess this nature [*xing* 性], it is nevertheless restricted by their physical structure... only the obstruction to a particular part of their nature is penetrated, just as light penetrates only a crack.[59]

Thus, if we accept a "unitary universal" reading of Zhu Xi's claims, his view would be equivalent to a constituent ontologist who believes that there is only one natural kind of material object.

The way to maintain the commitment to Zhu Xi being a relational ontologist, rather than a constituent one, is to return to Zhu Xi's claims that *li* is distinct. Instead of reading this claim as the view that *li* differs in virtue of different qualities of *qi* as such, one can modify the reading to conceive of *li* as essentially distinct in kind. This is to say that *li* would be a collection of distinct universals, in the way the properties "blue" and "charged" can be plausibly thought to be universals whose character is essentially different. David Tien echoes the sentiment of this reading: "since different things manifest different *li*... this implies that there is more than one *li*, or at least that the universal *li* is multi-faceted, which... amounts to much the same as saying that there is more than one *li*."[60] On such a reading of *li* as a collection of universals, speaking of a thing as being characterized by *li* in a general sense would only indicate that, if we did not refer to any specific "universal," that the thing is being characterized by *some universal or another*. Then it would be contingent whether any particular material thing was characterized by any specific universal.

However, for the same reason that the first reading was intuitive and natural in light of the texts, it cannot be the correct reading of Zhu Xi's metaphysics. Quite simply, Zhu Xi is very direct in stating: "the [*li*] received by things is precisely in the same degree as the [*qi*] received by them."[61] This would be inexplicable if *li* were not essentially unified in some way as to constitute degreed instances. Further, he employs quite extensively the implication that *li* is found according to different degrees. He explains differences among natural kinds by appeal to such facts. A student, for instance, is confused on the way in which it could be that everything "possesses" (*ju* 具) the one *li* of everything (*Taiji* 太极), and whether that entails that every material thing is therefore in possession of the fullness of *li*. Zhu Xi responds:

> To say that it is wholly [possessed] is possible, to say that it is partially [possessed] is also possible. When speaking of *li*, then nothing does not have its fullness. But, when speaking of *qi*,... [things] cannot be without partiality. For this reason,

[some thinkers] thought that the nature of some things approached closer to that of human nature, as cats are similar in kind to infants. Wen Gongji kept in his house a cat, and there was indeed still a great difference between them! There are thus in the world things with natures similar to that of humans.[62]

Zhu Xi appears here to account for kinds of things (animals, plants, humans) precisely by appeal to each kind of thing being some degree of *li* instantiation. Zhu Xi even uses the term "kind" (*lei* 类) in this passage in such a way as to imply that each is constituted by a distinct share in that one *li*. Similarly, in other contexts, Zhu Xi is explicit in accepting a qualified claim that animals and humans do not share the same nature. In the *Mencius*, Mencius attacks statements made by his opponent Gaozi that seem to imply humans and animals share the same nature (6A2). Zhu Xi comments on this passage:

> Whereas men receive the fullness of *li*, when speaking of [other non-human things], then they only receive it partially …. Still there are many differences of nature among everything under the Way of Heaven, as oxen themselves are of ox nature, and horses are themselves of horse nature, and dogs are themselves of dog nature, and certainly [their natures] are not the same.[63]

Very often, this is cast in a clearly *normative* sense, where the *qi* needs to be of "the right sort" in order to get the higher animals among the hierarchy of the natural kinds:

> Nature is like water: if it is flowing through a clear channel it is clear; if it flows through a dirty channel it is turbid. If the embodiment is clear and correct, one gets it completely and is a human; if the embodiment is turbid and partial, one gets it in a darkened manner and is a bird or beast. *Qi* can be clear or turbid. Humans get clear *qi*, while birds and beasts get turbid *qi*.[64]

Li as a Metaphysical Part

The two above readings of Zhu Xi as either holding that *li* resembles a unitary universal with graded instances, or a collection of universals, both fail to make sense of Zhu Xi's wider metaphysical commitments. While perhaps initially plausible in light of some of the analogies Zhu Xi uses to express his views, the assumptions on which Zhu Xi is operating indicate that he needs to hold that it is essential to *li* to characterize its instances in some particular sense, even while at the same time holding that it is not essential to *li* to characterize any material object in the general sense. Historically, this interpretive option has precedents; the Korean Neo-Confucian school, following Zhu Xi's thought, developed a similar distinction between universal and special senses of both *li* and *qi*.[65]

Some interpreters recognize these distinct senses. JeeLoo Liu recognizes the problem that "[Zhu Xi] is ambivalent on whether human nature is the same or distinct from other creatures' nature. On one hand, he wants to assert that everything in the world takes a partition of the supreme ultimate [*taiji*]; on the other hand, he does not want to deny the uniqueness of human nature."[66] She resolves the puzzle in accordance with the reading on which there is a particular sense of *li* which belongs essentially to certain kinds of wholes. "Particular [*li*] define the nature and functions for each kind of things …. the qualitative differences in creatures' mental capacities result from the physical differences in their constitution."[67] Thus, for example, we can distinguish senses of *li* to emphasize the way in which, despite each kind of thing having a distinct "nature," that can be described in a wider sense as being "natured" in some way: "Since humans and other creatures have different functions and normative duties, they have different [*li*] and hence cannot be attributed the same nature. However, in the sense that they all have their respective [*li*] and normative roles, they are all endowed with the same heavenly [*li*]."[68]

As the term *li* is then ambiguous between these two senses, the general and the particular, it would not be surprising if Zhu Xi were to draw a distinction in some contexts. Zhu Xi's distinction between *li* as instantiated in "material nature" (气质之性) and *li* as "fundamental nature" (本然之性) seem to me exactly such a disambiguation. A particular or specific sense of *li* is the "material nature" of a thing, and the general sense of *li* is that thing's "fundamental nature."[69] Zhu Xi uses that technical term "material nature" for the nature of a material thing when that nature exists in a particular instance, resulting from combining with some *qi*.[70] Liu therefore concludes that the appeal to "material nature" resolves how each individual object is constituted by a particular kind of nature, even if there is only one *li* considered in the general sense.[71]

The way the term "material nature" is used in the context of his metaphysics can appear to confirm an interpretation of Zhu Xi as a constituent ontologist, given that the other possible interpretations of Zhu Xi's metaphysics cannot plausibly be interpreted as relational. There is, however, one final step to characterizing Zhu Xi as a constituent ontologist. That requires that Zhu Xi believe not only that "material nature" is a particularized *li* in the sense that there are distinct natural kinds of material thing, but also that something on his account functions in a way to a *li-particular*, having a part-like relation to what it constitutes. Such texts, however, are not hard to find where Zhu Xi appears to refer explicitly to *li* as a part or with particularized terms.

Zhu Xi does not, nevertheless, distinguish clearly between two roles that a material nature plays in a material thing. One of these roles is that the material nature of a thing corresponds to a particularized sense of *li*, such that an individual belongs to something resembling a natural kind in virtue of the particular way their material nature possess to a higher or lesser share in the one *li*, in the general sense. Zhu Xi refers to *li* and to the natures of particular things as "this" (*ci* 此) *li* or nature, which seems to mean that an object has a *particular* nature or *li*: "In all under heaven, there is not any object lacking a nature. Rather, when there is *this* thing, then there exists *this* nature. If there is not *this* thing, then there is not *this* nature."[72] Another role that a material nature seemingly has to play is as that which individuates the kind of that object, in the sense of being an individual instance of the kind *as* characterized by *qi*. Zhu Xi often uses language implying *li* is "in" the things it informs: e.g., *li* is in the midst of objects (*zhi zhong* 之中).[73] Ordinarily, to be "in" something is to be in a spatial relation to something, but Zhu Xi also claims that *li* has no physical form (形) in itself—the claim would be unintelligible unless *li* were something analogous to a "metaphysical part" in a distinct sense from a "material" part.

The context of these remarks, in light of the qualifications I have made to rule out various other interpretations or readings, seems to me to require that "material nature" is playing both of these roles. The analogy with mixtures or combinations seems to imply that *li* and *qi* cannot be separated in the material object—wherever one is, there is the other. Further, with use of an image of mixture or combination, Zhu Xi also implies that the relationship of *li-qi* to the object is something like particular parts of that object, at least in the way that mixtures are composed of their ingredients. Zhu X's language clearly points to *li* and *qi* as something like "parts" of objects. This interpretation of Zhu Xi is buoyed by the other evidence that *li* can be a "particular this" when it exists in an object, "in" those objects, and that each object "partakes" of *li*. If we recall Zhu Xi's claims that *li* and *qi* are not themselves material objects, then these principles must presumably fall in some other category of things aside from material objects. The natural conclusion from this is that *li* and *qi* are supposed to be something akin to metaphysical parts of objects.

In fact, when seen through this lens, we have surprising coincidence between Zhu Xi and Aquinas on two points in how they think of material objects. Zhu Xi tantalizingly hints at what might be a theory on which *qi* functions like Aquinas' prime matter, such that *qi* has no intrinsic properties whatsoever apart from *li*:

> If we speak of the "nature" of Heaven and Earth, then we are speaking specifically of its *li*. If we are speaking of a "material nature," then we are speaking of what results from *li* and *qi* combining [lit. "mixing"]. If this *qi* does not exist, then this nature already exists. If *qi* were not to exist, it is still the case that nature always

exists. Even though in that place [*li*] is in the midst of *qi*, it is still the case that *qi* still is *qi*, and nature still is nature, even when they do not combine with each other. Consequently, if we speak of their place in the body [*ti* 体] of an object, there is no place where they are not; *nor can we speak of qi as being turbid or clear, if it has no li existing in it* [又不論氣之精粗，莫不有是理].⁷⁴

These two properties "turbid" and "clear" (or, "coarse" and "fine") are what Zhu Xi seems to take as exhaustive of all possible states of *qi*. If *qi* would have no such properties without *li*, then *qi* is "pure potentiality" for *li*. In a different context Zhu Xi drops another off-hand comment that indicates he shares a "pure potentiality" view of *qi*. Offering a further clarification of the "horse" and "rider" analogy which we saw earlier, Zhu Xi describes how it is that *qi* can "resist" *li*, even though *li* was described as the "rider" of *qi* in the earlier analogy:

> Although *qi is wholly produced by li* [是理之所生], once it has been produced, then *li* cannot wholly govern it. Once this *li* comes to be in many different *qi*, then the many different ways in which [*li*] is employed daily will depend on *qi*, as *qi* is strong whereas *li* is weak… this is like a father relating to his sons, but where the son is worthless, and then the father cannot govern him effectively.⁷⁵

The analogy seems to indicate that, even though *qi* is in itself not such as to constitute anything without *li*, once a material thing is constituted by the combination of *li-qi* in some particular circumstance, then it can be the case that there are particular qualities of the *qi* that comes to exist in that "material nature." If the *qi* of that compound is of poor or "turbid" quality, that material thing will not be able to exemplify or exercise the powers appropriate to its kind well or easily.

In addition, Zhu Xi objects to Buddhist views of reincarnation as contradicting the apparent facts: "The Buddhists say that after a man dies he becomes a ghost, and the ghost in turn becomes a man. If this were the case, the world would always have so many people coming and going. There would be no creation, and neither production nor reproduction. This is absolutely unreasonable."⁷⁶ To say that it is clearly the case, not merely illusion, that human beings cease to exist at death, and that they come into existence at birth, seems to mean that a human being could not *possibly* survive their death to become reincarnated. And the case of human beings is not unique among material things. Zhu Xi holds that all living things really cease to exist: "this is such for all the ten-thousand things' vitality [萬物之精]: that they die [or, 'are destroyed'] and [their parts] are scattered."⁷⁷

Interestingly, *jing* (精) is usually translated "essence"—I translate it as "vitality," indicating it is something relative (most likely) to living things, and to avoid equivocations that would too easily prove the point. Nevertheless, Zhu Xi's point seems, in fact, to make a claim about the *essence*, in the technical sense, of "living things" (no living thing is such that it will live forever); or, if we took *si* 死 to mean merely "destruction," it would qualify over all material things whatsoever. We might recall, however, that Aquinas held that substantial forms essentially compose their compounds and, although he offers a different explanation that allows human souls to survive death, he appeals to just such a thesis to argue transmigration of souls is impossible. The natural interpretation, in light of what has been said, is that Zhu Xi affirms that *li* – considered as a particular – can be essential to a material object it composes, as well as its *qi*. I do not think these parallels are mere coincidence.

"Participation" Metaphysics and Hylomorphism

I have shown that Zhu Xi distinguishes between *li* and *qi* as two fundamental explanatory principles of material things, where *li* is what accounts for the essential nature, properties, and powers associated with particular kinds of material thing. Further, it is necessarily the case that no material thing exists which is not characterized by *li*. And, there is a particular sense of *li*, namely, the "material nature" of a material thing, which composes that material thing in a way that Zhu Xi sometimes describes in a manner that resembles parthood closely. Finally, the material parts of that material thing, namely, that thing's *qi*, constitute that particular material thing in virtue of the composition of the "material nature." If *qi* had no *li* in it, no material thing would result. Consequently, it can be safely concluded not only that Zhu Xi is a constituent ontologist, but that Zhu Xi embraces a hylomorphic account of material objects. *Li* in the sense of the "material nature" of an object is such that resembles a particular part of the material things it characterizes, such that if any part of that object were not to be so characterized it would not constitute that object (or any object at all), and where "material nature" of a material thing is neither identical to that thing or any of its material parts.

There is one remaining point that might lead to some puzzlement: why did Zhu Xi engage in all these metaphors that seem to indicate that *li* is one, if he really is a hylomorphist about material objects? Specifically, Zhu Xi goes through a great deal of trouble to emphasize repeatedly that there is *one li* possessed by all the material things: "The [*li*] is in the *qi* like a bright jewel is in water. [*Li*] in clear *qi* is like a jewel in clear water: its brightness is fully visible. [*Li*] in turbid *qi* is like a jewel in turbid water: you cannot see its brightness outside."[78] When speaking of the virtues, Zhu Xi explicitly invokes this kind of presence of the whole *li* in every manifestation of a particular virtue:

> upon encountering the stimulus of a baby about to fall into a well, the [*li*] of humaneness responds, and the emotion of alarm-and-commiseration takes form; or when, upon encountering the stimulus of passing a temple, the [*li*] of propriety responds, and the emotion of respect takes form. From within, where the myriad [*li*] are all integrally and indivisibly possessed, individual [*li*] become distinctly manifest.[79]

In these cases, Zhu Xi seems to obviously be moving between different senses of the particular *li* of individual objects and relating them intimately to the one *li*, the *Taiji* or "Heavenly Li" of all things. This one *li*, and the fact that it is the "fundamental nature" of all things, is absolutely central to Zhu Xi's metaphysics, central to how he characterizes the "ranking" of material things in a chain of being from higher to lower. Zhu Xi thus affirms a student's statement that:

> The nature of man and the nature of things are in some respects the same and in other respects different. Only after we know wherein they are similar and wherein they are different can we discuss nature [*xing* 性]. Now, as *Taiji* [太極] begins its activity... the myriad transformations of things are produced. Both man and things have their origin here. This is where they are similar. But [material forces] in their fusion and intermingling, in their interaction and mutual influence, produce innumerable changes and inequalities. This is where they are different.[80]

The student then quotes Zhu Xi himself (in a commentary on the *Great Learning*) saying:

> From the point of view of [*li*], all things have one source, and of course man and things cannot be distinguished as higher and lower creatures. From the point of view of [*qi*], that which receives [*li*] in its perfection and is unimpeded becomes man, while those that receive it partially and are obstructed become [other things; e.g., animals]. Because of this, they cannot be equal, but some are higher and others are lower.[81]

The unity of all the material things in terms of their "fundamental nature" provides metaphysical grounds for the moral implications for the Neo-Confucian project, because all things are fundamentally united on a deep level. These claims all seem to be in stark contrast to a hylomorphic metaphysics of material composition.

Nevertheless, there are precedents in the Aristotelian metaphysical tradition for this way of speaking about the role that form can play in material objects. In fact, Thomas Aquinas is a precedent for combining the Aristotelian notion of an individual or particular substantial form with the Neo-Platonic metaphysics of a "participation" of each object in various grades of form. In the context of his commentaries on the Neo-Platonic *On the Divine Names,* Aquinas often employs language about form and matter that mirrors Zhu Xi's general sense of *li.* What is again the case for Aquinas is that he is able to employ both a specific sense of form as that which constitutes a particular object (that object's substantial form) and a generic sense of form in which all informed things participate. Particularly, Aquinas conceives of God as a subsistent form, complete in perfection, and all other existent things as receiving or participating in God's perfections. This closely parallels in many ways Zhu Xi's claims about individual material objects participating in one *li* to various degrees.

For example, Aquinas holds that, while God's own essence and nature cannot be communicated to a creature, all creatures are similar to God in virtue of their perfection: "in the procession of creatures [from God], the divine essence itself is not communicated to the creatures proceeding, but remains incommunicable and imparticable; but a similarity to Him, in virtue of what God gives to creatures, is propagated and multiplied in creatures."[82] God therefore contains in Himself the perfections of all the creatures He causes to exist: "[God as] the One, insofar as He is singular and that in which all things participate, singularly, i.e., indivisibly, contains within Himself, as in one principle, all existent things and everything wholly."[83] Aquinas consequently can appropriate the language of the Neo-Platonists to argue that every created thing is a limitation or restricted participation in the perfection of God.

Aquinas refers to this elsewhere as God's "exemplar causality" in regard to everything He creates. An exemplar cause is a type of "formal" cause, but, instead of the form of the exemplar informing all the instances as their substantial form, there is a relation of similarity between all instances and the exemplar.[84] God stands in a special relationship to all the particular forms that constitute objects, because "a thing is said to be similar to another by sharing a certain form; but all forms are from God. And not only is God the cause of similar things, but is even the cause of similarity itself."[85] God has a relationship that is quasi-formal to every other entity which participates in His formal perfection:

> [God] is that One which is the cause of all, not that one which is the a part of a multitude, because such a part would be partial and participated, but rather is before all multitude, not only in the order of time and of nature, but even in the order of causality because He determines all participable "oneness" and all

"multitude" by the way in which the participated determines through its form that which participates in it.[86]

Specifically, Aquinas thinks every created being exemplifies "perfection" to some degree but is not "perfection itself subsisting" (i.e., God): "God is the essentially self-subsisting Being... all beings apart from God are not their own being, but are beings by participation. Therefore it must be that all things which are diversified by the diverse participation of being, so as to be more or less perfect, are caused by one First Being, Who possesses being most perfectly."[87]

It is this relationship of similarity between all creatures and God which allows Thomas to enunciate his famous theory that we can draw analogies from creaturely perfections to the nature of God Himself: "whatever is said of God and creatures, is said according to the relation of a creature to God as its principle and cause, wherein all perfections of things pre-exist excellently."[88] Aquinas even holds, like Zhu Xi's *Taiji*, that God can be said to be wholly present in each creature: "one and the same seal wholly is present in each individual impression, but diverse participants make dissimilar impressions, [and all are] representations of one and the same principal form, by which they have the one form totally."[89] In Thomas, therefore, we have a parallel construction to Zhu Xi's *Taiji*: God is that in virtue of which any particular thing has any perfection at all, but there are various limited participations in that perfection by all the individual beings that exist. One could still, on this scheme, accommodate claims that individual species of animal—such as cats—all occupy the same "level" of participation in universal form, so that every animal of that species exemplifies the same nature in the sense of having the same particular kind of form.

Aquinas moreover claims that it is due to diversity in matter that things participate in God's perfection to varying degrees. For example, in the above analogy, Aquinas claims that the hardness or softness of different qualities of wax will lead to different appearances of the same seal, and distinct individual impressions of a seal, even if all individual forms in the wax are representations of the one form of the seal.[90] Yet Aquinas clarifies that this is not because matter is an opposing and equal principle that limits God's omnipotence. Rather, we have to recall that, for Aquinas, act and potency are functionally characterized, so that "form" is any kind of actuality and "matter" is any kind of potentiality. God intends His likeness to be reflected by different creatures in distinct ways—to be received differently in distinct kinds of finite creatures. Each of these creatures does not exhaust God's perfection and so limits or is in potentiality to all of God's perfection. Aquinas therefore compares God to an architect who not only has a design to build a house for a purpose, but his purpose involves distinct kinds of material parts. Similarly, the likeness to God is received differently in different parts of creation, according to the differences among those recipients, even though this "diversity is preordained by God according to His purpose."[91] That matter is limited means that a material being can only receive some limited participation in God's perfection, even though God Himself is not limited to create material things.

These claims of Thomas appear to parallel in many ways Zhu Xi's view that *qi* is what leads to speciation and individuation among individual objects. There are, obviously, differences. On one hand, Thomas' claims have a great deal more specificity in metaphysical classification than those of Zhu Xi. Aquinas' position involves larger background assumptions about the relation of a genus to its species both in logical and in metaphysical contexts, so that Thomas can draw complicated associations between how matter differentiates genera from each other, whereas forms account for species-specific differences among material objects.[92] Thomas' metaphysics relies on a well-defined logical distinction between genus and species, whereas the literature claiming that Zhu Xi holds that *qi* accounts for species differences does not make such a distinction. Yet, while it is unclear whether or how the scholastic distinctions could be mapped on to Zhu Xi's views, there remains a possibility in the Aristotelian tradition for at least similar way of understanding materiality as participating in formal perfection. I therefore take Aquinas' claim about exemplar causality only as an illustrative example that such a double sense of "form" has clear precedents in the Aristotelian tradition.

While I have only focused on the metaphysics Zhu Xi offers for material composition, Zhu Xi's *Taiji* might be revisited fruitfully in light of the distinctions I have drawn. Even if Zhu Xi's *Taiji* does not clearly have conscious intention, intellect, or a will that Aquinas attributes to God, *Taiji* might be, like Aquinas' God, a subsistent being and the root of all perfection in the universe by something like a "participation" relation.[93] Yet the lack of parallel here would not affect the overall hylomorphic interpretation of Zhu Xi. It would only show that Zhu Xi shares a great deal in common with Neo-Platonism alongside hylomorphism, and that, despite initial appearances to the contrary, such views can be compatible. It would still be perfectly reasonable of Zhu Xi, as a hylomorphist, to point to a dependence among all the different ways that things in the universe embody *li*, such that they form a "great chain of being" from higher to lower material things, even if *Taiji*, Zhu Xi's "Heavenly *Li*," were not subsistent (like Aquinas' God). As the discussion of Aquinas' commitments to very similar theories illustrate, Zhu

Xi's views on these matters are not incompatible with his hylomorphism. Thus, any worries one might have had that Zhu Xi's claims about every material object being composed of one *li* can be given a coherent and plausible interpretation; we should not be tempted to think that Zhu Xi is a relational ontologist merely because he makes such claims.

Conclusion: Confucian Hylomorphic Metaphysics

Looking back at the historical record from this perspective bolsters the case that Zhu Xi's metaphysics is fundamentally a hylomorphist one, as there are certain easy ways to misunderstand the claims that hylomorphism makes about metaphysical parts. Zhu Xi's theory prompted subsequent Confucians to raise objections that resemble common objections to hylomorphism, as these objectors might presume different models of metaphysical explanation or reject Zhu Xi's constituent approach to ontology.[94] Nevertheless, that Zhu Xi is a hylomorphist is not merely of historical interest. Rather, Zhu Xi illustrates a basic intuition about the nature of material composition shared by hylomorphists of various stripes. This intuition is that whatever accounts for the composition of some parts into a material composite whole—what I have been calling in this chapter, up to this point, a "material thing"—is a metaphysical part of that object. There would need to be such a part even in the extreme case of monism, or in the case that there are no distinct natural kinds of objects, or if there were no changes among the composite objects. But notice that my arguments in favor of a hylomorphic interpretation of Zhu Xi's claims about *li* also illustrate the reasoning that leads us from facts about whether composition is restricted— that is, material composites really exist, and that any material thing does not necessarily compose a composite whole—to certain conclusions about what composition must be like. As long as it is the case that facts about *what composes what* are mind-independent, a position that Zhu Xi clearly endorses, then it follows that whatever it is that accounts for when some material parts compose a whole will function relevantly like a wholly-overlapping "metaphysical part" of those objects.

What is salient, then, is that Zhu Xi's metaphysical intuitions help us build an argument that all restricted theories of material composition entail hylomorphism. In the final chapter, I will consider the ways in which one could deny the remaining assumption necessary to generate my conclusion: that truths about what things compose what, the facts of composition, do not require there to be any extra-mental particular "metaphysical part" of the wholes that are composed of proper parts. Kit Fine might represent one such view, holding that facts about composition of material objects could be or are entirely mind-dependent. Facts about material composition might be true in virtue of the way humans have introduced objects into their ontology, for example, and not in virtue of the way that the objects are. What I will argue is that those who hold that composition is restricted, and that substances cannot be parts of other substances, should also hold that facts about composition could not vary in this way without veering into mereological universalism or nihilism. Fine's theory thus resembles some of Zhu Xi's Buddhist interlocutors, and I will return to Zhu Xi's objections to Buddhism after showing why such assumptions about material objects would undermine the aim of providing a restricted theory of composition. Consequently, I will argue that, if facts about the composition of material objects could not be mind-dependent in this way, whatever makes the difference between a mere heap of things and a genuine material object composed of parts is something in virtue of which those parts are unified, functioning like a common part of all the material parts that compose a whole. Whatever serves the role of the "difference makers" will be, in short, nothing other than substantial forms.

5

Forms Matter

To recapitulate the journey up to this point, I started by reviewing three contemporary theories of material composition which accept the possibility that substances can have other substances as proper parts. These were the Neo-Aristotelian versions of hylomorphism proposed, respectively, by William Jaworski, Kathrin Koslicki, and Kit Fine. I employed these theories as illustrations of what it is to be committed to the possibility of substance-parts specifically on the assumption that material composition does not occur "automatically" between two or more arbitrary material things, that is, on which composition is "restricted." Instead, each of these theories posits a "structure" as that in virtue of which the xs compose y in cases where material composition occurs. There was, I argued, a conflict between these assumptions.

Specifically, I selected two of these theories, that of Koslicki and Jaworski, and argued that these exemplify the problem associated with attempting to construct a restricted theory of composition that accepts the possibility of substance-parts. What I characterized as the "grounding" problem that results from accepting the possibility of substance-parts is that, if the account accepts the stipulation that composition is "restricted," this entails conclusions which make the claims that one composite whole composes another as a proper part incoherent. The relevant conclusion that results from "restricting" composition is that a theory has to hold both that composition is a contingent matter—whether any two or more things compose a whole is a contingent matter—and that, if one is to meaningfully specify a set of conditions under which the material things *do* compose a whole, that has to be such that, *necessarily,* if the conditions are fulfilled, then the xs compose y. To make sense of the possibility of substance-parts in a way which respects these requirements that characterize what it is to be a "restricted" theory of composition, when one composite whole composes another as a proper part, these wholes must belong to different kinds of wholes.

The first issue is that Koslicki and Jaworski's account of composition specifies *particular* entities—structures—which characterize a set of each particular parts that compose a whole of a distinct kind. They must make such a stipulation about structure in order to account for the way in which one substance composing another will not entail that, by transitivity alone, the structure of the substance-part is not identical with the structure of the whole. Yet this entails unsavory, and ultimately incoherent, results for the appeal to structure to account for facts about which things form the composite wholes. Since particular structures must also come in kinds, such that they essentially compose wholes according to those kinds, the account cannot also be that each particular structure necessarily (essentially) composes each member of every kind of material whole, as that would entail mereological Universalism—every whole of any kind would be such that the parts necessarily compose it. They need to specify that any particular structure is *not* such that it necessarily or essentially composes any particular whole.

The problem that results, however, is that, if structures only characterize their wholes in this way—only that: necessarily, if the parts are structured, then they compose a whole—one does not get an account of composition which meaningfully makes "structure" that in virtue of which xs compose y. Each structure only is such that, when a whole is composed, a particular structure necessarily composes *that one*. Koslicki and Jaworski's respective accounts both end in incoherence due to the grounding problem that characterizes all restricted accounts of composition which accept the possibility of substance-parts.

It should now be apparent that the last chapter indirectly addressed in greater detail a possible response to the grounding problem only sketched in the second chapter. That possible response, recall, was similar to the way in which (I proposed) Peter van Inwagen addressed the general problem of material composition. That interpretation which read Zhu Xi as holding a "relational" metaphysics was one where whatever accounts for when two or more material things composes a whole is relatively like a universal rather than a particular. That is, whatever is the "explanatory factor" that correlates to the conditions under which two or more material things compose a whole, i.e., that in virtue of which composition occurs and the xs compose y, is such that it can be *exactly similar* across two numerically distinct instantiations of that same explanatory factor. Then the appeal to kinds to differentiate types of material whole would correspond to distinct kinds of (what act like) *universals* rather than particulars.

However, what I illustrated by appeal to texts from Zhu Xi is that this cannot be true of his metaphysics because he does not accept an assumption that is made by Peter van Inwagen: Zhu Xi, unlike van Inwagen, does not accept that *qi* (which serves a role like "matter" in Aristotelian theories) is inherently particulate. That is, Zhu Xi's *qi* is not like van Inwagen's simples, such that to be an instance of *qi* in this sense is for that material thing to necessarily lack parts. Indeed, Zhu Xi says *qi* by itself does not constitute a material thing at all (and mirrors Aquinas' own reasons for claiming that prime matter is "pure potentiality"). This latter claim is what ensures that Zhu Xi is a hylomorphist.

There is, nevertheless, one remaining way to attempt to rescue the possibility of one composite whole composing another as a proper part, which is to deny that an account of restricted composition strictly *needs* to hold that material composition is such that the facts about whether some particular parts compose a whole do not hold in virtue of *either* anything like a universal or a particular characterizing those parts. That is, it is not such that the xs composing y involves any "internal relation" existing among the xs and y. Just those same xs and y could exist in another possible universe, then, and not compose a whole, because the relation among them is an "extrinsic" one which does not hold necessarily between the xs and y. Notice this position is distinct from another in the conceptual environs. A meaningful account of restricted composition has to hold that: necessarily, if the conditions (specified by the theory) under which the xs compose y are satisfied by some particular xs and y, then those xs compose that particular y. The move instead is to claim that a meaningful account of composition does *not* need to thereby also affirm that: if the conditions under which composition occurs are satisfied, then those xs necessarily compose that y.

I deferred treatment of Kit Fine's theory of material composition to this final place in the book because, whereas Fine's theory resembles those of Jaworski and Koslicki in many respects, Fine's differs from theirs in a crucial respect. The other two thinkers, in keeping with van Inwagen, hold that a restricted theory of material composition is motivated by extra-mereological considerations that indicate there is a *real* difference between the things that compose a material whole and those that do not. Fine's theory of embodiments was criticized by the other two hylomorphists because, when two or more things are characterized by an embodiment, this does not entail (on Fine's theory) anything more than a certain kind of relation holds among them. I will argue in this chapter, first, that their perception of Fine's theory was accurate: specifically, Fine's theory makes it true that, even if the conditions under which composition occurs are satisfied, and the xs compose y, those xs *do not necessarily* compose that y. That is to say that Fine makes the final theoretical move which could appear to rescue the possibility of substances composing other substances as proper parts.

The issues at the forefront of this final chapter concern what we should be aiming for in giving an account of the unity of material objects and their parts. I will be arguing that accepting a theory of restricted material composition on which the particular xs do not compose a particular y necessarily (when conditions of composition are fulfilled), in the sense in which Fine affirms it, results in a more global kind of incoherence than that which affected the accounts of material composition offered by Koslicki and Jaworski. In order to show this, I will first appeal to Karen Bennett to explore the reasons we should hold that, necessarily, if the conditions on composition are satisfied by the xs and y, then those things compose a material whole. I will call these the "composition facts"—the facts about which things are parts of what wholes— and differentiate them from the "identity facts"—the facts about which things are identical with what. The way to avoid the conclusion that the particular xs *necessarily* compose y whenever they fulfill the restrictions on composition is to argue that the facts about identity and composition are identical. One way is by appeal to a view that "composition is identity." After showing that the first of these ways is insufficient by itself to block the conclusion that particular xs necessarily compose y, I turn to the other, which requires that identity is not a transitive relation (such that $x=y$ and $y=z$ does not entail $x=z$).

Graham Priest, adopting a Buddhist perspective, proposes a metaphysics of material objects on which identity is not transitive, and, by that fact, a theory of material composition on which the composition and identity facts are the same. Zhu Xi, in fact, argues exactly against that kind of Buddhist perspective from which Priest operates, and I will independently offer arguments that confirm Zhu Xi's analysis as to why such views are not accounts of restricted composition; such views render trivial the thesis that composition is restricted, in much the same way that Fine's account did. However, in rejecting this last option for showing how the possibility of substance-parts is compatible with offering a theory of restricted material composition, we have exhausted the ways in which to avoid the conclusion that the explanatory factor which accounts for when the xs compose y resembles in an important sense a particular. Then, combined with the other assumptions, it will be true that every coherent account of restricted composition will posit an explanatory factor (corresponding to when the restrictions on composition are satisfied) where the xs necessarily compose y when characterized by that factor, and where that explanatory factor itself characterizes the xs and y necessarily. Such an "explanatory factor" functions just like an overlapping part, overlapping all and only those material xs which compose y, and which accounts necessarily for the fact that those particular material parts compose that whole. This factor corresponds exactly to how I characterized a "substantial form."

Kit Fine's Theory of Things and Their Parts

On Kit Fine's ontology of composite material objects, the things that play the corresponding role that "structure" does in the theories of Koslicki and Jaworski, are identified as a species of relation, a "principle of embodiment"; the material objects constituted by these principles are termed "embodiments." Fine is explicit that there are no "special forces" associated with operations of composition, where an operation of composition is characterized as "the way that the constituents come together."[1] One thing Fine clearly seems to rule out, by characterizing his principles this way, is that these are not "parts" of the material objects in the same way that Jarworski characterizes structures as a kind of causal power for configuring the material parts into a composite whole. Rather, principles of embodiments account are a special kind of part: intensional or conceptual elements of the identity of a material composite and the parts: "there will be an intensional or conceptual element to the identity of many material objects… [these principles,] which are intensional or conceptual in nature, are directly implicated in the identity of the embodiments and hence also in the identity of the material things that are explained by their means."[2] Fine's account of objects therefore resembles Koslicki's in this respect, because structures are akin to "formal" parts of the composite wholes they constitute.

Nevertheless, there is a difference in how Fine understands "operation of composition." To be a material composite object is to be a thing that has an "explanation of its identity" in terms of some operation of composition, the latter being those operations by which the parts compose a whole, which is in turn associated with a definite kind of object.[3] Conversely, operations of composition are associated with distinct kinds of principles of embodiment that describe the appropriate relation among the parts of those objects. Fine notes that, on his approach, the operation of composition is the "primitive" in the theory, rather than the part-whole relation. This is what sets his theory apart from Universalism, because there are operations by which some constituents could come together aside from grouping the constituents together as member of one set (i.e., mereological fusion or summation); that is, coming together as members of one set is not necessarily the only way two or more material things could form a whole.[4] Yet, for Fine, the operation of composition is—unlike Aristotle's and (indeed) van Inwagen, Koslicki, and Jaworski's accounts of material composition—set up in such a way that Fine rules out any appeal to any extra-mereological considerations to fix which instances count as "material wholes."

When criticized by Koslicki that his theory is expanding the ways in which objects can exist such that the number of material objects will vastly outnumber those posited by mereological Universalism, Fine replied that his theory is agnostic whether there are extra-mental "natural" kinds of principles of embodiment or whether all such principles reflect mind-dependent ways human beings privilege certain things over others. He describes this position by appeal to cases in mathematics where certain kinds of objects, such as sets or irrational numbers, can be legitimately introduced into the mathematical ontology in various ways. For many domains of objects, such as these, what exists is "inevitably an arbitrary matter."[5] He also proposes that many of the material objects we ordinarily take to exist, such as tables or chairs, are "introduced" in such a manner and not ontologically privileged in any way over any of the objects posited by mereological Universalism.[6] Fine concedes that it may seem implausible that many material objects, e.g., electrons, exist only as a matter of being "introduced."[7]

He admits, then, the possibility that there is a difference between the objects that can be introduced by some mind-dependent operation of composition and the "given" or genuine material objects that are not introduced by such an operation. He believes his theory can accommodate this difference, however, although it does not require it:

> what goes for material objects in general will go for the rigid and variable embodiments of my theory in particular. Thus it might be supposed that some (perhaps all) of them are introduced while the others (perhaps none) are given. There will then be no special difficulty in making the theory consonant with our ordinary views as to what exists as long as the putative monsters of the theory are not among the embodiments that are taken to be given.[8]

What this implies is that Fine's principles of embodiment differ in an important way also from Koslicki's formal parts, because his principles are similar to universals insofar as they can characterize many different particulars in exactly the same way. This indicates, subsequently, that it is not essential to any principle that it characterizes any *particular* xs, and thus that these principles in general do not essentially characterize any instances of material composition. As a result, it is unproblematic for Fine's theory of principles that it might be contingent whether material objects are all introduced, i.e., counting or identifying the things that "come together" according to a merely arbitrary standard, such as the way that a new object can be "introduced" in mathematics.

Why Forms Matter

Of course, Fine is not asserting that there *are* no material things. That would seem on-its-face absurd for Fine to do in the context of offering an account of the material "things and their parts." What he is claiming is only that one can still satisfactorily resolve problems of material composition by considering the nature of what a "composition" relation would need to be like, without determining whether there are any "given" objects, that is, without determining whether there is a difference between "real" operations of composition and merely arbitrary ones. And he seems to claim, further, that it might be impossible to draw any such distinction between operations of composition in a satisfactory way: e.g., "there can be no theory that is internally satisfactory in providing a precise and principled basis for determining what exists and yet also externally satisfactory in being consonant with what we ordinarily take to exist."[9] Fine is only denying then that there is any *way to demonstrate* that our standards by which we group the objects together as wholes—the "operations of composition"—are the "given" and, in that sense, the "true" ones.

This is not the end of the story, however, because Fine makes much stronger claims elsewhere that "there is no such thing as *the* ontology, one that is privileged as genuinely being the sum-total of what there is. There are merely many different ontologies, all of which have the same right (or perhaps we should say no right) to be regarded as the sum-total of what there is."[10] Now, this claim would seem to contradict what Fine is doing in offering a theory of material composition if means that it is impossible to decide *whether material things* exist. I take it that we can interpret Fine in one of three ways. First, he might mean that we cannot offer any meaningful way to *say* that something "exists," that is, that all the ways we group objects in *any* context (outside of merely the way we group material things into wholes) cannot be given a meaningful characterization. This would seem to me far too strong in the context of how Fine deals with other problems in ontology.

Or, Fine might mean that there are limits (e.g., epistemic or logical) to what can be *known* about what exists. In which case the theory of material composition he offers is supposed to be meaningful whether or not any material things exist. In this case, Fine's theory is fundamentally just offering an account of the ways in which any things, of any sort, can be "parts" of other things, rather than a theory about the composition of material objects. These facts about how things can be "parts" will nevertheless be necessary truths of some sort, even if there are no ways to determine the truths about what material objects compose what wholes (i.e., if we cannot know the "composition facts"). Yet it seems hard to see the way in which we could know *those* necessary truths about the meaning of "part" without being able to say something about what exists, except if we could know all the necessary truths about what *could* exist *a priori* by a special faculty or way of knowing that does not require us to know anything about the things that actually do exist. It seems implausible to me that we have any such faculty. Finally, Fine could mean something similar to this claim, but more limited: we can know facts about *our own minds*, or mental operations, such as the possible ways that we reason about things, and we can deduce conditionally from these facts the constraints on what we could possibly mean by the word "part."[11]

While I think the last reading is most sympathetic to Fine's overall goals in philosophy of mathematics and logic, it is not critical to my purposes which of these readings is correct. The reason that I tried to disambiguate all three of these senses is to only show that, on all such readings of the way in which the facts about composition were contingent in the way Fine wants them to be, the point of commonality—that none of these readings abandon—is that there is nothing about the *identities* of material objects, either facts concerning the kinds of things or the particular things themselves, that would entail whether those objects compose a whole as proper parts. While some have therefore read Fine to be a mereological Universalist,[12] his position is quite distinct from Universalism because he is making no claim that he is making no claim that any given material object necessarily composes a whole. But Fine is not denying the general claim that *if* there were some things that *did* compose a whole, that this would be a *fact* (i.e., a proposition such that, necessarily, if a proposition is a "fact," it is a *true* proposition). Nevertheless, there is something resembling Universalism in Fine's commitments, insofar as Fine's account does not clearly hold that the occurrence of composition is an objective matter. Attacking Fine's position requires showing that there is something deeply problematic, or contradictory, in combining such a claim with an account of restricted material composition.

Making Restrictions on Composition Meaningful

Think back to our friendly exemplars of material composition: Goliath, a statue, and Lumpl, the lump of clay that composes Goliath. In our actual world, it is true that Lumpl composes Goliath. Now consider a world where, despite nothing at all differing in either Lumpl or Goliath, it is true that Goliath composes Lumpl rather than the other way around. Or, imagine a very similar world where it is neither that Goliath or Lumpl composes anything. Instead, both are merely spatially coincident objects, with neither Goliah or Lumpl as parts of the other. In these worlds, the facts about composition are not the same as in the actual world, but, apart from it being true that different composition relations characterize both objects, Goliath and Lumpl themselves vary in no other respect. In this case, what we have is an illustration of what composition would be like if composition were an *external* relation rather than an internal one holding among the compose and its parts. In cases such as these, clearly, the facts about the *essences* of Goliath or Lumpl do not account for why it is that a composition relation holds among them. What makes the case seem odd is that we have already specified that Goliath is a "[clay] statue" and Lumpl is the "clay" that composes Goliath. By setting the case up this way, we are identifying what Goliath and Lumpl are, that is to say, what kinds of thing they belong to. And then it could seem counterintuitive or odd to say that lumps of clay can have statues as proper parts or that a clay statue can have no clay as a proper part.

What I have constructed is a case where the identities of material objects—the facts about what is intrinsic to either object (what they are, their properties, etc.)—can come apart from whether those things compose anything as a proper part, i.e., that there are any "composition facts" about those things. This is not to say that they *do* in the actual world, because in our world clay statues are necessarily made of clay; the possibility envisioned by the case involves saying that it *could* happen that, in some possible world, clay statues are not made of clay. Affirming such a possibility entails that composition is an external relation—one determined in no way by the identities of the things doing the composing. I use "identity" here, rather than "essence," because I do not want to make it seem as if this way of thinking about composition is related to whether "essences" (in some technical sense of the term) exist, or whether the facts about composition hold in virtue of the "properties" of the things in question (or any other particular respect in which something could be characterized as having an "identity"). The "identity facts" about a particular material object are thus supposed to be, in what follows, a general term for facts about that object that are broadly such that they are intrinsic to it, but explicitly bracketing what it is for anything to be "intrinsic" to something else. (As the argument gets further along, it should become clear that I need no assumptions about what "intrinsicality" is like.)

In the above case of Lumpl and Goliath, one could imagine that facts about the identity of Goliath and Lump are unrelated to whether either composes anything because whether that object composes anything is mind-dependent. Or, one could imagine that facts about the identity of an object are only partially related to whether that object composes anything, but that they do not *by themselves* necessarily entail any facts about composition. There are some other facts that, combined with the facts about identity, account for the composition relation holding among an object and the other things it possibly composes.

The option that the composition relations were *entirely* unrelated to identities of the material objects means that whether something composes anything else is entirely mind-dependent. This is a strong claim. If it were taken to mean that we cannot *refer* to "material objects" (reference being impossible because, e.g., there really aren't any material objects to refer to), or that we cannot know anything about the material objects, then a theory of material composition is in principle impossible. There would be *no* "identity facts" about material objects.[13] Consequently, it more naturally means that, as the "mind-dependent" term indicates, that whether something composes another as a part is an extrinsic relation among which objects can do the composing: that is, the facts about our minds plus facts about the identities of the objects are what determine whether a composition relation holds among the material objects. For instance, one could not likely introduce a special kind of number without a clear and rigorous definition of such numbers that was compatible with the overall principles of our chosen mathematical system.[14] Similarly, while it might be impossible for a clay statue to fail to be composed of clay, this fact would be relative to our *actual* conceptual framework.

But then we can notice that the natural way to interpret the claim that composition is mind-dependent is not terribly far from the claim that facts about the identities of objects do not *by themselves* entail whether those things compose anything. The relevant difference is in the way that each characterizes the "third factor"—in addition to the identity facts—that entails these propositions about composition; namely, our minds or something else. Yet the mind-dependent view involves a problematic result. To highlight what is wrong with an entirely mind-dependent view of material composition, I turn to a principle advocated by Karen Bennett in the context of what she refers to as *building* relations. The building relation family encompasses relations such as grounding, causation, truthmaking, and, importantly for my purposes, composition. As Bennett conceives it, these relations all involve entities being "built" by other entities. Specifically, Bennett proposes that, whenever a building relation obtains among some things, something necessitates the building relations that obtain among them – this is what she calls "building determinism."[15] Without committing myself to the existence of building relations or these general claims Bennett makes about building, her claim strikes me as eminently plausible when restricted to the context of material composition. If two or more objects compose a whole, it looks like *something* necessitates this composition fact.

Why should we accept this requirement, though? Bennett gives two cases that I adapt to show why the more restricted claim about composition is plausible. The first case is that there are two worlds that are complete duplicates of each other. In world w_1 there are two entities a and b, but in world w_2 b does not exist or obtain. If both worlds are possible, Bennett proposes, then whether or not b obtains is merely a matter of luck or chance. Nothing makes it the case or accounts for the fact that b obtains. Clearly, then, "nothing a is doing (as it were) makes a difference between those worlds where [b] exists and worlds where it doesn't."[16] The entity b does not seem "built" at all by a – b is indiscernible from any other unbuilt entity. The conclusion of Bennett's argument is that it seems impossible that building relations should function in a similarly chancy way – otherwise, the built entities would differ in no important way from the unbuilt ones. My initial case with Goliath and Lumpl is analogous to this case, where Goliath and Lumpl stand for a, and the composition relations between them stands for b. (I am assuming, with Bennett, there is no other relation to c in virtue of which these facts hold). If duplicate worlds of the same sort were jointly possible for Goliath and Lumpl, such that the worlds otherwise differed in no way, it would seem similarly to be a matter of luck whether Lumpl composes Goliath.

Bennett's second case is to argue that, if the above worlds w_1 and w_2 are jointly possible, then b is modally recombinable with the rest of reality that is to say, b could obtain without a or anything else. But, "if something fails to supervene on the rest of reality, it is recombinable with the rest of reality; if it is recombinable in that way, it is fundamental; if it is fundamental, it is unbuilt."[17] While Bennett's case requires the intuition that a fundamental object is not a built object, the second case strikes me as providing a much stronger argument when restricted to composition. A denial of the claim would entail that Goliath, Lumpl, and the composition facts about their compositional relations are modally recombinable. This not only entails that it is possible for the composition facts about Goliath's relation to Lumpl to differ without the world differing in any way, but seems to entail that it is possible for composition facts about these objects to obtain *without Goliath and Lumpl existing*. While deniers of compositional determinism would likely hold it necessary that Goliath and Lumpl exist for there to be composition facts about these objects, it is hard to see how such a position is a principled one.

I take it that such a claim about composition facts being necessitated by *something* is also required to differentiate the thesis that composition is restricted from either mereological nihilism or universalism. A view on which composition facts are determined in no way by the world, or any object in it, but only by my conceptual schemes or the way I classify the material objects would similarly undermine the distinction between restricted views of composition and those on which composition does not occur. While it will be true that my conceptual scheme could be understood to necessitate truths about what things composed what other things as material parts, it is only my ideas that necessitate or determine whether something is a material object, or a part of one. Nothing about the objects or the world does so, by stipulation. But this makes the differences between Universalism, Nihilism, and restricted views of composition merely differences in which conceptual schemes we employ. Rejecting this requirement that something necessitates composition facts trivializes these divergent views concerning the nature of the composition relation, so that one would not be interestingly distinct from the other. If material objects are duplicates concerning the non-mereological facts, but worlds are possible where the mereological facts about these objects vary, such possibilities would seemingly trivialize metaphysical debates about composition relations.

If the denier of compositional determinism holds that the facts about composition are mind-dependent or merely pragmatic in this way, as I argued it might be for Fine, then I would propose such theories conflict with the assumption that material composition is restricted. Instead, on a theory where composition facts are mind-dependent, the *world* appears to differ in no non-mereological way from mereologically nihilist theories where composition does not occur. For this reason, on these theories that hold mereological facts are mind-dependent, it would not seem that composition is restricted in any non-trivial sense. Consequently, we should reject accounts of material objects and their composition similar to that which I am attributing to Fine, those on which composition facts are entirely mind-dependent.

Entirely mind-dependent theories of composition therefore fail to be meaningful as *restricted* theories of composition (I will return to this point below, in regard to Graham Priest's account of composition). All other theories that invoke a "third factor" aside from the facts about the identity of objects (if they aim to be meaningful) should not be "entirely mind-dependent" accounts in the sense that, whatever facts which, in combination with facts about human minds or conceptual schemes, necessitate the facts about composition will always include *other kinds* of facts that do not merely pertain to facts about our conceptual schemes. We can easily characterize the difference by saying that, on the "entirely mind-dependent" view, there are strictly speaking no *facts* about whether something composes something else as a proper part, but on all other "third factor" views, there would be composition *facts*, i.e., true propositions strictly entailed by the facts, rather than merely propositions about the possible nature of composition relations in general. Since the set of facts that entails the facts about composition necessarily includes facts *other* than facts about human minds aside from facts about the identities of the material objects that might possibly be composite wholes, call these "facts about the world."

Identity, in Two Flavors

The question at this point is whether we can make sense of the view that facts about the world, in addition to facts about the identities of the material objects, entail the facts about what material things compose others as proper parts. A number of prominent metaphysicians seem to think that the scenarios with Lumpl and Goliath are impossible not because of the way the objects are, but because of some other fact about the world.[18] For example, Ross Cameron, claims that: "once you settle the non-mereological facts, you thereby settle the mereological facts: there can't be two possible worlds indiscernible in all respects describable in non-mereological terms but which are mereologically discernible."[19] Nevertheless, he holds that the nature of composition itself is contingent.[20] Cameron envisions that, in our actual world mereological universalism is false and composition is in fact restricted, but, in another possible world, it could be the case that there are no composite objects at all and mereological nihilism is true.

We need to be careful, because Cameron's characterization is too general. In order for composition facts to be necessitated by the facts about the world and the identities of objects, we have to be careful not to presume that the facts about the composition of the objects are already among the facts about the *world*. Cameron's claim that the nature of the composition relation is contingent could mean either [1] it is a contingent matter whether there are any material objects or whether these objects are such that they would compose wholes under certain conditions or [2] it is a contingent matter whether the composition relation as such essentially involves what *we* call composition in this actual world.

Assuming we dismiss an equivocation between use and mention of the term "composition," the latter position is just identical to the claim I already have identified as problematic: where it is contingent (not necessarily the case) that, if some two or more things compose a whole, then those things compose that whole. But the first claim is too general by itself to conclude that we need any facts *other than* the facts about the identities of objects to arrive at the result that the composition relation is contingent. It could just be that facts about the particular objects are such that the material objects are characterized, in a different possible world, by distinct identities from that which they have in the actual one. Would that difference be in virtue of the facts that the *objects'* essences differ, as opposed to whether the *world's* essence does?

What we need to make the theory substantive, and to differentiate the facts about the identity of the objects relevant to composition from the facts about the world, is to invoke a way in which the identities about material objects are not already part of the identity of the "world." One way to do this is to think that (globally) the "world" has a distinct identity from that of all the material objects in it. Yet the world's identity cannot be such that the material objects are like proper parts of it *and* where the world's identity as a (very large) material particular entails facts about the identities of the objects that compose it. All of the problems I've already detailed for the possibility of substance-parts would recur if differentiating the essences of the material particulars from that of the whole involved positing that the world is a material composite in a different sense than the composite particular material objects composing it—the material substances would be substance-parts of the world, a composite material whole.

We might think instead that the world would have to be thought of as a common part—all the material objects *have* the world as a part, but are not identical with the world, and where facts about the identity of the world do not entail facts about identity of the material things. But this too runs into an infinite regress because we would need some other account as to why the identities of the material things, plus the identity of the world, entails any facts about the composition of the material things. The world, in other words, seems to be composing all of the other material objects only contingently, not necessarily; and so, we would need facts not only about the world's identity but its composing all the other material objects—the facts about the world's composition!—aside from the facts about the material objects' identity, in order that this set would entail the facts about what material objects compose what wholes. (Recall why substantial forms had to be such that, when they compose the material parts that they do, they *necessarily* compose precisely those parts.)

For this reason, the stalwart advocate of the position that the facts about the world are distinct from those of the material objects should not think of the "world" as itself having an identity. Instead, the "world" is nothing over-and-above *all of the things* that are in it, whatever these things in the world are, whether material particulars or universals. What the position involves is not that the facts about the identity of the world as a whole (distinct from the things in it) entail the facts about composition, but that the identities of all the material things and the facts about all the *other things* in the world, taken as having their own individual identity, entail facts about whether any particular material x composes y.

This is not quite mereological universalism because it does not require that composition is necessary among any two or more material things. Rather, the position is that, given the things that actually exist (of whatever kind), then their identities together entail all the *contingent* facts about composition. We might go the way, then, of Ned Markosian, who believes that it is "impossible for two worlds to be duplicates with respect to non-mereological universals but differ with respect to composition."[21] Markosian's "non-mereological universals" are then precisely the "other things" that can have an identity which is distinct from the facts about the identities of the material things, *insofar as* those identities entailed anything involving facts about their composition.[22] On his theory, however, composition is restricted but is a brute matter of fact, as there is no finitely long, true, and non-trivial account of the conditions under which the xs compose y.[23]

Markosian draws this conclusion on the basis of an argument by elimination. After rejecting Nihilism and Universalism as satisfactory accounts of material composition, as well as van Inwagen's view (because that view entails "vagueness of identity"), Markosian addresses a view on which we might appeal to different kinds of objects, revealed by natural science, to account for the (restricted set of) conditions under which the xs compose y. These "serial" responses are such that they hold: "There is an object composed of the xs iff *either* the xs are F1s and related by R1, *or* the xs are F2s and are related by R2, *or* ... the xs are Fns and related by Rn."[24]

He proposes that there are two reasons to reject that we can give any finite list of such conditions, because "the problem with moderate answers to SCQ is that they must identify some multigrade relation that is linked in the relevant way with the concept of composition.... The Finite Serial Response apparently compounds the problem because it requires identifying not just one multigrade relation that is linked to the concept of composition in the relevant way, but several."[25] We might put the matter a different way in saying that one needs to specify a way in which, if one posits a series of different kinds of material object, composition needs to be related to each of these kinds in such a way that the claims about the kinds relate to the facts about composition where the list of those conditions "express a proposition that is necessarily true," and he does not see a non-arbitrary way to identify the particular instances when the kinds *are* necessarily relevant to whether the xs compose y and when they are not.[26]

Markosian's options are limited to holding either that there is only a trivial way to delineate the conditions under which xs compose y (e.g., just whenever they do) or to an infinitely long list of such conditions. Yet this is in respect of the way that he characterizes what role the "kinds" of material object play in a series account: the kinds in the list are characterized by distinct kinds of composition relations (R1 ... Rn) to their instances. This follows from the assumption that the non-mereological universals are *non-mereological*, that is, that their identity does not entail or involve any properties relative to material composition, i.e., whether the material things *x*s compose *y*. Then adding together a list of the kinds, the circumstances under which *y* (of some kind or another) is essentially composed by *x*s, plus the non-mereological universals of how such kinds *could* relate to their material instances, does not provide us anything that necessitates or entails the facts about whether any particular *x*s compose a particular *y*—we would only have the facts about the identity of the universals and the kinds, but not about whether any particular material objects were characterized by (exemplified) those universals and kinds.

We can reject Markosian's assumption in regard to the identity facts about the things in the world, other than the composite material things, in the following way: holding that each individual material object has an identity such that that identity could include relational properties to other things.[27] In the context of these claims about how facts concerning the identity of the "other things" (i.e., things not themselves material composites) in the world, alongside the facts about the material objects, is akin to saying that the essences of some of these "other things" in the world could be "individual" in such a way that, by knowing the essences of *those* objects, one knows all the composition facts about the material object in question (because, knowing that individual essence, one knows whether it is essential to that object to compose another as a part). These objects would have to be particulars, since it is essential to them that they relate to certain particular wholes, but these "other things" could not be themselves composite material objects, since the whole point of maintaining that composition is an extrinsic relation (relative to the material objects) was precisely to hold that it is not essential to the material objects, merely in virtue of their existence, that any composition relations hold among them.

To review the way in which we got to this conclusion: there need to be "composition facts," truths about what material things compose other as proper parts, in order to maintain the position that composition occurs at and that we can state the limited conditions under which it occurs meaningfully; then, we need to maintain that the "world" is not something that has its own identity independent of the objects in the world; rather, the facts about the world which, in addition to the facts about the identity of the material things, would necessitate the composition facts about those material objects have to be such that there are objects, not themselves material objects, but whose essence is such that each particular object of this kind entails relational facts—that is, that they essentially relate to the identities of the material things. Then, by knowing the facts about these latter objects, alongside the facts about the material things' identities, these two would be sufficient to entail the composition facts about all the material objects and their parts (if there are any such facts).

Clearly, we are almost but not quite at a substantial form, because substantial forms are just one way of conceiving the nature of such particular objects—they are particular entities whose identities are such that those identities relate them essentially to particular material things, and then necessitate relations among those things such that the material things necessarily compose wholes of different kinds. In order to see whether this conclusion is really warranted, I need to show there is not some other assumption that is being made implicitly which would stop this inference. In the next two sections, I will review two ways in which one might conceive of composition in a nonstandard way. One such way is to claim that "composition is identity," which is to say that for the composition relation to hold among any two or more material things is for those things to be identical with each other. Normally, such a claim is taken to entail that composition is unrestricted, which is to say, that mereological Universalism is true. However, in recent metaphysics, some have illustrated ways in which this does not follow. When conceiving of composition as identity is understood in a way compatible with restricted theories of composition, the claim—modified in this way—does not necessarily stop the inference to substantial forms. Subsequently, I will review one last-ditch attempt to avoid substantial forms, by holding that the composition facts are identical with the facts about identity, but that dialethism is true—which is to say that identity is not transitive.

Identity as Composition, a Transitive Relation

On the thesis that composition is identity, for some xs to compose a y is nothing more than for those xs to be identical with y. One implication of conceiving of composition and identity in this way is that, whereas we typically either utilize identity claims in saying one thing is identical with another (or itself), or that many things are identical with many things, this thesis that composition is identity requires it to be possible that many things can be identical with one. For example, if Suzie the parrot has three parts, her feathers, her beak, and the rest of her body, then the whole parrot is simply identical with her feathers, beak, and body. Conversely, these three things (feathers, beak, and body) are identical with one thing (Suzie).

It could seem that this thesis that composition is identity would also rule out that composition is restricted. If what it is for some *x*s to compose a *y* is to be identical with that *y*, then whenever there are some *x*s, the *x*s compose that *y* as it were "automatically." "Composition as identity" therefore seems to entail that any given set of object/s always composes some whole, i.e., mereological universalism or unrestricted composition. Cameron has argued convincingly to the contrary that, even if composition were identity, composition could still be restricted. He points out the thesis composition is identity entails "that *when* there is a complex object, it is identical to its parts, and that *when* the many is identical to some one, they compose that one. But this doesn't tell us whether, given some Xs, they in fact compose; it only settles the biconditional: they compose iff there is some one to which the Xs is identical."[28]

Composition as identity only entails mereological universalism if one assumes that "for any collection of things, there is some one to which that collection of things is identical."[29] As Cameron points out, the thesis that composition is identity consequently leaves it open whether there are some *x*s that are *not* identical to one *y*. In fact, Cameron can then restate the thesis that composition is restricted and occurs only under certain circumstances in a way compatible with composition as identity. For composition to be restricted, on the thesis that composition is identity, would be for it to be the case both that some sets of many objects are identical to one object, and that some sets of many objects are identical to no one object.[30] On this restatement of what it is for composition to be restricted, Cameron points out we can still answer the question "when a plurality of things is identical to one thing."[31] For example, van Inwagen's own resolution of the Special Composition Question can be restated as the view that "there's only a one identical to the many when the many participate in a life ... ."[32]

Nevertheless, the thesis that composition is identity then has a very interesting consequence when it is modified to be compatible with restricted theories of composition. Cameron points out that the defender of composition as identity will be committed to a further principle about the circumstances under which a plurality of things are identical with one:

> Normally, of course, the essentially of individuality—that no one thing could have been a mere collection of things; i.e., that every individual is essentially an individual: essentially identical to some one thing—is an extremely attractive principle. But ... acceptance of [composition as identity] opens up room to doubt this principle: room for doubt that is lacking if we don't accept the coherence of many-one identity.[33]

Cameron argues that defenders of composition as identity cannot coherently accept that "individuality" is essential to any object, if they accept that composition is restricted.[34]

For example, imagine that we believe it is possible that an object in our actual world, such as Suzie the parrot, is identical with something in another possible world. Normally, this is one way to think about what belongs to an object essentially or contingently—to ask whether that object has a property in every possible world, or only some of them. Our ordinary way of conceiving of identity as a one-to-one relation would just entail that any object can bear at most *one* relation of identity with itself in another possible world; then, since Suzie is identical with herself in every possible world where she exists, and we assume that she is an individual in the actual world, it follows that Suzie is essentially that individual. However, if identity is possibly in some instances a many-to-one relation, as the view that composition is identity requires, then something which is identical with a singular or individual object in one world can be identical with a (mere) plurality in another. Thus, Suzie, who is an individual in our world, might be identical, in another possible world, with the mere collection of those things which compose Suzie in the actual world (e.g., her beak, feathers, etc.), i.e., such that that collection of stuff is not identical with any one individual "Suzie." Since we ordinarily think of what is essential to Suzie as what characterizes her in every possible world, yet Suzie in at least one possible world is not an individual, Suzie is not necessarily an individual.

In other words, if composition is identity, then it is possibly the case that *any* individual be identical with a plurality in another possible world; it is essential to no object that it is singular or individual.[35] This result undermines, however, the appeal to composition as identity. Composition as identity would get us too easily to conclusion that the identity of some objects necessarily entail relations to other objects, without appeal to a special class of particular objects, because, if identity is composition, then we could know what things compose what other things as parts merely by knowing the facts about the material objects themselves. But in order to arrive at an account of composition as compatible with an assumption that composition does not occur necessarily—such that any two or more material things do not necessarily compose a whole—we have to assume that identity can hold as a many-to-one relation. Only in this way is it possible to make sense of the idea that any two or more material things do not necessarily compose a whole: because the facts about what things are identical to what are contingent. Clearly, then, it will follow that the xs compose y, as they are identical to it in the actual world, but that those very same xs would be *not* identical with *y* in at least one possible world. And this even makes it possible that, over some period of time in the actual world, those very same *x*s could cease to be identical with *y*:

> the Xs can fail to compose at a time t but come to compose something at a later time t*. What has changed? A mere many has become a many-one. That's *all* that's changed .... Nothing new has come into being, and nothing exists at t* over and above what exists at t.[36]

The problem, then, is that we would still need some account of what it is in virtue of which the *x*s are *identical with* an individual *y* in this world rather than a mere plurality. "Composition as identity" alone would not help resolve this. Ross Cameron proposes that the change at t* must involve a change in the fundamental properties of the objects in question: "there is a fundamental property of *being an individual* that can be had by a collection of things, but need not be ... the individual is identical to the collection that existed before and lacked the property. It's just that these things are fundamentally a different way: they are now an individual whereas they weren't before."[37] Now, it could seem that the coming into existence of a new property is arguably a case of a new *entity* coming into existence at t*, such as a property characterizing the *x*s, even if there is no changes among what material objects exist at t*.

This would be to introduce some separate class of things, the objects in virtue of which a new property characterized the identity relations among the material things in question at t*, such that the identity of these entities entails that the material things have the property of "being an individual" at one time, when those entities exist, and "being a mere plurality" at others, when they do not exist. Such an entity, like the fundamental property of *being an individual*, cannot be identical with the objects so unified, but it needs to be *in* all of the objects unified (e.g., a *way* those objects exist). It seems obvious, on this account of composition as identity, a need for an entity functionally equivalent with substantial forms falls directly out of the account. Substantial forms will be those entities in virtue of which a plurality of things is identical with one thing.

By contrast, the defender of composition as identity will likely want to rule out that whatever it is in virtue of which the identity of an object makes it a singular thing could be an *entity* in any sense of the term. For example, one would need to claim that whether some objects possess or lack a fundamental property of *being an individual* does not involve any change in the facts about what exists. Whenever there is a change in the identity of some objects, nothing comes into or goes out of existence. Nevertheless, for the defender of composition as identity to make this move is self-defeating. If defenders of composition as identity hold that the facts about the identities of the material objects (i.e., what is identical with what) do not settle facts about composition, it is difficult to see how their account of composition will be able to give a meaningful account of restricted composition.

The account is not meaningful because, given their position on the nature of composition as identity, the facts about identity do not necessitate or settle the facts of composition. For example, if $a = b$, and we know that a is a mere plurality, we have not settled whether a composes a singular object; b could be a singular object, but it need not be. Then, if the defender of composition as identity also claims that what exists does not necessitate the identity facts, it is hard to see how the objects themselves are what necessitate the composition facts. Consider a world where $a = b$ and another where $a \neq b$. Nothing in these worlds changes except the identity relation, even though no new entity comes into existence and nothing about these objects change. If b is a singular object and a a plurality of objects, the composition facts about whether a composed b has changed merely in virtue of the identity relation being different. Yet nothing about the objects necessitates the identity relation being different. An account of restricted composition which adopted this explanation of the circumstances under which composition occurs would then be saying, again, nothing more than the xs compose y whenever those identity relations hold—and those identity relations hold whenever they just do. That looks very trivial as an account of composition.

The defender of composition as identity has only *one* other way to attempt to construct a meaningful restricted theory of material composition: denying that it is necessary that identity relations involve transitivity in every case. We could think this would save the theory, because we could appeal to such a fact to block many-to-one identity across possible worlds, as well as in the actual world. Thus, the fact that the xs are identical to z, and the z identical to the ys, does not entail that the xs are identical to the zs. We would arrive at a way in which the identity facts necessarily entail the facts about composition, because the facts about composition are just a subset of the facts about identity. And we could preserve the contingency of composition, as it will be contingent which things are essential to what other things (since identity is not transitive), alongside the attempt to provide meaningful restrictions on composition. All this without positing any special entities, such as substantial forms, that would be parts of what they constitute as material composites. The cost of this move, however, is clearly high, as it involves accepting that there can be true contradictions, i.e., dialethism. But I will argue it is not only the cost of admission that is too high; the defender of composition as identity would pay a steep price only to be redirected toward a destination far away from a restricted theory of material composition.

Identity as Contingently Transitive: Huayan Buddhism and Zhu Xi

To take stock, I have proposed that, if we accept as an assumption that composition is restricted, we should be committed to a couple of other theses. One of these was that these accounts require both that, necessarily, if the conditions under which xs compose y are satisfied in some particular instance, then the xs compose y; and that facts about composition need to be contingent in the sense that merely being among the material things does not necessitate facts about whether a material thing composes a whole (if they all do, Universalism; if none, Nihilism). Facts about the world would not be such, in addition to the facts of the identities of the material things, to necessitate the facts about what composes what, without some nonstandard theory of identity or without the assumption that there are a special class of entities such as substantial forms whose identity is such that it involves relational facts to the material objects that compose wholes. And I argued, further, that – as long as composition is restricted – not even the thesis that composition is identity would derail an argument to the conclusion that there are substantial forms. The only remaining option in avoiding that conclusion was to opt for a non-standard theory of identity. This latter step is to deny that identity is transitive. There is, in fact, just such a theory of material composition, which attempts to account for the restricted circumstances under which composition occurs by appeal to paraconsistent logics on which identity is not transitive.

Graham Priest is well known for defending dialethism, and he has also defended an application of dialethism in the context of the metaphysics of material composition. Priest presents his theory of material composition within the context of an infinite regress: when we ask what unifies a set of parts, or why they compose one material object, it does not do to invoke yet another material part to explain that unity. Priest however rejects the view that what accounts for the facts about composition could be an entity of a different *kind* from the material parts, such as a substantial form. He argues that, even if the unifying entity were not a material part, the problems of how a non-material entity itself forms an appropriate unity with the material parts is mysterious and poses serious problems.[38] Priest argues that the vicious regress "is generated by the thought that [the unifier] is distinct from each of the other parts."[39] What is needed is a unifier that is identical to all the parts *and which is not itself an entity*.

Priest's account appears initially to posit entities that are the same as my substantial forms, as he proposes that there are special entities, "gluons," which account for when some set of parts composes one material object. Priest's account of gluons requires that gluons, by contrast with substantial forms, are not parts; rather, each gluon is *identical* with some material things and necessitate that compose wholes in virtue of being identical with them: "Given a partite [i.e., composite] object, x, a gluon for x is an object which is identical to all and only the parts of x. By being identical to each of the parts and to only those, it unifies them into one whole."[40] Priest therefore accepts a version of composition as identity—but the identity in question is not among the parts, as identity with the gluon is not transitive. Even though the gluon is identical to each material part, it does not follow that the parts are identical to each other.[41]

Unlike the Thomistic account of substantial forms as actualities, where actualities are entities of a special type, Priest takes a very different position on whether gluons are entities. He argues that any account of composition will need to posit some intrinsically unified entity to explain the unity of a set of material parts.[42] Further, Priest thinks we need to quantify over gluons in discussing the identity of a material object. Nevertheless, he also argues that gluons *cannot* be entities. If they were entities, even of a special kind, Priest argues that they would not adequately resolve the regress. We could always ask what accounts for the unity between the gluon and the material parts it unifies.[43] Priest resolves this by appeal to his paraconsistent logic, arguing that it is true of gluons both that they are and are not entities—gluons, in sum, are *paraconsistent entities*.[44] This claim also resolves, he thinks, the worry that gluons will have the properties of the parts they unify, by being identical with those parts, even if these properties are contradictory.[45] As paraconsistent entities, he argues that gluons can have contradictory properties without incoherence.

Abstracting from whether paraconsistent logic is coherent, an interesting feature of Priest's account is that, unlike ordinary composition as identity, Priest is denying that being a singular or individual object is contingent. Instead, gluons are *intrinsically* or *essentially* singular or unified things. It is this fact that allows Priest to respond to a case that Jason Turner has proposed as a problem for Priest's theory of gluons: "Harry is a hair on my head; as a part of me, he is identical to the same gluon g that I am. Harry is then plucked from my head; he, I, and g all continue on, but [Harry] is no longer identical to g. The identity facts have changed, but the existence facts have remained the same."[46] Even though Priest does not hold that facts about the identity of any material object with any other necessitate facts about their composition, he does think that the facts about whether an entity exists or not, a subset of facts about their identity, can necessitate the facts about identity.[47] Thus, in response to Turner's case, Priest should not concede that the existence facts have remained the same. Rather, Priest could respond to Turner's case in a way that echoes Thomas Aquinas' account of substantial forms: a gluon of a particular whole ceases to be identical with a part precisely when that part ceases to exist. Thus, when Harry ceases to compose me, and thereby ceases to be identical with the gluon g that is me, then Harry ceases to exist. Given that Priest's notion of identity is not transitive, the whole can continue to exist even when the part ceases to do so.

Another chief difference between gluons and substantial forms, aside from holding that gluons are identical with their material parts, is that Priest's theory attempts to understand facts about the identity of objects *only* as facts about their composition. As Priest puts it, gluons do not "answer the question of what something *is*" in the same way that Aristotle's forms do.[48] Gluons only unify and do not account for or explain anything else about what an object is. In contrast with an Aristotelian account of forms, which constitute objects in a genus and species, Priest's objects have identities that are entirely constituted by their relations to other entities; "what it is that makes something one—namely, its gluon—is what it is that makes it empty, that is, its relatedness to all things."[49] Priest concludes that his theory then supports Buddhist metaphysics, claiming that all entities are lacking any intrinsic essence or quiddity, constituted only by relations to other things.[50]

That which unifies an object, the gluon, does not account for any other facts about that object's identity beyond facts about that object's composition, making facts about composition the same as the facts about identity. The set of facts as to whether a set of objects are identical or not identical with some particular individual whole (a gluon) is *all there is* to being a particular material object (there are other views in the metaphysical neighborhood of this kind of Buddhism, such as Super-Humeanism).[51] We can contrast the Aristotelian theory of objects and Priest's account according to the way in which they understand the identity of material objects. For an Aristotelian, whatever unifies the parts of an object also constitutes that object as having some determinate characteristics that could be shared or similar to other objects, e.g., a genus and species. Consequently, there are multiple dimensions of comparison between one object and another. For Priest, the identity of an object *only* involves facts about whether it is identical with or not identical with any other. Notice then that Priest's account resembles in important ways the "first interpretation of the Substance-Part Principle" that was outlined in the second chapter, in that it attempts to make sense of something like substance-parts without appeal to kinds of objects and instead merely to facts about numerical identity. The grounding problem for the first interpretation of SPP, described briefly in that chapter, was that there is something apparently stipulative about the sense of composition being employed, even if we can make sense of how something can be a part and a whole at the same time and same respect.

In sum, the problem for Priest's account is this: if all there is to the identity of an object is whether it is identical to another, then there is no need for the unifiers—gluons—at all. For instance, we might want to explain how a set of bricks comes to compose a house in some circumstances but not others. The natural claim is that the bricks need to be arranged in some way; when they lack the arrangement, they do not compose a house. "A unity… is more than the simple sum of its parts."[52] If we accept Priest's account of composition, the identity of the parts and the whole and the gluon itself are nothing more than *not* being identical with other things. Then why is arrangement of the bricks relevant to whether the gluon of the house exists or not? Why are *any* properties of any parts relevant to whether those parts are identical with a given gluon? If properties account for the identities of the objects, and when those objects compose something, then there is no need to propose a theory of gluons at all. The properties can account for facts about composition by themselves. If the properties of an object entirely result from identity with the gluon, then it seems like we are owed an explanation of how the parts acquire one of the many properties with which the gluon is identical. The problem of material composition merely becomes the problem of material *differentiation*—why the parts have distinct identities from the wholes they form.

We can put the problem the other way around. Priest claims, "any object is what it is in virtue of the properties it bears."[53] There are objects and there are the properties borne by objects, with the gluons accounting for an object bearing a given property. It is in virtue of being identical with some set of objects that the gluon constitutes them as one material object. The gluons therefore have all the properties of the objects that they are identical with, and so need to be identical with contradictory properties (and be such that identity is not transitive). Consider the bricks again. The bricks each have properties such as being rectangular and weighing (let's say) one pound each. The house is not a one-pound rectangular thing, but has its own properties of weight and shape resulting from the appropriate arrangement of the bricks.

Yet the bricks are supposed to compose the house in virtue of being identical with some gluon, where some particular gluon is identical to each of the bricks and with the house that results from their composition. The gluon therefore has the properties both of being one-pound and rectangular, and of weighing some X numbers of tons and being in the French country style of architecture. Even if we admit that identity is not transitive, so that the whole does not automatically acquire all of the properties of the bricks in virtue of being identical with the gluon, it is not clear why the parts have the properties that they do. Everything that exists is supposed to have a relational identity, such that "everything is what it is in relation to, and only in relation to, other things."[54] The relation of each brick to the gluon is supposed to *make* that object a "brick," having the properties it does, and similarly for the house. But why does the brick "get" one set of properties and the house "get" a different set? Identity has to be *intransitive in the right way* to get the results Priest needs. And that makes gluons look suspiciously *ad hoc* in solving problems of material composition in line with our intuitions that bricks compose houses and not, say, bananas.

Either something about the house, independent of its identity with the gluon, explains why it has the properties it does (and why it is not identical with the bricks), or the nature of the gluon explains why it gives "house" properties to some things identical with it and not to others. In either case, all you need (on Priest's theory) is for the thing having the identity in question to *exist* and all problems of composition are settled: the house, essentially such that it and its bricks have distinct properties; or the gluon, essentially identical with a particular house composed of bricks suitably arranged, having appropriately distinct properties. It is now unclear why we needed the gluon at all; all we need is for the house to be essentially composed of bricks such that, merely in virtue of the house existing, the nature of the house accounts for the properties and arrangement of the bricks. The bricks would not be the things that they are unless they composed precisely that house.

The concern about the gluon providing what look like selective facts about the properties of objects can be mitigated significantly if we disregard that gluons, or houses, or anything else, has an essence at all. Accounts which explain the unity of material objects by appeal to essences need, Priest argues, to explain not only how it is the case that the essence of a whole is such as to make it essentially the case that some kind of parts belong to that whole, but need more particularly to explain (further) a way in which it is necessarily true that *the particular parts* belong to that whole:

> Consider a pile of stones and a person's body. The former, it might be suggested, is not a true unity; the latter is. And what makes the difference is that the identity of the pile depends on the identity of its parts, the stones; whereas in the case of the body, it is the other way around: the identity of the parts depends on the

identity of the whole .... Thus, the thought continues, what explains the oneness of a partite genuine unity is the dependence of its parts on the whole .... The fact that in a unity the natures of the parts depend on the nature of the whole in no way explains how they cooperate to form a unity. For all their dependence, the parts are still parts; and facts about identity do not bear on cooperation. Granted, the parts would not be the parts they are unless they were parts of the whole. But that hardly explains how it is that the various parts do what they do to create the whole. We know, by their nature, that they are parts of that whole; but how is it that they have this nature?[55]

What such accounts need to posit, in addition to facts about the essences of wholes which make certain kinds of parts compose those wholes essentially, is provide a further story on which the *particular parts* have the nature that they do as a result of composing the whole. It is tempting for such accounts to appeal to the causal processes by which the parts came to compose those wholes but, Priest argues, these too are not explanatory in the right way:

> one might suggest that no explanation [of that in virtue of which the particular parts compose the whole] in the pertinent sense is called for. What constitutes the unity of a table? Simply that I take a piece of wood and nail four legs to it in appropriate places. There is nothing more to be said. This will not do, however. What we are being offered here is an explanation of how the unity came into being—the causal processes that brought it about. Now, explaining how something is brought about is not explaining what it is that has been brought about. To explain how to get married is not to explain what marriage is. One who nails the legs to a table top in the appropriate way has indeed brought the table into existence by certain causal processes. But causal processes are going on all around us, and only some of them bring objects into existence. So what is it that one which does so, actually does?[56]

Appeal to a causal process which explains the way in which those particular parts came to compose a whole are not explanatory in the right way, because appeal to such processes would assume precisely what it is that needs to be proved: we would need to identify the difference between those causal processes that result in the parts composing nothing at all and those which result in the parts composing precisely that whole. But this requires that these facts about causal processes need to be necessary truths about them, and this merely pushes the problem elsewhere. We still have not answered what makes it necessary for these particulars to compose that whole.

Priest's own solution might appear at first glance, then, to appeal to the essence of the gluon that accounts for why some parts are related to other parts in a composite whole appropriately, and, because the gluon is an entity to which transitivity of identity does not apply, the paraconsistent nature of the gluon explains why the parts are not identical with the others. But this is a mistake. Instead, a gluon's own identity is not the stopping point of explanation as to why that gluon has the identity it has. Gluons do not have essences at all, as, in Priest's metaphysics, *nothing* does. Rather, the identity of every gluon is dependent on the nature of the whole universe—the whole web of identity relations between that gluon and everything else (and nothing).[57] Thus, the parts of an object compose a given object not in virtue of the essence of a particular object, but in virtue of the way in which every object is bonded by its identity relations to every other thing in the universe. Even though such identity relations are not transitive, all the particulars are characterized by their place in the overall web of these relations, i.e., the way in which each thing is identical with one set of things but not with others.

Such a way of reading Priest's account is accurate to his inspiration, the Huayan ("Flower Garland" 华严) school of Buddhism. The Huayan school is an idealist school of Chinese Buddhism that develops insights from an earlier idealist school of Indian Buddhism, Yogācāra. The Huayan school's perspective on reality is one where all reality is inter-connected and inter-dependent, such that there are no individual entities or natures or substances, but only a grand web of relations. In the central text of the school, the *Huayan Jing* (华严经), the web of relations among all things is compared to the "Net of Indra," a vast mythical net of jewels, where each jewel is reflected in every other in the net.[58] Priest explicitly appeals to this as a predecessor of how he understands the "web of identity relations" according to which we can characterize any particular by its place in that web, without appeal to any essence of any member of the web.

The Huayan school is less focused on facts about composition, but argues for a similar conclusion to that advanced by Priest by appeal to causation. The school denies that any causal agent exercises causal power by itself, let alone being able to act or exist without any other cause. That is, anything involved in a causal sequence depends on causal conditions in order to bring about its effect, and every cause also depends on its effect in terms of what both are. An important patriarch of the school, Fazang 法藏, comments on the *Huayan Jing*, saying:

> All beings arise through causation, and being is necessarily manifested in many varieties… . [Yet] because they come into existence through causation, they surely have no nature of their own. Why? Because the dust is not self-caused but necessarily depends on the mind. Similarly, the mind does not come from itself,

but also depends on subsidiary causes. Since they depend on each other, they do not come into existence through any fixed causes.[59]

Fazang assumes that a particle of dust undergoes a change when it comes to be an object of my thought, but also that my mind undergoes a change when it comes to have the dust particle as object of thought. The point of the example is that the nature of both of these entities (the dust and my mind) depend on each other in order to be individuated as cause and effect. In fact, Fazang holds that their coming to be so related depends on the whole net of every causal sequence that has ever, presently, or will ever occur. Consequently, all causation never really involves existential dependence where one entity brings another into existence. Instead, every individual thing depends on everything else for its existence and character.[60]

It should appear that the account suffers from just those problems which I argued beset "entirely mind-dependent" accounts like that of Kit Fine. Quite simply, it looks as if there would be *no* "facts"—propositions being such that, necessarily, if a proposition is a "fact," it is true—about what material things compose wholes. What Priest does to avoid this problem is to appeal to dialethism such that any proposition about whether a thing is identical with another thing (or, composes another as a proper part) is, necessarily, only contingently true. (This is clearly what "stops" transitivity across identity relations as well.) Thus, it can be true both that [1] necessarily, if the xs are identical with y, then the xs compose y as proper parts; and, [2] necessarily, if the xs are identical with y, then the xs do not compose y are proper parts.

Priest's account denies that there are "facts" about composition, but that we can still give an infinitely long list of true conditions under which the xs compose y. Priest therefore concludes his account of material composition by proposing that claims about what things compose what wholes as proper parts can never be answered in a conclusive or satisfactory manner. Instead, the only right answer is to defer them infinitely. For example, he argues that the whole web of relations itself, the structure in which every object and property fits, i.e., the Net of Indra, is similar to a non-well-founded set that requires no proper foundation. Its identity is infinitely analyzable as depending on other things, and no part of the whole, or the whole, requires something having an intrinsic identity.[61] Priest's solution is then not to deny that material composition occurs, or deny that we can know anything about it, but to embrace an infinite regress: what makes it true of any x that it composes y is that *that y* composes z, and so on *ad infinitum*.

There are two considerations which should defeat Priest's account. One is that the account, while providing an infinitely long, true series of the conditions under which composition occurs, does not provide us with a *non-trivial* one. In fact, Fazang makes precisely the claim that, because we can see that causes and effects cannot be defined except in a circular way, that all truths about causation are trivial; this is the salvific import of Huayan: by recognizing "that after all nothing arises and there is nothing to be found, perturbed thoughts naturally cease and erroneous discriminations are annihilated."[62] Fazang's point is that, since Huayan is an *idealist* school of Buddhist metaphysics, distinctions between cause and effect can only be defined in a circular fashion because what it is to be a "cause" or an "effect" depend upon our mental activity in dividing the world. In other words, propositions or judgments about causation are "entirely mind-dependent" rather than facts about the world at all. These propositions or judgments are all trivial. And the *Huayan Jing* seems to draw this conclusion about judgments about *everything*.[63] All truths are only trivially true – including truths about composition, naturally.

Another more serious consideration is that, even if we accept Priest's conclusion that all accounts of material composition are necessarily trivial or incoherent, Priest thinks being an incoherent account of composition is what should push us to accept the trivial account he offers. Yet his own account ends up not only trivial but incoherent in exactly the same way. Imagine that what Fazang claims is in fact the correct view about composition and, indeed, all judgments about the world. Following, then, from the conception of the world as one in which *nothing at all* has an essence, then *all of the truths about anything* are contingent, such that there are no "facts" of any kind. This Huayan position would clearly conflict with the claim I defended above, on which *something* should necessitate the facts about composition. This *cannot* be and is not Priest's view of the material world, because, in order for his account of material composition to arrive at even trivial truths about composition, it has to be [1] that *not every* material thing composes a whole *necessarily,* and [2] it is *not* a necessary truth that material things do not compose anything. [1] is the whole motivation to apply non-transitive theories of identity to material parthood, because being identical with some gluon does not entail being identical with other things that are also identical with that gluon. [2] allows him to avoid mereological Nihilism. It is hard to see what it is in virtue of which these two truths *are facts*, since just what it is to be a fact is for something to be a proposition such that, if it is a "fact," it is a proposition such that it is true ('necessarily, if a proposition is a fact, then it is a true one'). If nothing were a fact (that is, if it were possible for a proposition to be both true and false), Priest could not hold that truths [1] and [2] were necessary conditions about what makes a theory of composition restricted and, consequently, his own account would be incoherent.

What I think that is going on is that Priest implicitly is making a distinction between: truths about anything that is what we can call an "object" and truths about other things. The truths about the *objects* includes things such as propositions, material objects, etc. because these are all the sort of things that can be the subject of a property in their own right. On the other side of the divide is anything that is not the sort of thing to be such a subject, such as the identity or composition relation (since relations are not things), as well as properties, qualities, and other things that are not subjects of predication; it is a circumlocution, of a sort, to say that a "property" *is* essentially a certain way, because properties are the sort of ways that subjects are, rather than being subjects of predication in their own right. But notice now an interesting, unintended point of commonality between Priest's account of composition and those of Thomas Aquinas and Zhu Xi: the things that are "objects" are all equivalent to "substances" in the sense of being the *primary* bearers of properties, whereas the "other things" belong to a different "ontological kind." Priest is implicitly assuming that there is such a distinction between the things that are such as to bear properties and those that are not, where it is *necessarily* true that these two categories are distinct. It would otherwise be incoherent to describe the identity relation as non-transitive, or even possibly non-transitive, if this description of the identity relation did not itself hold *necessarily* of that relation—in other words, unless it were essentially true of the identity relation that it was contingently transitive, the very truth "the identity relation is contingently transitive" would not be a fact about that relation.

This is why Huayan, being a more consistent development of Buddhism than Priest's account of material composition, denies that there *could* be any distinction between "objects" and the "other things" that would deliver the "facts" about the world. And Zhu Xi recognized this as the most serious problem with that theory. Zhu Xi, too, recognizes that it would be a superficial critique of Buddhist doctrines to portray their position as the view that all things "are literally nonexistent and contain nothing (*wu wu* 無物)."[64] He notes that the Buddhists hold that objects truly exist, even though they lack their own nature. But, then he claims that "the distinction between Confucianism and Buddhism lies only in the distinction between emptiness and concreteness.... The very sources of our doctrines are different: we Confucians hold that the myriad [*li*] are real, while the Buddhists hold that the myriad *li* are all empty."[65]

Zhu Xi's *li* does not account merely for facts about composition, and so the identity or nature of a material object is not constituted entirely by that object's relations to other things. Before *li* exists in composition with particular material *qi*, as i.e., the

Heavenly Li 天理, or the general sense of *li*, such "heavenly" *li* is not the "nature" (性) of any material object. Before it informs or is mixed with any particular *qi*, *li* is complete and the root or principle of every nature. When *li* composes a particular object as that object's nature, then *li* takes on particular characteristics associated with the *qi* of that object and its kind; a specific sense of *li* appropriate to some given kind of object. "Before people or things are born, we can speak only of [*li*] and not of the nature … when humans are born then this [*li*] has already fallen into the [material nature], and it is no longer completely the [principle of the nature]."[66] The problem is that the Huayan Buddhists hold that the natures of things are "empty and devoid of content,"[67] and this results in serious problems because it makes it the case that all the truths are trivial. However, even the Huayan Buddhist cannot consistently claim, again, that their construal of the world holds necessarily—i.e., there it is a *fact* that all the truths about things are trivial—unless they presume a distinction like that drawn by Priest between "objects" and "other things."

Zhu Xi hits on exactly where that distinction lies for the Huayan Buddhism. Buddhists, unlike Confucians, "don't at all concern themselves with heaven, earth, and the four directions, only with understanding a single [mind]."[68] Zhu Xi thinks that they practice meditation, introspection, and so forth in order to understand the true nature of reality as fundamentally contingent. But this requires the Huayan Buddhist to draw an implicit distinction between "objects/things" and the mind itself:

> We Confucians take the nature [性] to be real; the Buddhists take pattern [性] to be empty (*xu*), As for their doctrine that refers to nature as the mind, it is unacceptable … first we must recognize [what the mind is] before we can speak [of the nature]. Bida recorded that, "If you refer to that which has knowing and awareness as being the nature, [in fact] you are only talking about the word 'mind.' If there is the nature ordained by heaven then there will be [*qi* 气]. If you take the nature that is ordained by heaven to be based in the mind, then where will the [material nature] be placed?"[69]

For Huayan, truths about *the mind* are the facts, that is, they hold necessarily, and these facts about the mind are what necessitate the facts about everything else. This is what allows Huayan's doctrines to be developed in the direction of saying that all the truths about "objects and other things" are entirely mind-dependent and so trivial. If that is the case, however, there is going to be something that it is essentially to be a *mind*. And Zhu Xi thinks it is obvious that a human mind (*xin* 心) is not like a relation, belonging to a distinct ontological kind from the "objects and other things" but is itself something that essentially belongs to a certain kind of material composite. That is, the human mind is not essentially immaterial. Instead, however, the Buddhists focus on facts about the mind that are *not essential to it*, such as the way that humans typically draw distinctions in certain contexts, or engage in selective attention, and this is why their introspective meditation does not reveal what the Buddhists would hope it does: "Buddhists separate [mind *xin* 心] from *li*, presumably because their methods [of meditation, introspection, etc.] … reveal only the contents of their own contingent psychology … ."[70]

And, in fact, Zhu Xi agrees with Huayan and other Buddhists that all things are connected—and so appropriates the poetic claim from the Buddhists themselves that "*li* is not cut into pieces, but it is instead as if one moon shines in ten thousand rivers."[71] Zhu Xi explicitly opposed his theory of *li-qi* composition to schools of Buddhist Chan 禅 metaphysics, influenced by the same Huayan thought that inspired Priest, concerning the nature of *li*.[72] The Buddhists are inconsistent, Zhu Xi thinks, because they claim that everything lacks a nature, but then in fact appeal implicitly to the nature of the human mind as what accounts for how everything else appears (and to account for the meaningfulness of the position that all the truths about everything else are trivial). The Buddhists have not demonstrated that the world *is* dependent on the mind, because they have not yet demonstrated that *only the mind* is the sort of thing that can have an essence; what the Buddhists have demonstrated is that, *if* the world were entirely mind-dependent, then the truths about the world would be entirely trivial. But, if this is the right way to understand what Huayan Buddhism has done, then there is no principled reason to think that other things might not have essences too, including, for example, material objects. The one *Li*, the whole set of possible configurations of all the things that could exist, is going to be *packed full* of different essences, unlike the Buddhist theory on which there is precisely *one* thing that has an essence (the mind). This is then one way to read what Zhu Xi means by saying Confucians and Buddhists disagree on whether *li* is "real" versus "empty," respectively.

All Coherent Restricted Theories of Composition are Hylomorphic

If Zhu Xi's and my characterizations of Huayan are correct, Huayan is quite similar to hylomorphism. Since Huayan wants everything to be explained by facts about the mind, the Huayan Buddhists cannot think that *each human mind* is a distinct thing. Instead, the mind that unites all of the other things, explaining all of their characteristics, is one particular. Following their Yogācāra predecessors, Fazang and others of the Huayan school refer to a "One Mind" that underlines the varied and fantastical illusion of the phenomenal world that appears to us.[73] Fazang, in the commentary on the *Awakening of Faith in Mahayana,* note that the "One Mind" of the Yogacara school and the "buddha nature" (*tathagatagarbha*) by which all things are essentially characterized are identical with each other. This "One Mind" that underlies all things, according to an interpretation proposed by Van Norden and Jones,

> is neither an individual consciousness nor something that stands apart from or opposed to matter. It is, instead, the one and only source of all that exists, creating and sustaining the dharma-realm of dependent arising—albeit without separation from that realm. One Mind, for Fazang, is reality prior to any individual consciousness and prior to the objects of consciousness (whether mental or material). This priority is ontological, tracking the order with respect to which reality is structured into more or less fundamental components.[74]

All the other things therefore resemble parts or properties *of* that One Mind, as the One is a common part of all them. And the One Mind is precisely something that characterizes every other particular thing *just like a substantial form*, since it is in virtue of the mind that all the other things exist and have the apparent characteristics that they do. Huayan therefore is in fact quite like a version of hylomorphism, *except that* "materiality" is an illusion, and everything is therefore a part of something mental. Rather than a *material* monism, the view is akin to pantheism or an *immaterial* monism, since everything is a part of something that is essentially immaterial.[75]

Views such as Huayan, along with other entirely mind-dependent views of material composition, therefore conflict with the aim of offering a meaningful account of *material* composition as restricted. Huayan is not characterizing the world as material in the right way, because it implies that materiality is an illusion; it is not essential to the world, and the material objects in it, that they are material. This is what sets apart Aquinas and Zhu Xi as hylomorphists: they posit not only substantial forms or *li* as an entity belonging to a distinct ontological category from the material composite wholes, but they also therefore require a principle of "materiality"—*qi* or prime matter—as a distinct metaphysical part of each material object. And that *qi*/prime matter is *essential* to something counting as a "material thing"; that is precisely the role *qi*/prime matter plays in the metaphysics of material composition, as it allows both of these thinkers to characterize what it is to be a "material thing" across the different kinds of material things that there might be.

The lack of a metaphysical part such as "prime matter/*qi*" characterizes all of the views of material composition holding to the possibility of substance-parts.

Theories of material composition on which it is possible for one substance (or material composite) to compose another as a proper part need to characterize the material composites as being distinct kinds of wholes. Since each kind is associated with a distinct parthood relation, there is no transitivity such that, whatever makes substance a's parts compose a is not inherited by the substance b which a could possibly compose as a proper part. Otherwise, both would be the same material whole. All of the Neo-Aristotelians surveyed in the first chapter, Fine, Koslicki, and Jaworski, attempt to offer their own respective accounts as to how this is possible. But what all of them lack, in various ways, is a coherent answer as to how the class of the "material things" forms *one* class. For, if (as Peter van Inwagen does) one characterizes what it is to be a material object such that some kinds of "material thing" are essentially simple but others are not, and there is to be some reason why it is necessarily true that "material things" come in no more than these two kinds, one's theory implies that being a "material thing" is *essentially to be* mereologically simple. Hence, one gets the continuous impression from theories on which substances could compose other substances as proper parts that they are either mereologically Universalist or Nihilist. Either it is the case that "materiality" does not really describe anything in the world, and any two or more things necessarily compose a material whole (since it is arbitrary how to distinguish the "genuine material" objects), or "materiality" describes what essentially composes nothing at all.

In order to coherently affirm a theory of material composition on which it is not a necessary truth either that there are no material composites or that everything counts as such a composite, one needs to steer a course between these two truths, holding that there is some respect in which material things, in a general sense, need not compose anything, but where, in a particular sense, it is not contingent, when the xs actually *do* compose y, that those very same xs compose y. Substantial forms are the kind of thing that belong to their composites essentially, because they belong essentially to kinds of substances, but it is not essential to matter in the general sense that a substantial form belongs to it. If substantial forms were a special kind of material part of those objects, the account would seem to involve an infinite regress, because substantial forms are the same sort of thing we characterized as one which contingently composes a whole. Substantial forms therefore belong to some other ontological kind, distinct from material wholes, such that that kind of thing is exactly what we need to give a meaningful characterization of the circumstances under which the xs compose y, without inadvertently falling into either Nihilism or Universalism.

Given that I have ruled out all alternative answers, such as a mind-dependent theory of material composition, or where facts about the world globally make it the case that composition facts hold among some material parts, or even that a nonstandard account of identity could offer a unique alternative, we are left precisely with the conclusion outlined in the third chapter as a functional characterization of substantial forms. If it is the case that material composition occurs but it does not occur "automatically" between any two or more material things, that in virtue of which xs compose a whole will need to be [1] a particular that characterizes all of the things that compose that whole; [2] a particular essentially such that, when it characterizes the parts, those parts compose that particular whole (rather than any whole of that kind); and [3] a particular which is not identical with the whole or any of the material parts. For that reason, every coherent theory of restricted material composition is a version of hylomorphism.

The only remaining question is whether hylomorphism is really satisfactory or if it is a trivial account of composition. A substantial form can look like an entity that *just is* whatever unifies the material parts, since to say some parts form a whole "when they actually do" does not look informative. With Aquinas' theory of substantial forms in hand, we can see that considering substantial forms as "actualities" is not an *ad hoc* solution to problems of restricted composition. To the contrary, Aquinas' cashing out of material composition in terms of actuality-potentiality that avoids the danger of offering an *ad hoc* solution. The way in which a substantial form is characterized as an *actuality* allows Aquinas to thread the needle because his analysis presumes that forms are not the sort of thing that is in the "fundamental ontology" of a theory. What fundamentally exist are neither forms nor matter but "actualized things."

Aquinas' analysis is informative because failure to make a distinction of this sort in the theoretical structure of a theory of restricted composition can generate overdetermination worries in material composition. By way of illustration, Trenton Merricks characterizes overdetermination in this way: "an effect is overdetermined if the following are true: that effect is caused by an object; that object is causally irrelevant to whether some object—i.e., numerically distinct— object or objects cause that effect; and the other object or objects do indeed cause that effect."[76] Then consider some a causal effect, like the shattering of a window, and some whole with simple constituents, e.g., a baseball and its atoms. Merricks offers an argument against the possibility of simples composing a whole, with the example of a baseball composed of its atoms, then can be given as follows:

(1) The baseball, if it exists, is causally irrelevant to whether its constituent atoms, acting in concert, cause the shattering of the window.
(2) The shattering of the window is caused by those atoms acting in concert.

(3) The shattering of the window is not overdetermined.
Therefore,
(4) If the baseball exists, it does not cause the shattering of the window.[77]

Jaworski's version of hylomorphism, for example, *is* susceptible to such overdetermination worries, which come in the form of "bootstrapping" or "downward causation" objections to structure as a causal power that unites the parts by causally influencing them to act in concert some way. That is, the baseball is what bears the powers it has, and we cannot divide what it is to be a baseball from being a set of atoms arranged in a suitable way such as to form a member of that kind of thing, That makes it appear as if a baseball, assuming "baseball" were a substance, had some causal power for configuring its own atoms, even though the baseball is then acting upon itself to give itself a power (by configuring its parts to be the sort of thing that can bear powers). This is to explain composition in exactly the respect where we need an explanation of why the baseball's parts compose a whole which is the sort of thing to bear powers. Koslicki's account too suffers from the problem that she appeals to the essences of the parts as what accounts for why they compose wholes of a particular kind, but is unable to give a clear account why *any particular parts* compose the *particular* wholes that they do. Overdetermination worries arise from acceptance, in short, of an account on which different senses of "material whole" to make sense of the way in which something like an atom could still be a material whole even while it composes the baseball as a proper part. This is to accept the possibility of substances compose other substances as proper parts, while both remain substances in each of their distinct kind of "material whole," with distinct parthood relations characterizing each.

What sets apart substantial forms is that, when we speak of the "form" of a substance, we are only distinguishing one way in which that thing exists, namely, we are selectively considering the way in which that thing is an instance of *actualizing* a potentiality or set of potentialities, in the same way we characterize a causal power as intrinsically such that it is a power *for* a manifestation. There is then no clear way in which, by distinguishing a substantial form from its composite, we are setting up an infinite regress. It is just the same kind of distinction, for Aquinas, as one finds between properties and property-bearers,[78] or powers and their manifestations.[79] The distinction in all such cases is not between two actualized things, but between a power and an actuality that together constitute one actualized thing. As a distinct kind of actualization from that which we find among causal powers, the potential which substantial forms actualize is not the potential to bring about some effect but the potential "to be a material object" of a particular kind. This then requires Aquinas's distinction between two senses of the potential that is actualized by a substantial form in a material object: the general sense in which it is contingent that "matter" constitutes any particular material composite, since it is contingent whether any material objects exist at all, and the particular sense in which a substantial form actualizes some *kind* of object (having some essential properties or parts), since any particular substantial form only actualizes one way that the material parts or the whole could be configured.[80]

Consequently, on a hylomorphic theory, Merrick's argument has made a basic mistake by counting the baseball alongside its atoms. If a baseball *were* a substance, then the material parts would have ceased to be the sorts of things that could be counted in their own right as "actualized things" alongside the only "actualized thing" in the example: the baseball. (As Aquinas puts it, the material parts are "in potentiality" to the composite that they compose.) In other words, if the baseball were a substance, then (1) is false. The baseball is nothing over-and-above the parts suitably characterized by the substantial form of the whole.[81] On this picture, it makes no sense to think of the parts having their powers independently of the substance or of the substance having powers independently of its parts; the most that could be said is that the *baseball* was exercising a causal power to shatter the window *insofar as* it exercised that power by means of its material parts (since parts can bear powers in only a derivative sense).[82]

Nor does this overdetermination worry recur for substantial forms themselves, even in that special case where the human soul is thought to be the sort of substantial form that could survive the death of the human composite,[83] because a substantial form is counted among the parts of the whole. That is, the substantial form is a *metaphysical* part, but it is in potentiality to the composite in an analogous sense to that in which the material parts are. A substantial form does not compose a distinct "actualized thing" when it constitutes a composite material whole. While the substantial form actualizes the material parts, the substantial form only characterizes those particular parts (and so constitutes an object from them) because the composite whole exists; the substantial form is not a "necessary being" which would exist whether or not the composite does. The substantial form is rather "in potential" to the whole insofar as the whole is not a necessarily existent thing (in all cases of material wholes, for Aquinas), but was brought into existence by some causal process. The substantial form is the actualization that such a process brings about when that process successfully constitutes some xs as proper parts of a material whole y.

Aquinas therefore explicitly underlines multiple times that the human soul is essentially such *as to be the actuality of* a particular human material composite, which is why transmigration of souls is impossible; it is only that the human soul is not *essentially* the actualization of a particular material whole. This is a difference between saying: the soul is a part such that it necessarily characterizes the parts of a particular material whole; and the soul is such a part that it necessarily can *only* be a part of that material whole. Again, modal clarifications like these are important to avoid confusion. The human soul is not unlike other substantial forms in the first of these claims, because many material objects can survive a change of material parts. A substantial form of such composites that can change parts cannot be essential to the *particular material parts*, otherwise it would be false that the material object was of such a kind as to survive a change of parts! The only unique claim for the human soul is that the soul does not essentially characterize material parts.[84]

Whether this is true, Aquinas thinks, requires determining the causal process by which the soul was produced; Aquinas does not think material objects are such, as a class, able to produce the human soul (only God can) given that the soul has intellectual powers that are not essentially those of any possible material organ.[85] Even though the survival of human soul after death of the particular composite which it essentially composes is clearly supposed to be (even for Aquinas) an exceptional case, and one can disagree with his arguments as to why a soul can subsist after death, his claims illustrate an important respect in which both Confucian and Thomistic hylomorphism improve over other accounts of composition.

Conclusion: The Significance of Hylomorphism

Hylomorphic accounts of composition such as those presented by Thomas Aquinas and Zhu Xi are not alone in an intuition that there is a real, discernible, extra-mental difference between genuinely unified composite wholes, i.e., the substances, and other things. Kathrin Koslicki, Peter van Inwagen, and William Jaworski all refer to extra-mereological considerations that undergird the motivation for their restricted theory of composition, because there is a real difference between the genuine wholes and the pseudo-objects. Koslicki's earlier book, *The Structure of Objects*, explains the unity of genuine structured wholes by appeal to the fact that the parts of that whole satisfy the requirements of a natural kind. Koslicki there argued that belief in natural kinds is motivated by extra-mereological considerations. Natural kinds are frequently posited, she believes, in the context of natural science. These considerations from natural science reveal to us that certain classes of objects, the natural kinds, are genuine instances of structured wholes.[86] The objects belonging to natural kinds are "ontologically privileged" because there are independent reasons from scientific research to believe that there exist the objects that are members of natural kinds, such as dogs. This is a strike against mereological Nihilism, because these objects have parts.

By contrast, it is a strike against mereological Universalism that we have no reason to believe in the objects that would result from taking a principle of unrestricted composition. On mereological Universalism, any two or more things compose an object, and there would be infinitely many objects such as "trout-turkeys" (viz., an object composed of the head of a trout and the body of a turkey). But "such (alleged) objects, and the pseudo-kinds to which they belong, lack any significance with respect to the sorts of considerations that are invoked in regions outside of mereology to justify our belief in the existence in a particular kind of object."[87] We have good reason to believe the objects that are members of natural kinds are genuine material objects, or substances, whereas we have no extra-mereological grounds to believe that "trout-turkeys" are genuine objects.

In *Form, Matter, and Substance*, Koslicki specifies properties in virtue of which we can discover the natural kinds. Objects belonging to natural kinds have an internal principle of unity—a structure—which results in the parts of those wholes exhibiting a certain kind of behavior (and so belonging to the kinds). Natural kinds therefore are classes of objects that are distinguished by a high degree of *unity* in capacity and function.[88] Koslicki calls the relevant behavior that indicates a unified material object "lawful interactional interdependence" among its parts. Two objects exhibit such interactional interdependence when an object of some kind and another object of a different kind when the first has some capacities that can only be manifested in tandem with the capacities of the second object.[89] In other words, for Koliscki, a thing is a whole or unified material object, properly speaking, just when it is a thing having some unique set of causal powers, where its parts belong to different kinds, interacting together so that those parts manifest these powers in a law-like fashion.[90]

By contrast, the kind of hylomorphism proposed by Aquinas (and Zhu Xi) apparently suffer from a defect. They hold that, at the moment something comes to compose a substance as a proper part, that thing must undergo a change in kind membership. I argued that none of these kinds of changes need to be interpreted as mysterious "replacement" cases. The "classical" hylomorphist does not hold that, when a substance comes to compose another substance as a proper part, that the substance that becomes a part by being mysteriously "replaced" by a token substance-look-alike with all the same properties and powers. All that is required is that, in a case when one substance composes another substance as a proper part, what *was* a substance *becomes* a part. Aquinas' senses in which the particular matter of one kind of compound substance has a power to *become* a part of another substance. Aquinas can even distinguish ways in which parts *themselves* bear certain properties, albeit in a derivative way, which get preserved across substantial changes. All that is required in this claim, minimally, is that a substance cannot remain *exactly the same thing in all respects* when it comes to compose another substance as a proper part, or when a proper part of a substance decomposes that substance and becomes a substance in its own right.

What fills out the account is the way in which Aquinas thinks we discover and identify the natural kinds. Substantial forms are *actualities*, not actualized things, which are in potentiality both to their substances, in the respect that they are actualities *of* that substance, and to the causal process from which that substance resulted. Picking out the things with substantial forms thus requires us to identify *the causal process* by which some things are modified in order to become a whole. There are real differences among the causal processes that might produce distinct kinds of substances or parts. The account in fact rests the nature of what resolves the problem of material composition on the extra-mereological considerations that should lead us to hold that some causal processes produce (or lead to the destruction of) instances of a natural kind. A causal process produces a substance, for instance, when that process brings some things together as parts such that the things that are the parts of the resultant substance are no longer essentially the same as the things that became those parts. Conversely, the process that leads to a destruction of a substance is one in which that substance "loses" some essential part or property over the course of the change and, *ipso facto*, ceases to exist. Even a "brute" theory of composition on which there is an infinite series of conditions under which the xs compose y can be hylomorphic if those conditions are interpreted as corresponding to different natural kinds of object; there would be no conflict with hylomorphism's account of the nature of material composition if there were infinitely many natural kinds, even if there might be some other good reason to think it is impossible for there to be truly be an "infinite" number of such kinds.[91] The account of natural kinds therefore tells us which are the things that have substantial forms, and so are the "genuine material objects."

Aquinas and Zhu Xi give us good reasons to think an empirical, scientific method for identifying the substances by appeal to facts about such causal processes is a promising one. They share with Koslicki the perspective that substances are characterized by distinct essential properties, but they deny that a substance can be composed of substance-parts that have distinct essential properties from the whole. What it *means* for a thing to be unified is to be a member of a natural kind, to be a material object of a determinate nature.[92] Whether an atom comes to compose a molecule, for example, is determined by whether that atom's essential properties changed in virtue of becoming an apparent part. These give us those criteria in virtue of which there is unity among the molecule's atomic elements, quarks, and electrons. And those criteria for molecules are of a very different sort from the criteria for other substances. Different natural kinds exemplify different kinds of unified causal powers or activities among the parts; it would be impossible to determine what "lawful interactional dependence" consists in, in general, without a minimal account of the natural kinds. Different natural kinds exemplify different essential activities or properties or powers or structures.

In the Thomistic/Confucian picture, then, the role that the form has in unifying some parts into a whole depends on *the rights kinds of changes in virtue of which some object changes kind membership* and thereby becomes a part of another thing of a distinct kind. That is, if substances can never compose other substances as parts, things must cease to be members of one kind and become members of another kind at the time they become parts.[93] For human beings, the unity among our parts is explained by facts about our organic chemistry as animals of a special sort. Captain Hook is a living, organic thing of a particular natural kind *human being*, where his parts are unified by bio-chemical bonds and various bio-organizational interactions. That in virtue of which all of his material parts are of the same kind *human being* is what makes those parts belong to Hook, but Hook is neither identical with his kind (the essence of *human being*), nor is Hook merely that which makes him a member of the kind or all his parts human (his soul). Rather, Hook is a substance formed of his material parts, suitably informed and united by his soul. When Captain Hook loses his hand to the crocodile, then that hand ceases to compose Captain Hook *because* that action causes his hand to cease to have the right bio-chemical bonds and interactions, so that Hook's substantial form ceases to be something Hook shares in common with that piece of matter that formerly was his hand. When Captain Hook acquires a hook made of iron and wood, and puts the hook in the place of his hand, that hook is not a part of Captain Hook because the hook is not changed into the right *kind* of thing that could be a part of his living, organic body. His substantial form does not overlap with any material parts of the hook, because the substantial form just is that in virtue of which Hook is a biological organism of a kind, and the hook is not the right kind of thing to be part of a biological organism.[94]

In sum, on the Thomistic/Confucian theory, the only way to determine the way in which a substantial form accounts for the unity of the parts of a substance is to determine the nature of the substance in question. This seems the best reason to commend the Thomistic and Confucian account of substantial forms. Questions about the unity of material objects can be resolved to a certain degree at an abstract, metaphysical level, but are fundamentally a matter to be resolved through empirical investigation. Hylomorphism of the Thomistic and Confucian sort appeals to forms to explain material composition, but what and how a form accounts for the composition of a substance depends on the *kind* of the substance it informs. This reliance on natural kinds grounds answers to the Special Composition Question soundly on empirical concerns; the question of what kinds there are, or their properties, can be given a fully satisfactory answer only in tandem with scientific investigation.

In the end, if it turns out that all those theories of material composition on which composition is restricted are hylomorphic at their core, then hylomorphism is not merely another answer among others to the Special Composition Question. Rather, *all* consistent answers to that question are hylomorphic. This view of the situation becomes more plausible if it is true that philosophers on either side of the planet, with no access to each other's writings and living in very different cultural, linguistic, social, and religious contexts, arrived at an explanation of the material universe on which forms, or *li*, matter.

Notes

Introduction

1 Lu Meipo 盧梅坡, "雪梅·其一," (translation mine) Chinese text taken from *Poems of the Chinese Masters* (Port Townsend, WA: Copper Canyon Press, 2003), 358. [有梅無雪不精神, 有雪無詩俗了人。日暮詩成天又雪, 與梅並作十分春。]
2 Peter van Inwagen, *Material Beings* (Ithaca, NY: Cornell University Press, 1990), 21.
3 Michael Rea, *Metaphysics: The Basics* (New York: Routledge, 2014), 132.
4 Omitting works of the three hylomorphists I survey in this chapter, some prominent works include: Simon Evnine, *Making Objects and Events: A Hylomorphic Theory of Artifacts, Actions, and Organisms* (Oxford: Oxford University Press, 2016); Verity Harte, *Plato on Parts and Wholes: The Metaphysics of Structure* (Oxford: Clarendon Press, 2002); Mark Johnston, "Parts and Principles: False Axioms in Mereology," *Philosophical Topics* 30 (2002): 129–66; Mark Johnston, "Hylomorphism," *The Journal of Philosophy* 103 (2006): 652–98; E. J. Lowe, "Form Without Matter," in *Form and Matter: Themes in Contemporary Metaphysics*, edited by David Oderberg (Oxford: Blackwell, 1999), 1–21; Anna Marmodoro, "Hylomorphic Unity," in Ricki Bliss and James Miller (eds.), *The Routledge Handbook of Metametaphysics* (New York: Routledge Taylor & Francis, July 2020), 284–99; Daniel D. Novotný and Lukáš Novák (eds.), *Neo-Aristotelian Perspectives in Metaphysics* (New York: Routledge, 2014); David Oderberg, *Real Essentialism* (New York: Routledge Taylor & Francis, 2007); Michail Peramatzis, *Priority in Aristotle's Metaphysics* (New York: Oxford University Press, 2011); Michael Rea, "Hylomorphism Reconditioned," *Philosophical Perspectives* 25 (2011): 341–58; Thomas Sattig, *The Double Lives of Objects* (Oxford: Oxford University Press, 2015); Eleonore Stump, "Emergence, Causal Powers, and Aristotelianism in Metaphysics," in *Powers and Capacities in Philosophy: The New Aristotelianism*, edited by Ruth Groff and John Greco (New York: Routledge, 2013), 48–68; Patrick Toner, "On Hylemorphism and Personal Identity," *European Journal of Philosophy* 19 (2011), 454–73; Patrick Toner, "Hylemorphic Animalism," *Philosophical Studies* 155 (2011): 65–81.
5 David Oderberg, "Is Form Structure?" in *Neo-Aristotelian Perspectives in Metaphysics. Routledge Studies in Metaphysics*, edited by Daniel Novotny and Lukas Novak (New York: Routledge Taylor & Francis, 2014), 164–80; c.f., Jeremy

Skrzypek, "Three Concerns for Structural Hylomorphism," *Analytic Philosophy* 58, no. 4 (December 2017), 360–408.
6   I am not using this term "entity" in anything more than a generic sense as referring to "anything that exists."

Chapter 1

1   van Inwagen, *Material Beings*, 17.
2   Here I am closely following a rough formulation of the SCQ given in van Inwagen, *Material Beings*, 19.
3   Rea, *Metaphysics*, 105.
4   See Dean Zimmerman, "Theories of Masses and Problems of Constitution," *The Philosophical Review* 104, no. 1 (Jan. 1995): 53–110.
5   See Rea, *Metaphysics*, 103–4.
6   Ibid., 102–3.
7   Ibid., 104.
8   van Inwagen, *Material Beings*, 30. van Inwagen offers clarification on how this formula is to be read esp. on pgs. 25–30 of the same, which is particularly helpful for understanding that x and y are "plural variables," so that the phrase should be read as "when is it true of any things whatever that they$_x$ are such that they$_x$ are all parts of they$_y$ and no two of them$_x$ overlap [i.e., have a common part] and every part of them$_y$ overlaps at least one of them$_x$?"
9   Ibid., 29.
10 Ibid., 72.
11 Achille Varzi, "Mereology," in *The Stanford Encyclopedia of Philosophy* (Winter 2016 Edition), edited by Edward N. Zalta. Available at: https://plato.stanford.edu/archives/win2016/entries/mereology/, 44.
12 David Lewis, *Parts of Classes* (Oxford: Blackwell, 1991), 7.
13 van Inwagen, *Material Beings*, 72.
14 Ibid., 74.
15 Ibid., 74.
16 Ibid., 72.
17 For further objections against either of these extreme views, see Ross Inman, *Substance and the Fundamentality of the Familiar* (New York: Routledge, 2018); Daniel Z. Korman, "Ordinary Objects," in *The Stanford Encyclopedia of Philosophy*, (Spring 2014 Edition), edited by Edward N. Zalta. Available at: http://plato.stanford.edu/archives/spr2014/entries/ordinary-objects/; Daniel Z. Korman, "Unrestricted Composition and Restricted Quantification," *Philosophical Studies* 140 (2009): 319–34; Daniel Z. Korman, *Objects: Nothing Out of the Ordinary* (Oxford: Oxford University Press, 2016).

18 van Inwagen, *Material Beings*, 31.
19 Most classical hylomorphists hold that organisms have substantial forms, but how to understand the forms of artifacts, like Goliath, is controversial.
20 Here I summarize from Varzi, "Mereology," 2.1.
21 Ibid., 4.5
22 Kit Fine, "Things and Their Parts," *Midwest Studies in Philosophy* 23, no. 1 (1999): 63.
23 Ibid.
24 Ibid., 69. In fact, Fine complicates the example by considering the car as a variable embodiment of rigid embodiments, but I simplify here.
25 Ibid., 65.
26 Ibid.
27 Ibid., 64.
28 Fine, "Response to Kathrin Koslicki," *Dialectica* 61, no. 1 (Mar. 2007): 162.
29 Fine, "Things and Their Parts," 73.
30 Fine notes that the operation of rigid embodiment is *sui generis*, and we can wonder whether the same might be true of the relation by which principles of embodiment are parts of objects; c.f., "Things and Their Parts," 66.
31 Kit Fine, "Towards a Theory of Part," *The Journal of Philosophy* 107, no. 11 (Nov. 2010): 569.
32 Kit Fine, "Aristotle on Matter," *Mind*, New Series 101, no. 401 (Jan. 1992): 38.
33 Fine, "Aristotle on Matter," 38.
34 Fine, "Towards a Theory of Part," 589.
35 Fine, "Things and Their Parts," 63.
36 Kathrin Koslicki, *The Structure of Objects* [SO] (Oxford: Oxford University Press, 2008), 83.
37 SO, 169.
38 Fine, "Things and Their Parts," 73.
39 Fine, "Response to Koslicki," 162–3.
40 SO, 86.
41 SO, 85, fn. 9.
42 Kit Fine, "Relatively Unrestricted Quantification," in *Absolute Generality*, edited by Agustín Rayo and Gabriel Uzquiano (Oxford: Oxford University Press, 2006), 38–9.
43 Fine, "Response to Kathrin Koslicki," 165.
44 Ibid., 163.
45 Ibid., 164.
46 Ibid., 164–5.
47 Ibid.
48 Ibid.
49 Ibid.

50 Fine explicitly links this to operations of composition in "Towards a Theory of Part," op. cit.
51 Fine, "Things and Their Parts," 73.
52 Fine, "Response to Koslicki," 164–5.
53 Fine, "Things and Their Parts," 69: "In contrast to the case of a rigid embodiment $a, b, c, \ldots$? R, the matter of a variable embodiment is not given independently of the form or principle, but is itself specified by means of that principle."
54 Kit Fine, "Compounds and Aggregates," *Nous* 28, no. 2 (Jun. 1994): 151.
55 Fine, "Things and Their Parts," 71–2.
56 SO, 171.
57 SO, 7.
58 SO, 168–9.
59 SO, 172–86.
60 Ibid.
61 SO, 187. This is the third non-temporal relative rephrasing of the principle.
62 SO, 185.
63 She also proposes that each of these principles can be temporally-relativized, if necessary; SO, 190.
64 SO, 169.
65 SO, 174, 176–9.
66 SO, 174.
67 SO, 233.
68 SO, 204–10.
69 SO, 180.
70 SO, 181.
71 SO, 183.
72 SO, 167–8.
73 SO, 183.
74 Her formal definition of my paraphrase of Leibniz's Law is: "If $x = y$, then every property of x is a property of y." SO, 45.
75 SO, 180.
76 SO, 181.
77 SO, 180.
78 SO, 180.
79 SO, 251.
80 SO, 253–4.
81 SO, 253.
82 Kathrin Koslicki, "Aristotle's Mereology and the Status of Form," *The Journal of Philosophy* 103, no. 12 (Dec. 2006): 733.
83 Ibid., 734.

84 Kathrin Koslicki, *Form, Matter, Substance* [FMS] (Oxford: Oxford University Press, 2018), 164–7.
85 For a further example, see SO, 151.
86 SO, 197.
87 Koslicki does admit the possibility that the matter of a composite could be mereologically simple, but takes no stand whether or not these kinds of parts are metaphysically necessary or even possible.
88 FMS, 191.
89 For her defense of the existence of natural kinds, see SO, 200–34.
90 In the definition of generic interactional dependence given at FMS 211–12, Koslicki explicitly sees the members of some interactional dependence as both individually members of natural kinds.
91 SO, 147.
92 SO, 147.
93 William Jaworski, "Hylomorphism and Part-Whole Realism," *Ancient Philosophy Today: Dialogoi* 1, no. 1 (2019): 112. DOI: 10.3366/anph.2019.0007
94 William Jaworski, *Structure and the Metaphysics of Mind* (Oxford: Oxford University Press, 2016), 104.
95 Ibid., 106.
96 Ibid., 3, 97.
97 Ibid., 104.
98 Ibid., 94.
99 Ibid., 96.
100 Ibid., 94.
101 Ibid., 28.
102 Jaworski, "Hylomorphism and Part-Whole Realism," 118.
103 Jaworski, *Structure and Metaphysics of Mind*, 95.
104 Ibid., 38.
105 Jaworski, *Structure and Metaphysics of Mind*, 29–30.
106 Jaworski, "Hylomorphism and Part-Whole Realism," 118–19.
107 Jaworski, *Structure and Metaphysics of Mind*, 55–6.
108 Ibid., 65.
109 Ibid., 63.
110 Ibid., 63.
111 Ibid., 118.
112 Ibid., 121–3.
113 Ibid., 120–2.
114 Ibid., 332.
115 Ibid., 106.
116 Ibid., 116–17.
117 Ibid., 116.

118 Ibid., 120.
119 Ibid., 27.

Chapter 2

1   Varzi, "Mereology," 4.4.
2   Notice that neither mereologically simple entities without parts, e.g., electrons, nor an immaterial object such as God, would be substances on this characterization.
3   I could qualify that the *xs* have to be structured *in the right way* because, for some, like Jaworski, only some structures account for substances (e.g., individual-making structures).
4   As noted in the first chapter, Koslicki's qualifications that perhaps nothing is a substance *simpliciter* do not prevent her from identifying exemplar unified instances of material objects; FMS, 191.
5   I am not presuming that material objects are concrete, even if that would be sensible, because Koslicki holds that some abstract things might be objects. Abstract objects, like sets, are "particular things" in my general sense.
6   For example, if electrons compose a material object, e.g., a quantum state, when they become entangled with each other, then SPP would entail that, even if these electrons are indiscernible, they are numerically distinct substances that are "the same particulars" before, during, and after being entangled.
7   In the fifth chapter, I address a case where identity relations might be many-to-one, and so where there might be "plural" identities. Here, I am assuming that identity is one-to-one. See Harold Noonan and Ben Curtis, "Identity," *The Stanford Encyclopedia of Philosophy* (Summer 2018 Edition), edited by Edward N. Zalta. URL = https://plato.stanford.edu/archives/sum2018/entries/identity/, sec. 8.
8   This remains true in *Form Matter Substance,* as in FMS, 217–20.
9   SO, 147.
10 SO, 170.
11 The reason each of these thinkers opts for the second interpretation of SPP is probably because the first interpretation likely requires one to hold a fairly thin view of material composition, if not a trivial one, because it ties composition not to criteria like kind membership but rather numerical identity. (NB: this kind of account, however, is distinct from a *brutal* account of composition, as will be discussed in chapter five). For something to be identical with something else in this way seems to either preclude composition, to require the view that composition is identity (which we had to rule out), or to make compositional restrictions trivial. Consider, in regard to the latter, the view that the *xs* compose a *y* if and only if there is a *y*. That seems very close to saying the *xs* compose a *y* if and only if *they just do,*

if nothing else is added, or merely that the composite exists whenever the parts do. All of three of the hylomorphists I survey claim that composition does not occur merely in virtue of the existence of the parts [See Fine, "Things and Their Parts," 63–4; SO, 169–90; Jaworski, *Structure and the Metaphysics of Mind*, 120].

12. See Ricki Bliss and Kelly Trogdon, "Metaphysical Grounding," *The Stanford Encyclopedia of Philosophy* (Winter 2016 Edition), edited by Edward N. Zalta. URL = https://plato.stanford.edu/archives/win2016/entries/grounding/; Tuomas E. Tahko and E. Jonathan Lowe, "Ontological Dependence," *The Stanford Encyclopedia of Philosophy* (Winter 2016 Edition), edited by Edward N. Zalta. URL = https://plato.stanford.edu/archives/win2016/entries/dependence-ontological/. Whereas Karen Bennett holds grounding relations are part of an overarching natural class of building relations in her *Making Things Up* (Oxford: Oxford University Press, 2017), I am, in fact, skeptical that "grounding" refers to any such one or natural class of relations; James Dominic Rooney, "Grounding Relations Are Not Unified," in *International Philosophical Quarterly* (2019): https://doi.org/10.5840/ipq201912125. Here I agree with Koslicki, who holds grounding is too coarse-grained to be of help in metaphysics [See Kathrin Koslicki, "The Course-graineness of Grounding," in *Oxford Studies in Metaphysics*, vol. 9, edited by K. Bennett and D. Zimmerman (Oxford: Oxford University Press, 2015), 306–41].

13. See van Inwagen, *Material Beings*, 8.

14. It would be difficult to see the way in which appealing to a universal would be able to get the result that we need, as universals are not "in" their instances except by some further relation—generating another regress. See EJ Lowe, "A Neo-Aristotelian Substance Ontology," in *Contemporary Aristotelian Metaphysics*, edited by Tuomas Tahko (Cambridge: Cambridge University Press, 2012), esp. 231–7; EJ Lowe, "Form without Matter," in *Form and Matter*, edited by David Oderberg (Oxford: Blackwell, 1999), 7–9; Peter van Inwagen, "Relational vs. Constituent Ontologies," *Philosophical Perspectives* 25, no. 1 (Dec. 2011): 393–6.

15. Peter van Inwagen holds one "life" cannot overlap another except in cases where they are subordinated to each other. See *Material Beings*, 89.

16. Jaworski, *Structure and the Metaphysics of Mind*, 104.

17. van Inwagen, *Material Beings*, 81.

18. Ibid., 81–2.

19. Jaworski, "Hylomorphism and Part-Whole Realism," 118.

20. Jaworski, *Structure and the Metaphysics of Mind*, 3.

21. Ibid., 4.

22. Ibid., 4–5.

23. Ibid., 107–8.

24. Ibid., 4.

25. Travis Dumsday, "Natural Kind Essentialism, Substance Ontology, and the Unity Problem," *Dialectica* 70, no. 4 (2016): 620.

26 Jaworski, *Structure*, 621.
27 Even though a worry would likely remain. Compare the view of Michael Rea, who argues that substances can have a structural power-property that unites the cooperative manifestation of the powers of their proper parts: "one power P unites some other powers just in case that P is so connected to the other powers that its manifestation depends upon the cooperative manifestation of the united powers and, furthermore, the latter do not confer any powers on the object has P that are both intrinsic to the object and independent of P," [Michael Rea, "Hylomorphism, Reconditioned," *Philosophical Perspectives* 25 (2011): 348–9]. Anna Marmadoro questioned whether Rea's structural power "P" that unifies the manifestations of other powers "is a power at all, and if so, what it is that makes *it* a power too, over and above the powers that is supposedly unifies. What is it that differentiates P from a structure of powers? In what sense is the manifestation of P over and above the manifestation of its constituent powers?" [Anna Marmodoro, "Aristotle's Hylomorphism without Reconditioning," *Philosophical Inquiry* 36, nos. 1–2 (Winter–Spring 2013): 14].
28 Jaworski, *Structure and the Metaphysics of Mind*, 27–9.
29 Ibid., 28.
30 Ibid., 333.
31 John Heil, "Hylomorphism: What's Not to Like?" *Synthese* (2018): 8, https://doi.org/10.1007/s11229-018-1792-x.
32 Jaworski, *Structure and the Metaphysics of Mind*, 124–5.
33 Ibid., 201–5, 281–5.
34 Ibid., 123.
35 Ibid., 278.
36 Ibid., 162, 199.
37 "Necessarily, for any structured individual, x, if x has the power to engage in activity A at time t, then ... necessarily, for any individual z and time t^*, if z has proper parts at t^* exactly similar to x's at t, then z has the power to engage in A-ing at t^*," (Ibid., 182).
38 Ibid., 199–200.
39 Ibid., 277–8.
40 Ibid., 140.
41 Ibid., 252.
42 Ibid., 9.
43 Thanks to Jeremy Skrzypek for the formulation of the point here.
44 SO, 180.
45 Marmodoro, "Aristotle's Hylomorphism without Reconditioning," 11.
46 Katarina Perovic, "Bradley's Regress," *The Stanford Encyclopedia of Philosophy* (Winter 2017 Edition), edited by Edward N. Zalta. URL = https://plato.stanford.

edu/archives/win2017/entries/bradley-regress/, esp. sec. 2.1–2.2.3. Paoletti also argues for a different account of modes; Ibid., 10–11.
47. Ibid.; but, c.f., Francesco Orilia, "Bradley's Regress and Ungrounded Dependence Chains: A Reply to Cameron," *Dialectica* 63, no. 3 (2009): 333–41.
48. FMS, 116.
49. FMS, 99, 102.
50. FMS, 100.
51. FMS, 121.
52. FMS, 108.
53. FMS, 120.
54. FMS, 119.
55. See SO, 256–7.
56. Alan Sidelle, "Does Hylomorphism Offer a Distinct Solution to the Grounding Problem?" *Analysis* 74, no. 3 (2014): 402.
57. FMS, 123.
58. FMS, 121.
59. SO, 186–8.
60. And further: if essences were mereologically complex, an essence will itself need a principle in virtue of which that essence is one thing—in virtue of which the parts of that essence compose one essence. For a development of these objections, see for example Andrew Arlig, "Multiplex Composition and the Prospects for Substantial Unity," in *Hylomorphism and Mereology*, Proceedings of the Society for Medieval Logic and Metaphysics, vol. 15, edited by Gyula Klima and Alex Hall (Newcastle upon Tyne: Cambridge Scholars Publishing, 2018), 1–20. By contrast, if essences were simple in such a way that they avoid that problem, then the account, again, seems to avoid the whole problem of material composition by accepting a view equivalent to Nihilism. That makes structures explanatorily vacuous within an account of material composition. See, for example, Michele Paolini Paoletti, "Structures as Relations," *Synthese* (2018), 15, https://doi.org/10.1007/s11229-018-01918-8. She holds that a whole which is produced by the structure and the parts is not a complex, composite entity composed of other substances at all. Instead, the whole produced by structured parts is a simple entity.

Chapter 3

1. I got this joke from Richard Garnett, "Mild and Equitable Establishments," *First Things* (April 2019), https://www.firstthings.com/article/2019/04/mild-and-equitable-establishments.
2. E.g., Eleonore Stump, *Aquinas* (New York: Routledge, 2003), 42.

3   Aquinas held that it is impossible to offer a formally adequate definition of "substance;" see Gregory Doolan, "Aquinas on *Substance* as a Metaphysical Genus," in *The Science of Being as Being*, edited by G. Doolan (Washington, DC: CUA Press, 2012), 99–128; John Wippel, *Metaphysical Thought of Thomas Aquinas* (Washington, DC: CUA Press, 2000), 228–37.
4   Thomas Aquinas, *Quaestiones Quodlibetales* [QQ] (Taurini edition, 1956), IX, q. 3, ad. 2 (Unless cited, all translations that follow are my own) [substantia est res cuius naturae debetur esse non in alio.]
5   It may be noted, first, that Aquinas' characterization involves a normative dimension ("to which it belongs"/*debetur*). Aquinas requires this normative qualification to address certain miraculous cases where things that ordinarily are substances exist as parts (e.g., Christ's human nature), and cases where things that ordinarily are properties of substances exist without inhering in any substance (e.g., Eucharistic accidents). As my discussion of substances is limited to non-miraculous cases of material composition, I have eliminated any normative dimension in characterizing substances.
6   Aquinas himself holds that there are immaterial substances of various kinds, and I will allude at various times to Aquinas' claims about immaterial substances, but I only appeal to these more global commitments about immaterial substances to illustrate Aquinas' general metaphysics.
7   For a helpful overview, see Christopher Brown, *Aquinas and the Ship of Theseus* (New York, NY: Continuum, 2005), esp. 98–112.
8   Robert Pasnau, *Metaphysical Themes 1274–1671* (Oxford: Oxford University Press, 2011), 35–40.
9   Stump, *Aquinas*, 37.
10 *Pace* Jaworski, *Structure and the Metaphysics of Mind*, 332.
11 See *De Substantiis Separatis*, c. 6.
12 ST I, q. 77, a. 1, ad. 2. See also, Wippel, *Metaphysical Thought*, 319.
13 *Pace* Travis Dumsday, "Can a Relational Substance Ontology Be Hylomorphic?" in *Synthese* (2019), 5, https://doi.org/10.1007/s11229-019-02173-1. See further ST I, q. 66, resp.
14 ST I, q. 66, a. 1. C.f., Quodlibet III, q.1, a. 1, resp.
15 Anna Marmodoro and Ben Page, "Aquinas on Forms, Substances and Artifacts," *Vivarium* 54, no. 1 (2016),12.
16 ST I, q. 77, a. 1, ad. 2. [actus ad quem est in potentia materia prima, est substantialis forma.]
17 Thomas Aquinas, *De Principiis Naturae* (Leonine edition, 1972), caput 1, 5.
18 Stump, *Aquinas*, 38.
19 Robert Pasnau, "Mind and Hylomorphism," in *The Oxford Handbook to Medieval Philosophy*, edited by John Marenbon (Oxford University Press, 2012), 492.
20 SLM, 775.

21 QDA, a. 9, resp.
22 QDA, a. 1, ad 5.
23 *In II Sent.*, dist. 18, q. 1, art. 2, corp. [trans. J. Wippel, in "Thomas Aquinas and the Unity of Substantial Form," in *Philosophy and Theology in the Long Middle Ages: A Tribute to Stephen F. Brown*, edited by K. Emery Jr.,R. Friedman, and A. Speer (Leiden: Brill, 2011), 122).
24 QDA, a. 10, resp. (Trans. John Patrick Rowan, St. Louis & London: B. Herder Book Co., 1949)
25 *De Principiis Naturae*, c. 1, 8.
26 Ibid.
27 ST I, q. 65, a. 4, resp. (Trans. English Dominican Fathers).
28 Wippel, "Thomas Aquinas and the Unity of Substantial Form," 124.
29 A claim derived from Aristotle; Michail Peramatzis, *Priority in Aristotle's Metaphysics* (Oxford: Oxford University Press, 2011).
30 ST I, q. 76, a. 7, resp. (Trans. English Dominican Fathers).
31 NB: Aquinas claims one cannot give a general definition of actuality and potentiality; e.g., SLM, 1826: "it is possible to make clear by examples that of which we wish to speak, that is of actuality, by way of examples in the case of singular things … [Yet] it is not possible to define the first simple things, for such a thing is not in definition, but would go on into infinity. And 'actuality' is among the first simple things. So to define it is not possible."
32 If one accepts a "pure process" ontology, that activity would not be the form of the substance, but the *substance* itself.
33 Peter van Inwagen, "Being, Existence, and Ontological Commitment," in *Metametaphysics,* edited by D Chalmers, D Manley, and R Wasserman (Oxford: Clarendon Press, 2009), 477.
34 Thomas Aquinas, *Summa Contra Gentiles* [SCG] (Taurini edition, 1961) II, cap. 58, no. 8. A similar argument is made concerning the composition of immaterial substances, so that their powers (e.g., intellect) cannot be the same as their form; e.g., QDSC, q. 1; ST I, q. 77, a. 1; SCG II, caput 52-54.
35 QDA, a. 10, ad. 18.
36 *Super Boethium De Trinitate*, (trans. Rose E. Brennan, S.H.N.; Herder, 1946), q. 5, ad. 4.
37 ST I, q. 75, a. 5.
38 John Heil, "Hylomorphism: What's Not to Like?," 8.
39 Thomas Aquinas, QQ, IX, q. 3, ad. 2.
40 John Heil, *The Universe as We Find It* (Oxford: Oxford University Press, 2012), 21.
41 Ibid.
42 Compare: EJ Lowe, *The Four Category Ontology,* (Oxford: Oxford University Press, 2005), 101–18, esp. 111.
43 QDA, a. 2, sed contra (trans. John Patrick Rowan, op. cit.)

44 See discussion in Michael Loux, *Metaphysics,* 3rd edition (New York: Routledge, 2006), 84–120.
45 Compare: Graham Renz, "Form as Structure: It's Not So Simple," in *Ratio* (new series), XXXI (Mar. 2018), 20–36.
46 QDA, a. 9, resp. (trans. John Patrick Rowan, *The Soul,* St. Louis & London: B. Herder Book Co., 1949).
47 Heil, *The Universe as We Find It,* 18–19.
48 Ibid., 19–22. See also John Heil, *From an Ontological Point of View* (Oxford: Oxford University Press, 2003), 177–92.
49 Heil, *The Universe as We Find It,* 107.
50 Aquinas, QQ IX (translated by Robert Pasnau, *Metaphysical Themes 1274–1671,* 624), q. 2, a. 2, resp.
51 SCG I, c. 21.
52 Aquinas, *De Ente et Essentia* (L. Baur edition, 1933), c. 3. Also, Gaven Kerr, *Aquinas's Way to God* (Oxford: Oxford University Press, 2015).
53 ST I, q. 50, a. 2, ad. 3.
54 Heil, *The Universe as We Find It,* 107. See also EJ Lowe, *Possibility of Metaphysics* (Oxford: Oxford University Press, 1998), 196.
55 C.f., ST III, q. 2, a. 1, resp.
56 ST I, q. 76, a. 8, resp.
57 Robert Pasnau, *Metaphysical Themes 1274–1671,* 624.
58 George Molnar, *Powers,* ed. Stephen Mumford (Oxford: Oxford University Press, 2003), 99–101.
59 *In De Anima,* Bk II, Ch. 1, #233.
60 Stump, *Aquinas,* 197. Compare: David Oderberg, "Hylomorphic Dualism," in *Personal Identity,* edited by E. F. Paul, F. D. Miller, and J. Paul (Cambridge: Cambridge University Press, 2005): 76: "the intrinsic incomplete constituent principle in a substance which actualizes the potencies of matter and together with the matter composes a definite material substance or natural body."
61 C.f., Alexander Bird and Emma Tobin, "Natural Kinds," *The Stanford Encyclopedia of Philosophy* (Spring 2018 Edition), edited by Edward N. Zalta. URL = <https://plato.stanford.edu/archives/spr2018/entries/natural-kinds/>.
62 Stump, *Aquinas,* 196–7.
63 Ibid., 43.
64 Marmodoro and Page, "Aquinas on Forms," 4.
65 *Pace* Theodore Scaltas, *Substances and Universals in Aristotle's Metaphysics* (Ithaca: Cornell University Press, 1994). C.f., SLM, 1674, (trans. John P. Rowan, Chicago, 1961.). Compare: Markku Keinänen & Jani Hakkarainen, "Kind Instantiation and Kind Change—A Problem for Four-Category Ontology," *Studia Neoaristotelica* 14, no. 2 (2017): 139–16; Markku Keinänen, "Instantiation and

Characterization: Problems in Lowe's Four-Category Ontology," in *Studies in the Ontology of E.J. Lowe*, edited by Timothy Tambassi (Neunkirchen-Seelscheid: Editiones Scholasticae, 2018), 109–24.

66 ST I, q. 76, a. 8, resp.: "an act is in that of which it is the actuality: wherefore the soul must exist in the whole body, and in each of its parts."
67 By reflexivity, every part is a part of itself. The form is thus a metaphysical part of itself, itself that in virtue of which it composes the whole as a metaphysical part.
68 Brown, *Aquinas and the Ship*, 79–83.
69 Marmodoro and Page, "Aquinas on Forms," 17–18.
70 QDA, a. 10, resp.
71 Ibid. [neque oculus neque caro neque aliqua pars remanet nisi aequivoce.]
72 SO, 147.
73 This remains true in FMS, 217–20.
74 SLM, 1632-3.
75 Aquinas, QQ IX, q. 2, a. 2, resp.
76 SO, 147.
77 I have made the case more specific; Jaworski, *Structure and the Metaphysics of Mind*, 118.
78 For example, see Hans van Kessel et al, "2.4 Proteins—Natural Polyamides," in *Nelson Chemistry 12* (Toronto: Thomson, 2003), 122.
79 Kerry McKenzie has written extensively in criticism of the view that particles are fundamental entities; see "Priority and Particle Physics: Ontic Structural Realism as a Fundamentality Thesis" in *British Journal for the Philosophy of Science*, (2014): doi:10.1093/bjps/axt017; McKenzie and F. A. Muller, "Bound States and the Special Composition Question," In *Recent Developments in the Philosophy of Science— EPSA15 Düsseldorf*, edited by Michela Massimi, Jan-Willem Romeijn, and Gerhard Schurz (Cham, Switzerland: Springer, 2017); "Arguing against Fundamentality," *Studies in the History and Philosophy of Physics* 42, no. 4 (Nov. 2011): 244–55.
80 Timothy Pawl and Mark Spencer, "Christologically Inspired, Empirically Motivated Hylomorphism," *Res Philosophica* 93, no. 1 (January 2016): 138.
81 Aquinas draws this very contrast between properties and parts. Properties, accidents, are not "particular things." But parts, even though they too are dependent entities like properties, can be considered particular things in ways that properties cannot (QDA, a. 1, ad. 9).
82 See further Patrick Toner, "Emergent Substance," in *Philosophical Studies* 141, no. 3 (Dec. 2008): 281–97.
83 Pasnau, *Metaphysical Themes*, 585.
84 QQ I, q. 4, a. 1 (trans. Sandra Edwards, *Quodlibetal Questions 1 and 2*. Mediaeval Sources in Translation, 27. Toronto: Pontifical Institute of Mediaeval Studies, 1983).
85 *De Ente et Essentia*, c. 5.
86 *Pace* Pawl and Spencer, "Christologically Inspired," 144.

87 I am speaking generally because a detached heart is likely not a substance, but a collection of individual substances (cells).
88 See the case study of carbon monoxide poisoning in Jeffrey Gaffney and Nancy Marley, *General Chemistry for Engineers* (Amsterdam: Elsevier, 2018), 233–4.
89 QDA, a. 1, ad. 3 & ad. 9.
90 Gyula Klima, "Aquinas' Balancing Act," *Bochumer Philosophisches Jahrbuch für Antike und Mittelalter* 21 (2018): 29–48, esp. 35.
91 SCG II, c. 83-84.
92 Compare: SO, 253–4.
93 Lowe, *Possibility of Metaphysics*, 196.
94 This follows Varzi, "Mereology," sec. 2.2, who defines overlap formally as: $Oxy =_{df} \exists z(Pzx \land Pzy)$. C.f., van Inwagen, *Material Beings*, op. cit., 29: "A thing *overlaps* a thing—or: they overlap—if they have a common part. If no two of the xs overlap, we shall sometimes say that the xs are disjoint."
95 On this point, my presentation of form contrasts with the view of Jeffrey Brower, who argues that forms are parts in some non-literal sense of part; Jeffrey Brower, *Aquinas' Ontology of the Material World* (Oxford: Oxford University Press, 2014), 72–3. For a good treatment of an Aristotelian account of these parthood relations, see Sally Haslanger, "Parts, Compounds and Substantial Unity," in *Unity Identity and Explanation in Aristotle's Metaphysics*, edited by T. Scaltsas, D. Charles, and M. L. Gill (Oxford: Clarendon Press, 1994).
96 Authors defending multiple primitive parthood relations are, e.g., R. Sharvy, "A More General Theory of Definite Descriptions," *Philosophical Review* 89 (1980): 607–24; DH Mellor., "Wholes and Parts: The Limits of Composition," *South African Journal of Philosophy* 25 (2006): 138–45.
97 For example, I have refrained from explaining exactly how substantial form relate to properties of various kinds, as I did not discuss Aquinas' account of properties, but only how they are implicated in material change. This would have overly complicated my discussion of material composition. See, e.g., ST I, q. 54, a. 3, ad. 2.
98 Pasnau, *Metaphysical Themes*, 574–87.
99 Ibid., 35–52.
100 I leave undecided how to classify those theories which identify the form with the whole object. In these theories, the form *could* be considered to overlap each material part as an improper part. It should also be clear from the context of my account of forms that forms need to wholly overlap the integral parts of a substance as if the form itself is a *part* of that substance. This helps distinguish hylomorphic metaphysics from, for example, a relational ontology where universals characterize but do not *compose* substances.
101 Kris McDaniel, "Modal Realism with Overlap," *Australasian Journal of Philosophy* 82 (2004): 137–52.

102 Kris McDaniel, "Structure-Making," *Australasian Journal of Philosophy* 87 (2009): 251–74.
103 David Armstrong's "How Do Particulars Stand to Universals?," *Oxford Studies in Metaphysics* 1 (2004): 139–54; *Truth and Truthmakers* (Cambridge: Cambridge University Press, 2004).
104 Peter van Inwagen's "lives" are, or are similar to, parts which overlap every simple that composes an organism; "lives" are "jealous," such that "only in certain special cases can two lives overlap: Only in certain special cases can there be *x*s and *y*s such that the activity of the *x*s constitutes a life and the activity of *y*s constitutes a life and the *x*s are not identical with the *y*s and, for some *z*s, the *z*s are among both the *x*s and the *y*s" [*Material Beings* (Ithaca, NY: Cornell University Press, 1990), 89].

Chapter 4

1 All citations of Zhu Xi, unless otherwise indicated, are from *Zhuzi Quanshu* 《朱子全书》, 27 vols (上海古籍出版社, 安徽教育出版社, 2002). I will refer primarily to "Zhuzi Yulei" 朱子语类 (vols. 14–18) [YL] or from "Gongwenji" 公文集 [WJ], followed by *juan:page*. Translations too are my own unless otherwise indicated.
2 YL 5:216 [性只是此理⋯生之理谓性]
3 YL 5:215 [理則就其事事物物各有則者言之]
4 YL 4: 182 [天下無無性之物。蓋有此物, 則有此性; 無此物, 則無此性。; 4: 189曰: 「是他合下有此理, 故云天下無性外之物」
5 YL 4:114 [氣以成形, 而理亦賦焉]
6 YL 4:194 [人之所以生, 理與氣合而已。天理固浩浩不窮, 然非是氣, 則雖有是理而無所湊泊。⋯ 凡人之能言語動作, 思慮營為, 皆氣也, 而理存焉]
7 YL 4:114 [有此理, 便有此天地; 若無此理, 便亦無天地, 無人無物, 都無該載了!⋯天下未有無理之氣, 亦未有無氣之理]
8 My translation adapts slightly the translation of Yung Sik Kim, "Another Look at Yi Hwang's Views about Li and Qi," in *Traditional Korean Philosophy*, edited by Youngsun Back and Philip Ivanhoe (New York: Rowman and Littlefield, 2017), 31–2; original from *Zhu Wengong Wenji* 朱文公文集 (Sibu Beiyao 四部備要 edition), 46:24a [所谓理与气此决是二物但在物上看, 则二物混伦, 不可分开各在一处。然不害二物之各为一物也。若在理上看, 则虽未有物而已有物之理。然亦但有其理而已未尝实有是物也。]
9 YL 1:114 [豈無先後! 理無形, 氣便粗, 有渣滓]
10 YL 4:115 [然必欲推其所從來, 則須說先有是理。然理又非別為一物, 即存乎是氣之中; 無是氣, 則是理亦無掛搭處]

11 John Krummel, "Transcendent or Immanent? Significance and History of *Li* in Confucianism," *Journal of Chinese Philosophy* 37, no. 3 (September 2010), 424.
12 WJ 70:3403 [且天地乃本有之物，非心所能生也]
13 Eiho Baba collects these examples together in "*Li* as Emergent Patterns of *Qi*," in *Returning to Zhu Xi*, edited by David Jones and Jinli He (New York: SUNY Press, 2015), 211–12. For example, YL 5:215 [理則就其事事物物各有則者言之]
14 See the discussion of the role of *gewu*, "investigation into things," in Yung Sik Kim, *The Natural Philosophy of Zhu Xi* (Philadelphia: American Philosophical Society, 2000), 21–5; or, Stephen Angle and Justin Tiwald, *Neo-Confucianism* (Malden, MA: Polity Press, 2017), Kindle edition, loc. 3983.
15 E.g., YL 15:473 [問：「致知，是欲於事理無所不知；格物，是格其所以然之故。此意通否？」曰：「不須如此說。只是推極我所知，須要就那事物上理會」
16 For example, see the discussion of Zhu Xi's account of moral knowledge in JeeLoo Liu, *Neo-Confucianism* (Hoboken, NJ: Wiley Blackwell, 2018), 228-235.
17 Zhang Liwen notes that Zhu Xi characterizes *li* as "所以然之故"; see Zhang Liwen, "Zhu Xi's Metaphysics," in *Returning to Zhu Xi*, translated by Andrew Lambert, edited by David Jones and Jinli He (New York: SUNY Press, 2015), 27.
18 YL 5:216 [性只是此理 … 生之理谓性。]
19 E.g., YL 1:116 [假如耳便是体，听便是用；目是体，见是用]; 6: 239 [體是這箇道理，用是他用處。如耳聽目視，自然如此，是理也；開眼看物，著耳聽聲，便是用]
20 C.f., Chen Lai, 《朱熹哲学研究》, 88–99, 144–8.
21 Stephen Angle, "Tian as Cosmos in Zhu Xi's Neo-Confucianism," *Dao* 17 (2018): 176–7.
22 JeeLoo Liu, *Neo-Confucianism*, 100–1.
23 Ibid., 128.
24 Ibid., 126.
25 Ibid., 128; "Based on its particular structure, each thing has its specific operation and usability."
26 E.g., David L. Hall and Roger T. Ames, *Thinking through Confucius* (Albany: State University of New York Press, 1987), 11–21, 131–8; David L. Hall and Roger T. Ames, *Thinking from the Han: Self, Truth, and Transcendence in Chinese and Western Culture* (Albany: SUNY Press, 1998).
27 As in the prior section, when Zhu Xi speaks of "affairs" as characterized by *li*, he seems to explain them in terms of the nature of the "things" engaging in the affair, not in terms of their own unique natures; he does not therefore seem to mean that an affair is anything more than a performance or activity *of* the "things."
28 Johanna Seibt, "Process Philosophy," *The Stanford Encyclopedia of Philosophy* (Summer 2020 Edition), edited by Edward N. Zalta. URL = https://plato.stanford.edu/archives/sum2020/entries/process-philosophy/, sec. 3.

29 Peter van Inwagen, "Relational versus Constituent Ontologies," *Philosophical Perspectives* 25, no. 1 (2011): 390.

30 See further, William Vallicella, "Constituent versus Relational Ontology," *Studia Neoaristotelica: A Journal of Analytical Scholasticism* 10, no. 1 (2013), 99–115.

31 E.g., YL 4:114 [問理與氣。曰: 「伊川說得好, 曰: 『理一分殊。』合天地萬物而言, 只是一箇理; 及在人, 則又各自有一箇理。」]

32 Russell Hatton, "A Comparison of Li and Substantial Form," in *Journal of Chinese Philosophy* 9, no. 1 (1982): 62.

33 Hatton, "A Comparison of Li and Substantial Form," 62. C.f., Russell Hatton, "A Comparison of Ch'i and Prime Matter," *Philosophy East and West* 32, no. 2 (Apr. 1982): 168.

34 Some have made the claim that Zhu Xi is a monist explicitly; C.f., John Makeham, "Monism and the Problem of the Ignorance and Badness in Chinese Buddhism and Zhu Xi's Neo-Confucianism," in *The Buddhist Roots of Zhu Xi's Philosophical Thought*, edited by John Makeham (Oxford: Oxford University Press, 2018), DOI:10.1093/oso/9780190878559.003.0006.

35 Zhu Xi's "Treatise on Ren," translated and complied by Wing-tsit Chan, *A Sourcebook in Chinese Philosophy* (Princeton: Princeton University Press, 1963), 595.

36 Melanine Jameson, "South-returning Wings: Yang Shih and the New Sung Metaphysics," a dissertation at the University of Arizona (1990) https://repository.arizona.edu/handle/10150/185201: Esp. 32–34.

37 Ibid., 596. This implication was drawn from Zhu Xi's treatise both by classical Korean (Toegye) and modern commentators (Kalton and Chan). See Michael Kalton, trans., *To Become a Sage* ["Ten Diagrams on Sage Learning" by Yi T'oegye] (New York: Columbia University Press, 1988), 151–2; also, Chan, *"Lun Chu-tzu jen-shuo,"* in *A Sourcebook in Chinese Philosophy,* (op. cit.), 391.

38 Justin Tiwald and Bryan van Norden, (eds.), *Readings in Later Chinese Philosophy* (Cambridge: Hackett Publishing Co., 2014).

39 Stanislaus Lokuang, "Chu Hsi's Theory of Metaphysical Structure," in *Chu Hsi and Neo-Confucianism*, op. cit., 66–69. The famous modern commentator Mou Zong San 牟宗三 is perhaps a source for this claim. Mou argues that Aristotle's forms are "class concepts," and as a consequence Zhu Xi's *li*, being one, cannot serve the same metaphysical role. The assumption Mou is making seems to be that a class is only meaningful in contradistinction to another class. If there aren't multiple classes, the concept of "class" becomes meaningless; e.g., Mou Zong San (牟宗三) 《一心体与性体》, in 《牟宗三先生全集》, vol. 5 (台北: 聯經出版事業有限公司, 2003), 43–4.

40 E.g., David Tien, "Metaphysics and the Basis of Morality in the Philosophy of Wang Yangming," in *Dao Companion to Neo-Confucian Philosophy,* edited by John Makeham (New York: Springer, 2010), 297.

41 YL 1:123[節復問：「這箇莫是木自是木，火自是火，而其理則一？」先生應而曰：「且如這箇光，也有在硯蓋上底，也有在墨上底，其光則一也。」]

42 YL 94:3167[不是割成片去，只如月映萬川相似。]

43 Chan, *A Sourcebook in Chinese Philosophy*, 637, no. 113. [References to Zhu Wengong Wenji 朱文公文集，四部倍要 edition, 49:8a]

44 "There actually was simply [*li*] before Heaven and Earth existed" and "… if somehow all the mountains, rivers, and the earth itself should vanish, [*li*] would still be here," translated in Tiwald and van Norden, (eds.), *Readings*, 183.

45 See further: Christopher Hughes, "Matter and Individuation in Aquinas," *History of Philosophy Quarterly* 13, no. 1 (Jan. 1996): 1–16.

46 See, for example, Chan, *A Sourcebook in Chinese Philosophy*, 641, no. 119. [WJ 49:14a]

47 YL 94:3129 [問「動靜者，所乘之機」。曰：「太極理也，動靜氣也。氣行則理亦行，二者常相依而未嘗相離也。太極猶人，動靜猶馬；馬所以載人，人所以乘馬。馬之一出一入，人亦與之一出一入。蓋一動一靜，而太極之妙未嘗不在焉。此-所謂『所乘之機』，無極、二五所以『妙合而凝』也」] C.f., Stephen Angle, *Sagehood: The Contemporary Significance of Neo-Confucianism* (Oxford: Oxford University Press, 2012), 43.

48 Chan, *A Sourcebook in Chinese Philosophy*, 641, no. 119. [Zhu Wengong wenji, 49:14a.]

49 Tiwald and van Norden, *Readings*, 180–2.

50 YL 94: 3131-3132 [氣質是陰陽五行所為，性即太極之全體。但論氣質之性，則全體墮在氣質之中，耳非別有一性也。]

51 YL 4:196 [論天地之性，則專指理言；論氣質之性，則以理與氣雜而言之。]

52 YL 6:237 [只是這箇理，分做四段，又分做八段，又細碎分將去。]

53 YL 18:619 [是一箇道理，界破看，以一歲言之，有春夏秋冬；。。。以一日言之，有旦晝暮夜。]

54 See Paul W. Kroll, *A Student's Dictionary of Classical and Medieval Chinese*, revised edition (Leiden: Brill, 2017), 122.

55 Hatton, "A Comparison of *Li* and Substantial Form," 56–7.

56 Chen Lai, 《朱熹哲学研究》, 117.

57 Ibid., 131–5.

58 Tiwald and van Norden, *Readings*, 174

59 Chan, *A Sourcebook in Chinese Philosophy*, 621, no. 57. [Zhu Wengong Wenji 42:27a-b]

60 David Tien, "Metaphysics and the Basis of Morality in the Philosophy of Wang Yangming," in *Dao Companion to Neo-Confucianism* (op. cit.), 297.

61 Chan, *A Sourcebook in Chinese Philosophy*, 620, no. 56. [Zhu Wengong Wenji 42:26b–27a]

62 YL 4:184 [又問：「物物具一太極，則是理無不全也。」曰：「謂之全亦可，謂之偏亦可。以理言之，則無不全；以氣言之，士毅錄作「以不能推言之」。則不能無偏。故呂與叔謂物之性有近人之性者，如貓相乳之類。溫公集載他家一貓，又更差異。人之性有近物之性者。」如世上昏愚人。]

63 YL 59:1876 [惟人得是理之全，至於物，止得其偏。…卻道天下是有許多般性，牛自是牛之性，馬自是馬之性，犬自是犬之性，則又不是。]

64 Tiwald and van Norden, *Readings*, 177.

65 See the discussion of the Korean schools mentioned in Youngchan Kim, "The LI-Qi 理气 Structure of the Four Beginnings and the Seven Emotions and the Aim of the Four-Seven Debate," *Traditional Korean Philosophy*, op. cit., 49–66.

66 Liu, *Neo-Confucianism*, 127.

67 Ibid., 127.

68 Ibid., 128.

69 c.f., Chen Lai, 《宋明理学》 第二版，(生活读书新知三联书店, 2011), 137.

70 Although the term is perhaps more perspicuously translated as the "nature of *qi*-of-a-particular-quality."

71 Liu, *Neo-Confucianism*, 131.

72 YL 4:182 [天下無無性之物。蓋有此物，則有此性；無此物，則無此性]

73 YL 94:3124 [便有氣；既有氣，則理又在乎氣之中]; 62: 2024[然這形而下之器之中，便各自有箇道理，此便是形而上之道]

74 YL 4:196 [論天地之性，則專指理言；論氣質之性，則以理與氣雜而言之。未有此氣，已有此性。氣有不存，而性卻常在。雖其方在氣中，然氣自是氣，性自是性，亦不相夾雜。至論其遍體於物，無處不在，則又不論氣之精粗，莫不有是理]

75 YL 4:200 [氣雖是理之所生，然既生出，則理管他不得。如這理寓於氣了，日用間運用都由這箇氣，只是氣強理弱… 又如父子，若子不肖，父亦管他不得。]

76 Wing-Tsit Chan, *Chu Hsi: New Studies* (Honolulu: University of Hawaii Press, 1989), 117.

77 YL 3: 157-162. E.g., 3: 162 [此皆萬物之精，既死而散也。]

78 Tiwald and van Norden, *Readings*, 174

79 WJ 58: 2779 (translation by Stephen Angle and Justin Tiwald, in *Neo-Confucianism*, loc. 1986-2008): [所以外邊纔感，中間便應，如赤子入井之事感，則仁之理便應，而惻隱之心於是乎形；如過廟過朝之事感，則禮之理便應，而恭敬之心於是乎形。蓋由其中間衆理渾具，各各分明。]. C.f., AC Graham, "What Was New in the Ch'eng-Chu Theory of Human Nature?" in *Studies in Chinese Philosophy and Philosophical Literature* (Singapore: Institute of East Asian Philosophies, 1986), 433.

80 Chan, *A Sourcebook in Chinese Philosophy*, 621–2.

81 Ibid., 622.

82 Thomas Aquinas, *Super De Divinis Nominibus* [DN], (Taurini edition, 1950), caput 2, lec. 3.

83 DN, caput 13, lec. 2 [unum, inquantum est singulare, in omnibus participatum, singulariter idest indivisibiliter coaccepit in se, sicut in principio uno, omnia existentia, et tota omnia,]
84 For example, Thomas Aquinas, *Summa Theologiae* [ST], trans. English Dominican Fathers (New York: Benzinger Bros., 1920) I, q. 44, a. 3.
85 DN, caput 9, lec. 3
86 DN, caput 13, lec. 2.
87 ST I, q. 44, respondeo.
88 ST I, q. 13, a. 5, resp. (Trans. English Dominican Fathers).
89 DN, caput 2, Lec. 3. [sigillum unum et idem totum se ingerit unicuique expressioni, sed diversitas participantium facit dissimiles expressiones, idest repraesentationes, unius et eiusdem principalis formae, quae totaliter habet formam.]
90 Ibid.
91 DN, caput 4, lec. 16.
92 See further Aquinas' claims in the commentary on the *De Trinitate* of Boethius, q. IV, a. 2. There, Aquinas makes clear the way in which forms account for species distinctions but matter (understood as *informed* matter) accounts for differences among genera.
93 Controversially, Julia Ching has argued that Zhu Xi's *Taiji* is relevantly subsistent like Aquinas' God; Julia Ching, *Religious Thought of Chu Hsi* (Oxford: Oxford University Press, 2000), 56. Further, it is noteworthy that this is how JeeLoo Liu and Feng Youlan read Zhu Xi's immediate predecessor, Cheng Yi. They argue Cheng Yi held that the one *li* is subsistent and eternal; see Liu, *Neo-Confucianism*, 93–4.
94 Subsequent Confucians took Zhu Xi's emphasis on *li* as problematic, and a number of Qing-Ming era Confucians rejected any priority of *li* to *qi* in objects. They held that *li* would either be reducible to a special physical force (*qi*) or merely a descriptive principle that served no ontological role. At least one of these critics, Wang Fuzhi (王夫之), appears to offer an objection to Zhu Xi's account of *li* that mirrors the grounding problem from Chapter Two. (Aside from in her *Neo-Confucianism*) JeeLoo Liu develops a reconstruction of Wang Fuzhi's objections to Zhu Xi's metaphysics in: JeeLoo Liu, "The Status of Cosmic principle in Neo-Confucian Metaphysics," *Journal of Chinese Philosophy* 32, no. 3 (Sept. 2005): 391–407; "Wang Fuzhi's Philosophy of Principle (Li) Inherent in Qi," in *Dao Companion to Neo-Confucian Philosophy*, edited by, Makeham, John (New York: Springer, 2010), 355–80.

Chapter 5

1 Kit Fine, "Aristotle on Matter," 38.
2 Kit Fine, "Things and Their Parts," 73.

3   Kit Fine, "Towards a Theory of Part," 589.
4   Ibid., 565.
5   Kit Fine, "Response to Kathrin Koslicki," 163.
6   Fine, "Things and Their Parts," 73.
7   Kit Fine, "Response to Koslicki," 164. He rejects the possibility of most material objects being thus introduced in Kit Fine, "The Question of Ontology," in *Metametaphysics*, edited by D. Chalmers, D. Manley, and R. Wasserman (Oxford: Oxford University Press, 2009): 164, fn. 2.
8   Fine, "Response to Koslicki," 164–5.
9   Ibid., 162–3.
10 Fine, "Relatively Unrestricted Quantification," 40.
11 On the last reading, doing ontology is then an exercise in giving "transcendental arguments" in a nearly Kantian sense.
12 This is how Korman appears to read Fine, as illustrated in the fact that Korman ranks Fine among mereological Universalists; see Daniel Korman, *Objects*, 14, fn. 1.
13 For problems with such a theory, see further Eliot Michaelson and Marga Reimer, "Reference," *The Stanford Encyclopedia of Philosophy* (Spring 2019 Edition), edited by Edward N. Zalta. URL = https://plato.stanford.edu/archives/spr2019/entries/reference/, esp. 2.1.
14 E.g., Fine, "The Question of Ontology," 157–77, esp. 163–4.
15 Karen Bennett, *Making Things Up*, (Oxford: Oxford University Press, 2017), 30–47, 51. The formal statement of this claim is that, for any x and y, if x fully builds y, then there is some z ($\neq y$) such that, necessarily, $z \to y$. In short, "if something is built, something necessitates it." (I have slightly modified Bennett's principle not to index the claim to any particular building relation.
16 Bennett, 50.
17 Ibid.
18 Zimmerman constructs a dialectical argument that resembles my own in this section: Dean Zimmerman, "Criteria of Identity and the Identity Mystics," *Ekenntnis* 48, no. 2/3 (1998): 281–301.
19 Ross Cameron, "Parts Generate the Whole but They Are Not Identical to It," in *Composition as Identity*, edited by Aaron Cotnoir and Donald Baxter (Oxford: Oxford University Press, 2014), 91.
20 See Ross Cameron, "The Contingency of Composition," *Philosophical Studies*, 136 (2007): 99–121. DOI 10.1007/s11098-007-9144-6.
21 Ned Markosian, "Brutal Composition," *Philosophical Studies* 92 (1998): 216–17.
22 Amie Thomasson shares a similar approach to these questions in her *Ontology Made Easy* (Oxford: Oxford University Press, 2014). See a critique of that view, similar to what I propose against Markosian, by Benjamin Marschall, "Easy Ontology, Quantification, and Realism," *Synthese* 198 (2021): 6281–95, https://doi.org/10.1007/s11229-019-02463-8.

23 Ibid., 214.
24 Ibid., 230.
25 Ibid., 231.
26 Ibid., 229.
27 See, e.g., Lynne Rudder Baker, "Why Constitution Is Not Identity," *Journal of Philosophy* 94, no. 12 (Dec. 1997): 599–621.
28 Ross Cameron, "Composition as Identity Doesn't Settle the Special Composition Question," *Philosophy and Phenomenological Research* LXXXIV, no. 3 (May 2012): 533.
29 Ibid.
30 Ibid., 534.
31 Ibid., 535.
32 Ibid.
33 Cameron, "Composition as Identity," 542.
34 Although Cameron qualifies that the argument would work with weaker relations, such as counterparthood, as well (Ibid., 542, fn. 17).
35 Ibid., 542.
36 Cameron, "Composition as Identity," 549–50.
37 Ibid., 550–1.
38 Graham Priest, *One: Being an Investigation into the Unity of Reality and of Its Parts Including the Singular Object which Is Nothingness* (Oxford: Oxford University Press, 2014), 10–12.
39 Ibid., 16–17.
40 Ibid., 20. When Priest contrasts his account explicitly with Aristotelian forms, he takes forms to be universals and gluons to be particulars (42). Nevertheless, on my mereological model, substantial forms are not universals.
41 Ibid., 17.
42 Ibid., 11.
43 Ibid., 15.
44 Ibid.
45 Priest calls gluons having the properties of every proper part *prime* gluons; Ibid., 21–2. Claudio Calosi uses the implication of composition as identity, that wholes often exemplify contradictory properties, as an argument against the coherence of the theory in, "Is Parthood Identity?" *Synthese* (2018), https://doi.org/10.1007/s11229-018-02057-w.
46 Jason Turner, "Review of Graham Priest, *One*," *Notre Dame Philosophical Reviews* (Sept. 15, 2015), https://ndpr.nd.edu/news/one-being-an-investigation-into-the-unity-of-reality-and-of-its-parts-including-the-singular-object-which-is-nothingness/. Turner poses a similar problem to theories on which composition is identity in his "Existence and many-one identity," *The Philosophical Quarterly* 63 (2013): 313–29.
47 This possibility for a theory of composition as identity is pointed out by Cameron, "Composition as Identity," 552.

48 Priest also argues that forms are universals—whereas substantial forms, as I have characterized them, are particulars. Priest, *One*, 42.
49 Ibid., 202.
50 Ibid., 167–93.
51 Notice that accepting composition as identity generally commits one to a similar position as Priest's, such that being a genuine whole is a matter of identity with some things and not others. The Super-Humean position shares much in common with the Huayan Buddhist, being defined by these two axioms: "(1) There are distance relations that individuate simple objects—namely matter points. (2) The matter points are permanent, with the distances between them changing" in Michael Esfeld & Dirk-Andre Deckert, *A Minimalist Ontology of the Natural World* (New York: Routledge, 2017), 21.
52 Priest, *One*, 8.
53 Ibid., 172.
54 Ibid., 182.
55 Ibid.
56 Priest, *One*, 13–14.
57 Ibid., esp. 179–81.
58 See Bryan Van Norden and Nicholaos Jones, "Huayan Buddhism," *The Stanford Encyclopedia of Philosophy* (Winter 2019 Edition), edited by Edward N. Zalta. URL = <https://plato.stanford.edu/archives/win2019/entries/buddhism-huayan/>., sec. 1.3.
59 Chan, *A Sourcebook in Chinese Philosophy*, 414–16.
60 Jay Garfield, *Engaging Buddhism* (Oxford: Oxford University Press, 2015), 76–79. See also Dushun, "Huayan Fajie Guan Men," translated by Alan Fox, in *Buddhist Philosophy*, edited by W. Edelglass and J. Garfield (Oxford: Oxford University Press, 2009), 76–7.
61 Priest, *One*, 189–93.
62 Chan, *A Sourcebook in Chinese Philosophy*, 418.
63 For example [from Thomas Cleary, trans., *The Flower Ornament Scripture* (Boston & London: Shambala Publications Inc., 1993)]: "All things have no differentiation; No one can know them ... Just as gold and gold color / Are in essence no different, / So also phenomena and nonphenomena / Are in essence no different" (448), and "If people want to really know / All Buddhas of all times, / They should contemplate the nature of the cosmos: / All is but mental construction" (452), " ... in all worlds there only exists verbal expression and verbal expression has no basis in facts" (462).
64 Justin Tiwald, "Zhu Xi's Critique of Buddhism," in *The Buddhist Roots of Zhu Xi's Philosophical Thought*, edited by John Makeham (New York: Oxford University Press, 2018), 150.

65 Zhu Xi, *YuLei*, 124: 2975-2976 [from *Zhu Xi: Selected Writings*, ed. Philip Ivanhoe, trans. Ellen Neskar and Ari Borrell (Oxford: Oxford University Press, 2019), chapter X, no. 16].

66 John Jorgensen "The Radiant Mind: Zhu Xi and the Chan Doctrine of Tathagatagarbha" in *The Buddhist Roots of Zhu Xi's Philosophical Thought*, edited by John Makeham (New York: Oxford University Press, 2018), 63, citing *YL* 95:2430. [人物未生時, 只可謂之理, 說性不得, 此所謂【在天曰命】也。…便是人生以後, 此理已墮在形氣之中, 不全是性之本體矣]

67 Ibid.

68 Tiwald, "Zhu Xi's Critique of Buddhism," 153, citing *Zhuzi Yulei*, 126:3013.

69 Ibid., 63; citing YL 4:64 [吾儒以性為實，釋民以性為空。若是指性來做心說，則不可。…須是先認得，方可說。必大錄云：若指有知覺者為性，只是說得【心】字。如有天命之性，便有氣質。如以天命之性為根于心，則氣質之性又安頓在何處！]

70 Tiwald, "Zhu Xi's Critique of Buddhism," 153.

71 YL 94:3167 [不是割成片去，只如月映萬川相似]]

72 For the history and players in Zhu Xi's own intellectual history, see both John Jorgensen "The Radiant Mind: Zhu Xi and the Chan Doctrine of Tathagatagarbha," in *The Buddhist Roots of Zhu Xi's Philosophical Thought*, edited by John Makeham (New York: Oxford University Press, 2018), 36–121; Brook Ziporyn, "The Ti-Yong Model and Its Discontents: Models of Ambiguous Priority in Chinese Buddhism and Zhu Xi's Neo-Confucianism," in *The Buddhist Roots of Zhu Xi's Philosophical Thought*, edited by John Makeham (Oxford: Oxford University Press, 2018), 193–276.

73 See Alan Fox, "The Huayan Metaphysics of Totality," in *A Companion to Buddhist Philosophy*, edited by S. Emmanuel (Malden, MA: Wiley-Blackwell, 2013), 187–8.

74 Van Norden and Jones, "Huayan Buddhism," sec. 4.2.

75 The challenge for these pantheistic views is to give a coherent account of how an immaterial thing, such as God or the One Mind, is the kind of thing that could have "parts," and, if they do, what it is in virtue of which that *those* parts compose God/the One Mind. This is, in fact, Aquinas' own underlying reason for holding his controversial doctrine that God is absolutely simple, such that He cannot bear any properties at all. God would not be the right kind of thing to explain the facts about everything else necessarily unless He is simple in that way, because there would be some other explanatory factor to which we would appeal to explain what it is that God's properties characterize Him (even if all of these properties were "essential" ones). If the properties are not identical with God's essence, then another regress starts, exactly such as we have seen many times. For the Huayan Buddhist, the challenge is to say whether the mental distinctions are identical with the One Mind or, if distinct, what makes them parts that compose precisely that Mind.

76　Trenton Merricks, *Objects and Persons* (Oxford: Oxford University Press, 2001), 58.
77　Ibid., 56.
78　E.g.,CB Martin, "Substance Substantiated," *Australasian Journal of Philosophy* 58 (Mar. 1980): 9.
79　C.f., Jeffrey Brower, *Aquinas' Ontology of the Material World*, 72–3.
80　See Dean Zimmerman, "Material People," in *Oxford Handbook of Metaphysics*, edited by Michael J. Loux and Dean W. Zimmerman (Oxford: Oxford University Press, 2003), 517: "If the matter now constituting my body is not the same as the matter that ceased to be as it came to constitute me, what is it and where did it come from? Either there is really no such thing as the matter now constituting me; or else 'the matter constituting my body' is just another name for my body ... ." Zimmerman argues that the dilemma can be resolved in a way like this, by appeal to different senses of "matter".
81　See a similar response to Merrick's argument by Patrick Toner, "Emergent Substance," 281–97.
82　Here I am not trying to determine a convoluted question as to whether wholes are "prior" to parts.
83　I'm not saying "human being" merely to avoid taking a side here on a controversial issue in Thomistic scholarship, which is whether a human being or person can survive their death. Stump holds, controversially, that humans can survive their death; *Aquinas*, 192–3, 200–2.
84　Aquinas is clear that, while souls are the kind of thing that can subsist (become individuals that compose no other thing as a proper part), disembodied human souls are not "complete" substances. C.f., *Quaestiones de Anima*, a. 1, ad. 3: "the human soul is not a particular thing as a substance having a complete species, but as a part of [something] having a complete species". What Aquinas seems to mean is that there is no *natural kind* associated with "separated human soul."
85　E.g., ST I, q. 90, a. 2, resp. & q. 75, a. 6.
86　SO, 200–34.
87　SO, 234.
88　Recall Koslicki's criteria do not arrive at saying that natural form-matter composites *are* completely unified objects, or substances. Rather, natural form-matter composites are functionally distinguished as *more* unified than other sets of things in the world.
89　FMS, 211.
90　FMS, 212. Koslicki offers the following example of an eye as a part that engages in such lawful interactional interdependence with a whole host of other proper parts of a living organism: "While the eye is part of the living organism, it is able to contribute to the living organism's ability to see by manifesting certain of its capacities. But the eye cannot accomplish this alone ... the eye's activities must

be coordinated in the right sort of way with the activities carried out by other components of the organism's visual system.... an eye which exists in a state separated from any such suitable surroundings is not able to manifest those of its capacities by means of which it can contribute to a living organism's ability to engage in visual perception. In turn, a living organism which is missing one of its eyes is not able to manifest its capacities for visual perception to the same extent as it would if the missing eye were present" (FMS, 209–10).

91 Ned Markosian, "Restricted Composition" in *Contemporary Debates in Metaphysics*, edited by Hawthorne, Sider, and Zimmerman, (Malden, MA: Blackwell Publishing, 2007), 19.

92 One should note the way this account is similar to the way in which Jansen criticizes and modifies Kit Fine's account of embodiments around the notion of a sortal: see Charles Jansen, "De-Fining Material Things," *Dialectica* 73, no. 4 (2019): 459–77. DOI: 10.1111/1746-8361.12280.

93 Koslicki recognized this implication, where she notes that accepting Aristotle's Homonymy principle requires that, if a substance becomes a part, "any such transformation would essentially involve a change in *kind membership*... " (SO, 147).

94 E.g., a human being *could* digest iron and make it part of its organism, but the hook as-is has not been digested or appropriately modified to form part of Hook's body. The same would be true of any sophisticated prosthetic; as long as these are such that they are not "biologically continuous" with the human organism, they are not parts of that organism except in perhaps an extended or metaphorical sense. By contrast, if we created a biological replica of Hook's hand, growing a cloned set of Hook's cells and structuring them in an appropriate way, then attaching such a biological prosthetic *would* be able to become part of Hook's body (if it was not rejected by his immune system, etc.).

Bibliography

Angle, Stephen. *Sagehood: The Contemporary Significance of Neo-Confucianism.* Oxford: Oxford University Press, 2012.
Angle, Stephen and Tiwald, Justin. *Neo-Confucianism.* Malden, MA: Polity Press, 2017.
Angle, Stephen. "Tian as Cosmos in Zhu Xi's Neo-Confucianism." *Dao* 17 (2018): 169–85.
Aquinas, Thomas. [All Latin editions obtained from those hosted at https://www.corpusthomisticum.org/, courtesy of the University of Navarre.]
De Ente et Essentia (L. Baur edition, 1933).
De Principiis Naturae (Leonine edition, 1972).
De Substantiis Separatis (Leonine edition, 1968).
Expositio Libri De Hebdomadibus (Taurini edition, 1954).
In libros Physicorum (Leonine edition, 1954).
In librum Aristotelis de Generatione et corruptione expositio (Leonine edition, 1886).
Quaestio Disputata De Anima (Taurini edition, 1953; translated by John Patrick Rowan, St. Louis & London: B. Herder Book Co., 1949).
Quaestio disputata de spiritualibus creaturis (Taurini edition, 1953).
Quaestiones Disputatae De Potentia (Taurini edition, 1953).
Quaestio Disputata De Unione Verbi (Taurini edition, 1953).
Quaestiones Disputatae De Veritate (Leonine edition, 1970).
Quaestiones Quodlibetales (Taurini edition, 1956; *Quodlibetal Questions 1 and 2*, translated by Sandra Edwards, *Mediaeval Sources in Translation*, 27, Toronto: Pontifical Institute of Mediaeval Studies, 1983).
Sententia libri Metaphysicae (Taurini edition, 1950; translated by John P. Rowan, Chicago: Regnery Co., 1961).
Summa Contra Gentiles (Taurini edition, 1961).
Summa Theologiae (Leonine edition, 1888; translated by the English Dominican Fathers, New York: Benzinger Bros., 1920).
Super Boethium De Trinitate (Lugduni edition, 1959; translated by Rose E. Brennan, S.H.N.; Herder, 1946).
Super De Divinis Nominibus (Taurini edition, 1950).
Aristotle. *Metaphysics.* In The Complete Works of Aristotle. Revised edition. Edited by Jonathan Barnes, Translated by W. D. Ross. Oxford: Clarendon Press, 1994.
Arlig, Andrew. "Multiplex Composition and the Prospects for Substantial Unity." In *Hylomorphism and Mereology.* Edited by Gyula Klima and Alex Hall. Newcastle upon Tyne: Cambridge Scholars Publishing, 2018, 1–20.
Armstrong, David. "How Do Particulars Stand to Universals?," *Oxford Studies in Metaphysics* 1 (2004): 139–154.

Armstrong, David. *Truth and Truthmakers*. Cambridge: Cambridge University Press, 2004.
Austin, C. and Marmadoro, Anna. "Structural Powers and the Homeodynamic Unity of Organisms." In *Neo-Aristotelian Perspectives on Modern Science*. Edited by R. Koons, N. Teh, and W. Simpson. New York: Routledge, 2017, 282–307.
Baba, Eiho. "Li as Emergent Patterns of Qi." In *Returning to Zhu Xi*. Edited by David Jones and Jinli He. New York: SUNY Press, 2015, 197–225.
Baker, Lynne Rudder. "Why Constitution is Not Identity." *Journal of Philosophy* 94, no. 12 (Dec. 1997): 599–621.
Bennett, Karen. *Making Things Up*. Oxford: Oxford University Press, 2017.
Bird, Alexander and Tobin, Emma. "Natural Kinds." In *The Stanford Encyclopedia of Philosophy* (Spring 2018 Edition). Edited by Edward N. Zalta. URL =
Bliss, Ricki and Trogdon, Kelly. "Metaphysical Grounding." In *The Stanford Encyclopedia of Philosophy* (Winter 2016 Edition). Edited by Edward N. Zalta. URL = https://plato.stanford.edu/archives/win2016/entries/grounding/.
Brower, Jeffrey. *Aquinas' Ontology of the Material World*. Oxford: Oxford University Press, 2014.
Brown, Christopher. *Aquinas and the Ship of Theseus*. New York: Continuum, 2005.
Calosi, Claudio. "Is Parthood Identity?" *Synthese* (2018): https://doi.org/10.1007/s11229-018-02057-w.
Cameron, Ross. "Composition as Identity Doesn't Settle the Special Composition Question." *Philosophy and Phenomenological Research* LXXXIV, no. 3 (May 2012): 531–54.
Cameron, Ross. "Parts Generate the Whole but They Are Not Identical to It." In *Composition as Identity*. Edited by Aaron Cotnoir and Donald Baxter. Oxford: Oxford University Press: 2014, 90–108.
Cameron, Ross. "The Contingency of Composition." *Philosophical Studies* 136 (2007): 99–121.
Chan, Wing-tsit. *A Source Book in Chinese Philosophy*. Princeton: Princeton University Press, 1963.
Chan, Wing-tsit. *Chu Hsi, New Studies*. Honolulu: University of Hawaii Press, 1989.
Chen Lai (陈来)。《朱熹哲学研究》。中國社会科学出版社出版发行, 1987.
Chen Lai [陈来]。《宋明理学》。 第二版。 生活读书新知三联书店, 2011.
Ching, Julia. *The Religious Thought of Csu Hsi*. Oxford: Oxford University Press, 2000.
Cleary, Thomas, translator. *The Flower Ornament Scripture*. Boston & London: Shambala Publications Inc., 1993.
Doolan, Gregory. "Aquinas on Substance as a Metaphysical Genus." In *The Science of Being as Being*. Edited by G. Doolan. Washington, DC: CUA Press, 2012, 99–128.
Dumsday, Travis. "Natural Kind Essentialism, Substance Ontology, and the Unity Problem." *Dialectica* 70, no. 4 (2016): 609–26.
Dumsday, Travis. "Can a Relational Substance Ontology Be Hylomorphic?" in *Synthese* (2019): https://doi.org/10.1007/s11229-019-02173-1.
Dushun. "Huayan Fajie Guan Men." In *Buddhist Philosophy*. Edited by W. Edelglass and J. Garfield and Translated by Alan Fox. Oxford: Oxford University Press, 2009, 73–81.

Esfeld, Michael and Deckert, Dirk-Andre. *A Minimalist Ontology of the Natural World.* New York: Routledge, 2017.

Evnine, Simon. *Making Objects and Events: A Hylomorphic Theory of Artifacts, Actions, and Organisms.* Oxford: Oxford University Press, 2016.

Fine, Kit. "Aristotle on matter." *Mind*, New Series 101, no. 401 (Jan. 1992): 35–57.

Fine, Kit. "Compounds and Aggregates." *Noûs* 28, no. 2 (Jun., 1994): 137–58.

Fine, Kit. "Things and Their Parts." *Midwest Studies in Philosophy* 23, no. 1 (1999): 61–74.

Fine, Kit. "Relatively Unrestricted Quantification." In *Absolute Generality.* Edited by Agustín Rayo and Gabriel Uzquiano. Oxford: Oxford University Press, 2006, 20–44.

Fine, Kit. "Response to Kathrin Koslicki." *Dialectica* 61, no. 1 (Mar. 2007): 161–6.

Fine, Kit. "The Question of Ontology." In *Metametaphysics.* Edited by D. Chalmers, D. Manley, and R. Wasserman. Oxford: Oxford University Press, 2009, 157–77.

Fine, Kit. "Towards a Theory of Part." *The Journal of Philosophy* 107, no. 11 (Nov. 2010): 559–89.

Fox, Alan. "The Huayan Metaphysics of Totality." In *A Companion to Buddhist Philosophy.* Edited by S. Emmanuel. Malden, MA: Wiley-Blackwell, 2013, 180–9.

Gaffney, Jeffrey and Marley, Nancy. *General Chemistry for Engineers.* Amsterdam: Elsevier, 2018.

Garfield, Jay. *Engaging Buddhism.* Oxford: Oxford University Press, 2015.

Graham, A. C. "What Was New in the Ch'eng-Chu Theory of Human Nature?" In *Studies in Chinese Philosophy and Philosophical Literature.* Singapore: Institute of East Asian Philosophies, 1986, 138–57.

Hall, David L., and Ames, Roger T. *Thinking through Confucius.* Albany: State University of New York Press, 1987.

Hall, David L., and Ames, Roger T. *Thinking from the Han: Self, Truth, and Transcendence in Chinese and Western Culture.* Albany: SUNY Press, 1998.

Harte, Verity. *Plato on Parts and Wholes: The Metaphysics of Structure.* Oxford: Clarendon Press, 2002.

Haslanger, Sally. "Parts, Compounds and Substantial Unity." In *Unity, Identity and Explanation in Aristotle's Metaphysics.* Edited by T. Scaltsas, D. Charles, and M. L. Gill. Oxford: Clarendon Press, 1994, 129–70.

Hatton, Russell. "A Comparison of Ch'i and Prime Matter." *Philosophy East and West* 32, no. 2 (Apr. 1982): 159–75.

Hatton, Russell. "A Comparison of Li and Substantial Form." *Journal of Chinese Philosophy* 9, no. 1 (1982): 49–76.

Heil, John. "Hylomorphism: What's Not to Like?" *Synthese* (2018). https://doi.org/10.1007/s11229-018-1792-x.

Heil, John. *From an Ontological Point of View.* Oxford: Oxford University Press, 2003.

Heil, John. *The Universe as We Find It.* Oxford: Oxford University Press, 2012.

Hughes, Christopher. "Matter and Individuation in Aquinas." *History of Philosophy Quarterly* 13, no. 1 (Jan. 1996): 1–16.

Inman, Ross D. *Substance and the Fundamentality of the Familiar*. New York: Routledge, 2018.

Jameson, Melanine. "South-returning Wings: Yang Shih and the New Sung Metaphysics," a dissertation at the University of Arizona, (1990): https://repository.arizona.edu/handle/10150/185201.

Jansen, Charles. "De-Fining Material Things." *Dialectica* 73, no. 4 (2019): 459–77.

Jaworski, William. *Structure and the Metaphysics of Mind: How Hylomorphism Solves the Mind-Body Problem*. Oxford: Oxford University Press, 2016.

Jaworski, William. "Hylomorphism and Part-Whole Realism." *Ancient Philosophy Today: Dialogoi* 1, no. 1 (2019): 108–27.

Johnston, Mark. "Parts and Principles: False Axioms in Mereology-+." *Philosophical Topics* 30, no. 1 (Spr. 2002): 129–66.

Johnston, Mark. "Hylomorphism." *The Journal of Philosophy* 103, no. 12 (Dec. 2006): 652–98.

Jorgensen, John. "The Radiant Mind: Zhu Xi and the Chan Doctrine of Tathagatagarbha." In *The Buddhist Roots of Zhu Xi's Philosophical Thought*. Edited by John Makeham. New York: Oxford University Press, 2018, 36–121.

Kalton, Michael, translator and commentator. *To Become a Sage* ["Ten Diagrams on Sage Learning" by Yi T'oegye]. New York: Columbia University Press, 1988.

Keinänen, Markku. "Instantiation and Characterization: Problems in Lowe's Four-Category Ontology." In *Studies in the Ontology of E. J. Lowe*. Edited by Timothy Tambassi. Neunkirchen-Seelscheid: Editiones Scholasticae, 2018, 109–24.

Keinänen, Markku and Hakkarainen, Jani. "Kind Instantiation and Kind Change—A Problem for Four-Category Ontology." *Studia Neoaristotelica* 14, no. 2 (2017): 139–61.

Kerr, Gaven. *Aquinas's Way to God*. Oxford: Oxford University Press, 2015.

Kim, Youngchan. "The LI-Qi 理气 Structure of the Four Beginnings and the Seven Emotions and the Aim of the Four-Seven Debate." In *Traditional Korean Philosophy*, op. cit., 49–66.

Kim, Yung Sik. *The Natural Philosophy of Chu Hsi*. Memoirs of the American Philosophical Society, 2000.

Kim, Yung Sik. "Another Look at Yi Hwang's Views about Li and Qi." In *Traditional Korean Philosophy*. Edited by Youngsun Back and Philip Ivanhoe. New York: Rowman and Littlefield, 2017, 25–67.

Klima, Gyula. "Aquinas' Balancing Act." *Bochumer Philosophisches Jahrbuch für Antike und Mittelalter* 21 (2018): 29–48.

Korman, Daniel Z. "Unrestricted Composition and Restricted Quantification." *Philosophical Studies* 140 (2009): 319–34.

Korman, Daniel Z. "Ordinary Objects." In *The Stanford Encyclopedia of Philosophy*, (Spring 2014 Edition). Edited by Edward N. Zalta. Available at: http://plato.stanford.edu/archives/spr2014/entries/ordinary-objects/.

Korman, Daniel Z. *Objects: Nothing Out of the Ordinary*. Oxford: Oxford University Press, 2016.

Koslicki, Kathrin. "Aristotle's Mereology and the Status of Form." *The Journal of Philosophy* 103, no. 12 (Dec. 2006): 715–36.

Koslicki, Kathrin. *The Structure of Objects*. Oxford: Oxford University Press, 2008.

Koslicki, Kathrin. "The Course-grainedness of Grounding." In *Oxford Studies in Metaphysics*, vol. 9. Edited by K. Bennett and D. Zimmerman. Oxford: Oxford University Press, 2015, 306–41.

Koslicki, Kathrin. *Form, Matter, Substance*. Oxford: Oxford University Press, 2018.

Kroll, Paul W. *A Student's Dictionary of Classical and Medieval Chinese*. Revised edition. Leiden: Brill, 2017.

Kronen, John; Menssen, Sandra, and Sullivan, Thomas. "The Problem of the Continuant." *The Review of Metaphysics* 53 (Jun. 2000): 863–85.

Krummel, John. "Transcendent or Immanent? Significance and History of *Li* in Confucianism." *Journal of Chinese Philosophy* 37, no. 3 (Sep. 2010): 417–37.

Lewis, David. *Parts of Classes*. Oxford: Blackwell, 1991.

Liu, JeeLoo. "The Status of Cosmic Principle in Neo-Confucian Metaphysics." *Journal of Chinese Philosophy* 32, no. 3 (Sept. 2005): 391–407.

Liu, JeeLoo. "Wang Fuzhi's Philosophy of Principle (Li) Inherent in Qi." In *Dao Companion to Neo-Confucian Philosophy*. Edited by John Makeham. New York: Springer, 2010, 355–80.

Liu, JeeLoo. *Neo-Confucianism: Mind, Metaphysics, and Morality*. Hoboken, NJ: Wiley-Blackwell, 2017.

Livingstone-Banks, Jonathan. "In Defense of Modal Essentialism." *Inquiry* 60, no. 8 (2017): 816–38.

Lokuang, Stanislaus. "Chu Hsi's Theory of Metaphysical Structure." In *Chu Hsi and Neo-Confucianism*. Edited by Wing-tsit Chan. Honolulu: University of Hawaii Press, 1986, 58–78.

Loux, Michael J. *Metaphysics: A Contemporary Introduction*. 3rd edition. New York: Routledge Press, 2006.

Lowe, EJ. *The Possibility of Metaphysics*. Oxford: Oxford University Press, 1998.

Lowe, EJ. "Form without Matter." In *Form and Matter: Themes in Contemporary Metaphysics*. Edited by David Oderberg. Oxford: Blackwell, 1999, 1–21.

Lowe, EJ. *The Four-Category Ontology*. Oxford: Oxford University Press, 2005.

Lowe, EJ. "A Neo-Aristotelian Substance Ontology." In *Contemporary Aristotelian Metaphysics*, edited by Tuomas Tahko. Cambridge: Cambridge University Press, 2012, 229–48.

Lowe, EJ, and Tahko, Tuomas E. "Ontological Dependence." In *The Stanford Encyclopedia of Philosophy* (Winter 2016 Edition). Edited by Edward N. Zalta. URL = https://plato.stanford.edu/archives/win2016/entries/dependence-ontological/.

Makeham, John. "Monism and the Problem of the Ignorance and Badness in Chinese Buddhism and Zhu Xi's Neo-Confucianism." In *The Buddhist Roots of Zhu Xi's Philosophical Thought*. Edited by John Makeham. Oxford: Oxford University Press, 2018.

Markosian, Ned. "Brutal Composition." *Philosophical Studies* 92, no. 3 (1998): 211–49.

Markosian, Ned. "Restricted Composition." In *Contemporary Debates in Metaphysics*. Edited by Hawthorne, Sider, and Zimmerman. Blackwell, 2007, 341–63.

Marmodoro, Anna. "Aristotle's Hylomorphism without Reconditioning." *Philosophical Inquiry* 36, nos. 1–2 (2013): 4–22.

Marmadoro, Anna and Page, Ben. "Aquinas on Forms, Substances and Artifacts." *Vivarium* 54, no. 1 (2016): 1–21.

Marmadoro, Anna. "Aristotelian Powers at Work." In *Causal Powers*. Edited by Jonathan Jacobs. Oxford: Oxford University Press, 2017, 57–76.

Marmodoro, Anna. "Potentiality in Aristotle's Metaphysics." In *The Handbook of Potentiality*. Edited by Engelhard and M. Quante. Dordrecht, Netherlands: Springer, 2018, 15–43.

Marmodoro, Anna. "Hylomorphic Unity." In *The Routledge Handbook of Metametaphysics*. Edited by Ricki Bliss and James Miller. London: Routledge, 2020, 284–99.

Marschall, Benjamin. "Easy Ontology, Quantification, and Realism." *Synthese* (2021) 198: 6281–95.

Martin, C.B. "Substance Substantiated." *Australasian Journal of Philosophy* 58 (Mar. 1980): 3–10.

McDaniel, Kris. "Modal Realism with Overlap." *Australasian Journal of Philosophy* 82 (2004): 137–52.

McDaniel, Kris. "Structure-Making." *Australasian Journal of Philosophy* 87, no. 2 (Jun. 2009): 251–74.

McKenzie, Kerry. "Arguing against Fundamentality." *Studies in the History and Philosophy of Physics* 42, no. 4 (Nov. 2011): 244–55.

McKenzie, Kerry. "Priority and Particle Physics: Ontic Structural Realism as a Fundamentality Thesis." *British Journal for the Philosophy of Science* (2014): doi:10.1093/bjps/axt017.

McKenzie, Kerry and Muller, F. A. "Bound States and the Special Composition Question." In *Recent Developments in the Philosophy of Science—EPSA15 Düsseldorf*. Edited by Michela Massimi, Jan-Willem Romeijn, and Gerhard Schurz. Cham, Switzerland: Springer, 2017, 233–41.

Mellor, D. H. "Wholes and Parts: The Limits of Composition." *South African Journal of Philosophy* 25 (2006): 138–45.

Merricks, Trenton. *Objects and Persons*. Oxford: Oxford University Press, 2001.

Michaelson, Eliot and Reimer, Marga. "Reference." In *The Stanford Encyclopedia of Philosophy* (Spring 2019 Edition). Edited by Edward N. Zalta. URL = https://plato.stanford.edu/archives/spr2019/entries/reference/.

Molnar, George. *Powers*. Oxford: Oxford University Press, 2007.

Mou Zong San (牟宗三)《一心体与性体》, in《牟宗三先生全集》, vols 5–7。台北:聯經出版事業有限公司, 2003.

Mumford, Stephen and Anjum, Rani Lill. *Getting Causes from Powers*. Oxford: Oxford University Press, 2011.

Oderberg, David S. "Hylemorphic Dualism." In *Personal Identity*. Edited by Ellen Frankel Paul, Fred D. Miller, Jr., and Jeffrey Paul. Cambridge: Cambridge University Press, 2005, 70–99.

Oderberg, David S. *Real Essentialism*. New York: Routledge, 2007.

Oderberg, David. "Is Form Structure?" In *Neo-Aristotelian Metaphysics*. Edited by Daniel Novotny and Lukas Novak. New York: Routledge, 2014, 164–80.

Orilia, Francesco. "Bradley's Regress and Ungrounded Dependence Chains: A Reply to Cameron." *Dialectica* 63, no. 3 (2009): 333–41.

Paoletti, Michele Paolini. "Structures as Relations." *Synthese* (2018): https://doi.org/10.1007/s11229-018-01918-8.

Pasnau, Robert. "Mind and Hylomorphism." In *The Oxford Handbook of Medieval Philosophy*. Edited by John Marenbon. Oxford: Oxford University Press, 2012, 486–504.

Pasnau, Robert. *Metaphysical Themes: 1274-1671*. Oxford: Oxford University Press, 2011.

Pawl, Timothy and Spencer, Mark K. "Christologically Inspired, Empirically Motivated Hylomorphism." *Res Philosophica* 93, no. 1 (Jan. 2016): 137–60.

Peramatzis, Michail. *Priority in Aristotle's Metaphysics*. Oxford: Oxford University Press, 2011.

Perovic, Katarina. "Bradley's Regress." In *The Stanford Encyclopedia of Philosophy* (Winter 2017 Edition). Edited by Edward N. Zalta. URL = https://plato.stanford.edu/archives/win2017/entries/bradley-regress/.

Priest, Graham. *One: Being an Investigation into the Unity of Reality and of Its Parts, Including the Singular Object Which Is Nothingness*. Oxford: Oxford University Press, 2014.

Rea, Michael C. "Hylomorphism Reconditioned." *Philosophical Perspectives* 25, no. 1 (Dec. 2011): 341–58.

Rea, Michael C. *Metaphysics: The Basics*. New York: Routledge, 2014.

Red Pine [aka Bill Porter], translator. *Poems of the Chinese Masters*. Port Townsend, WA: Copper Canyon Press, 2003.

Renz, Graham. "Form as Structure: It's Not so Simple." *Ratio* XXXI (March 1, 2018): 20–36.

Rooney, James Dominic. "Grounding Relations Are Not Unified." *International Philosophical Quarterly* 59, no. 1 (2019): 57–64.

Sattig, Thomas. *The Double Lives of Objects*. Oxford: Oxford University Press, 2015.

Scaltsas, Theodore. *Substances and Universals in Aristotle's Metaphysics*. Ithaca, NY: Cornell University Press, 1994.

Seibt, Johanna. "Process Philosophy." In *The Stanford Encyclopedia of Philosophy* (Summer 2020 Edition). Edited by Edward N. Zalta. URL = https://plato.stanford.edu/archives/sum2020/entries/process-philosophy/.

Sharvy, R. "A More General Theory of Definite Descriptions." *Philosophical Review* 89 (1980): 607–24.

Sidelle, Alan. "Does Hylomorphism Offer a Distinct Solution to the Grounding Problem?" *Analysis* 74, no. 3 (2014): 397–404.
Skrzypek, Jeremy. "Three Concerns for Structural Hylomorphism." *Analytic Philosophy* 58, no. 4 (Dec. 2017): 360–408.
Stump, Eleonore. *Aquinas*. New York: Routledge, 2003.
Stump, Eleonore. "Emergence, Causal Powers, and Aristotelianism in Metaphysics." In *Powers and Capacities in Philosophy: The New Aristotelianism*. Edited by Ruth Groff and John Greco. New York: Routledge, 2013, 48–68.
Thomasson, Amie. *Ordinary Objects*. Oxford: Oxford University Press, 2007.
Tien, David. "Metaphysics and the Basis of Morality in the Philosophy of Wang Yangming." In *Dao Companion to Neo-Confucianism*. Edited by John Makeham. Springer Netherlands, 2010, 295–314.
Tiwald, Justin. "Zhu Xi's Critique of Buddhism." In *The Buddhist Roots of Zhu Xi's Philosophical Thought*. Edited by John Makeham. New York: Oxford University Press, 2018, 122–55.
Tiwald, Justin and Van Norden, Bryan, editors. *Readings in Later Chinese Philosophy*. Cambridge: Hackett Publishing Co., 2014.
Toner, Patrick. "Emergent Substance." *Philosophical Studies* 141, no. 3 (Dec. 2008): 281–97.
Toner, Patrick. "Hylemorphic Animalism." *Philosophical Studies* 155, no. 1 (Aug. 2011): 65–81.
Toner, Patrick. "On Hylomorphism and Personal Identity." *European Journal of Philosophy* 19 (2011): 454–73.
Turner, Jason. "Existence and Many-one Identity." *The Philosophical Quarterly* 63 (2013): 313–29.
Turner, Jason. "Review of Graham Priest, One." *Notre Dame Philosophical Reviews* (Sept. 15, 2015): https://ndpr.nd.edu/news/one-being-an-investigation-into-the-unity-of-reality-and-of-its-parts-including-the-singular-object-which-is-nothingness/.
Vallicella, William. "Constituent versus Relational Ontology." *Studia Neoaristotelica: A Journal of Analytical Scholasticism* 10, no. 1 (2013): 99–115.
van Inwagen, Peter. *Material Beings*. Ithaca, NY: Cornell University Press, 1990.
van Inwagen, Peter. "Being, Existence, and Ontological Commitment." In *Metametaphysics*. Edited by D Chalmers, D Manley, and R Wasserman. Oxford: Clarendon Press, 2009, 472–506.
van Inwagen, Peter. "Relational vs. Constituent Ontologies." *Philosophical Perspectives* 25, no. 1 (Dec. 2011): 389–405.
van Kessel, Hans, et al. *Nelson Chemistry 12*. Toronto: Thomson, 2003.
van Norden, Bryan, and Jones, Nicholaos. "Huayan Buddhism." In The Stanford Encyclopedia of Philosophy (Winter 2019 Edition). Edited by Edward N. Zalta. URL = https://plato.stanford.edu/archives/win2019/entries/buddhism-huayan/.
Varzi, Achille. "Mereology." In *The Stanford Encyclopedia of Philosophy* (Winter 2016 Edition). Edited by Edward N. Zalta. URL = https://plato.stanford.edu/archives/win2016/entries/mereology/.

Wippel, John. "Thomas Aquinas and the Unity of Substantial Form." In *Philosophy and Theology in the Long Middle Ages: A Tribute to Stephen F. Brown*. Edited by K. Emery Jr., R. Friedman, and A. Speer. Leiden: Brill, 2011, 117–54.

Wippel, John. *The Metaphysical Thought of Thomas Aquinas*. Washington, DC: CUA Press, 2000.

Zhang Liwen. "Zhu Xi's Metaphysics." In *Returning to Zhu Xi*. Translated by Andrew Lambert. Edited by David Jones and Jinli He. New York: SUNY Press, 2015, 15–50.

Zhu Xi (朱熹). *Zhu Xi: Selected Writings*. Edited by Philip Ivanhoe. Translated by Ellen Neskar and Ari Borrell. Oxford: Oxford University Press, 2019.

Zhu Xi (朱熹). 《朱子全书》 [*Master Zhu's Complete Works*] 27 vols. 上海古籍出版社, 安徽教育出版社, 2002.

Zimmerman, Dean W. "Theories of Masses and Problems of Constitution." *The Philosophical Review* 104, no. 1 (Jan. 1995): 53–110.

Zimmerman, Dean W. "Criteria of Identity and the 'Identity Mystics.'" *Erkenntnis* 48, no. 2/3, Analytical Ontology (1998): 281–301.

Zimmerman, Dean W. "Material People." In *Oxford Handbook of Metaphysics*. Edited by Michael J. Loux and Dean W. Zimmerman. Oxford: Oxford University Press, 2003, 491–526.

Ziporyn, Brook. "The Ti-Yong 体用 Model and Its Discontents: Models of Ambiguous Priority in Chinese Buddhism and Zhu Xi's Neo-Confucianism." In *The Buddhist Roots of Zhu Xi's Philosophical Thought*. Edited by John Makeham. Oxford: Oxford University Press, 2018, 193–276.

Index

Locators followed by "n." indicate endnotes

actuality 67–9, 84, 147, 159–60, 165, 180 n.66
   of composite 92, 162
   intrinsic 79
   of matter 80–2
   and potentiality 69, 88, 92, 121, 160, 178 n.31
   primary 75, 80
   secondary 75, 84
   substantial forms as essentially 71–6
   of whole 84
Angle, Stephen 101
Aquinas, Thomas 4, 34, 42, 64, 94, 116, 120–1, 148, 155, 158, 162–6, 177 n.3, 178 n.31, 181 n.97. *See also* actuality; substantial forms
   De Trinitate of Boethius 187 n.92
   forms 64–5, 69, 79–80, 91–5, 122
   God as subsistent form 120–2, 187 n.93, 191 n.73
   immaterial substances 78–9, 177 n.6, 178 n.34
   metaphysics 65, 69, 78, 81, 83, 90, 94, 177 n.6
   normative dimension 177 n.5
   prime matter 67–9, 80, 83, 116, 127
   properties and parts 180 n.81
   souls 83, 92, 118, 162–3, 192 n.82
   substance 66, 73
   substantial changes 81, 88, 91–2, 165
Aristotle 2–3, 13, 15 16, 24, 27, 80, 90, 108, 129, 148, 181 n.95
   form and matter 13–14, 26, 107, 148, 184 n.39, 189 n.38
   Homonymy Principle 26, 193 n.91
   metaphysical tradition 119, 122
   soul 80
   unity and indivisibility 24
Armstrong, David 95
Awakening of Faith in Mahayana 158

Baba, Eiho 183 n.13
Bennett, Karen 128
   Making Things Up 174 n.12
blobject 68
Boyd, Richard 21
Brower, Jeffrey, *Aquinas' Ontology of the Material World* 181 n.95
Buddhism 124, 148, 152, 155. *See also* Huayan Buddhism/Buddhist

Calosi, Claudio 189 n.43
Cameron, Ross 137, 142–4, 189 n.32, 189 n.45
causal process 151, 162, 165–6
Charybdis of triviality 92
Cheng 104, 106, 111
Chen Lai 101, 111–12
Ching, Julia 187 n.93
class, concept of 184 n.39
classical hylomorphism/hylomorphists 4, 15, 56, 164–5, 170 n.19
composition as identity 37, 128, 140–6, 173 n.11, 189 nn.43–5, 190 n.49
   fundamental property 144
   individuality 142
   many-to-one relation 143
composition facts 57, 128, 132–7, 140–1, 145, 160
composition principles 12
Confucianism 155
counterparthood 189 n.32

debtor 8, 11–12
Dumsday, Travis 48

embodiments, principles of 13–14, 16–18, 20, 39, 62, 114, 127, 129
   criticism 193 n.90
   extra-mental natural 130
   genuine whole 16, 19

intensional/conceptual parts 14, 129
  kind of 38, 129–30, 136
  metaphysical and integral parts 15
  rigid embodiment 13, 16–19, 130, 170 n.24, 170 n.30
  variable embodiment 13–14, 18–19, 39, 130, 170 n.24, 171 n.53
  whole's descriptive character 15
essence 38–9, 44, 57–60, 71, 79–80, 117–18, 133, 150, 176 n.60
essentialism 81
explanatory factor 56, 61–2, 126, 128, 191 n.73
external relations 55, 81, 133

Fazang 152–3, 158
Fine, Kit 3, 7, 12, 17, 24, 27–8, 33–5, 39–40, 62, 65–6, 124–5, 127–31, 136, 153, 159, 170 n.24, 170 n.30, 188 n.12, 193 n.90
  atomism 19
  car-bouquets 18
  embodiments (*see* embodiments, principles of)
  "explanation of the identity" 16, 19, 129
  ham sandwich (example) 13, 16
  operations of composition 15–16, 18, 129–31, 171 n.50
  point of commonality 132
  star-groupings, "constellations" 18–19
  "Things and Their Parts" 13, 129–31, 171 n.53
  "Towards a Theory of Part" 16, 171 n.50
Finite Serial Response 139
forms matter 131–2
free-floating oxygen atom 86–7

generic interactional dependence 172 n.90
genuine material objects 1, 33–4, 36, 38, 41–2, 46, 52, 62, 64, 66, 124, 130, 164, 165
genuine whole 15–16, 19, 25, 54, 163, 190 n.49
gewu, role of (investigation into things) 101, 183 n.14
gluons, theory of 147–52, 154, 189 n.38, 189 n.43
Godehard (irreducible power) 52–3

Goliath and Lumpl case 7–8, 12, 22, 57–8, 132–3, 135, 170 n.19
grounding 40, 125, 174 n.12
  problem for SPP 8, 39–46, 61, 149

Hatton, Russell 105–6, 111–12. *See also* radical monism
"heaven and earth" (material objects) 98, 100, 107, 110, 116, 185 n.44
"heavenly *li*" (Zhu Xi) 110, 119, 122, 156
Heil, John 29, 49, 73–4, 77–8
homonymy principle 26, 83, 90–1, 193 n.91
Hook, Captain 166, 193 n.92
Huayan Buddhism/Buddhist 146–57, 190 n.49, 191 n.73
  One Mind 158, 191 n.73
Huayan Jing 152, 154
Huayan school 152, 158
hylomorphic metaphysics 5, 94, 119, 123–4, 181 n.100
hylomorphic theory of material composition 94–5, 97
  matter and form 65–6
hylomorphism 2–3, 7, 11–12, 15, 46, 54, 57, 62, 67, 94, 123, 160–61. *See also* structural hylomorphism
  Neo-Aristotelian versions 125
  proponents 3 (*see also specific proponents*)
  and restricted composition 32
  significance of 163–7
  substantial forms 4–5
hylomorphists 72, 104, 109, 168 n.4, 174 n.11
  classical 4, 15, 56, 164–5, 170 n.19
  metaphysical and integral parts 72

identity 19, 133–4
  as composition 37, 42, 128, 140–6, 173 n.11, 189 nn.43–5, 190 n.49
  as contingently transitive 146–57
  facts 128, 133–4, 139, 145, 148
  many-to-one relations 173 n.7
  of material objects 8, 14, 131–3, 137, 146, 148
  of material things 14, 129, 138, 140
  non-transitive relation 154
  one-to-one 143, 173 n.7

plural 144, 173 n.7
theory of properties and powers 29–30
in two flavors 137–41
whole web 152
immaterial monism 158
improper parts 9, 92–3, 181 n.100
internal relation 55–6, 102, 112, 127

Jaworski, William 3, 7, 12, 27, 33–5, 39–40, 47, 53–4, 62, 65, 85, 87, 125–30, 159, 161, 163, 173 n.3
bearing powers 48, 50–2
bootstrapping 49, 53–4, 161
exhaustive decomposability 52
H$_2$O molecule generation (case) 30–1
hylomorphic account 28
identity theory of properties-powers 29–30
individual-making structures 28–9, 31, 46, 48, 51, 173 n.3
material part 58
numerically identical 30, 91
part, causally influencing 49
powerful quality view (properties) 29
prime matter 31
"sparse" theory of properties 29
substances and parts 49–50
substances and powers 48
"Thomist" view of parts 30
trope 29, 48
variations of hylomorphism 32
Jones, Nicholaos 158

Korman, Daniel Z. 188 n.12
Koslicki, Kathrin 3, 7, 12, 16–17, 27–8, 33–5, 37–40, 46, 53, 62, 65–6, 72, 81, 83–4, 125–30, 159, 161, 163–4, 156, 172 n.87, 172 n.90, 173 n.5, 192 n.86, 192 n.88, 193 n.91
formal parts 23–4, 54–5, 57, 129–30
formal principles of material objects 20–1
Form, Matter, and Substance 25, 164
Goliath-Lumpl case 22, 58
hylomorphic composites 25–6
kind membership 38, 54, 58–9, 193 n.91
lawful interactional dependence 81, 164, 166, 172 n.90, 192 n.88

NAT 21
objects as structured wholes 20
objects, distinction 58
simpliciter, substances 25–6, 173 n.4
structural relation 56
The Structure of Objects 163
structures, proper parts (considerations) 21–4
substancehood, criteria 25–6
substance-parts, possibility 26–7, 83, 125–6
Krummel, John, interpretation 100

lawful interactional interdependence 81, 164–5, 172 n.90, 192 n.88
Leibniz's Law 171 n.74
Liu, JeeLoo 102, 115, 187 nn.93–4
li (Zhu Xi's principle) 98–9, 155, 157, 182 n.8, 183 n.17, 183 n.27, 184 n.39, 185 n.44, 187 nn.93–4
distinct 108, 111, 113–14
as fundamental/material nature 115–16
Li as Emergent Patterns of *Qi* 183 n.13
as metaphysical part 114–18
nature 102
particular sense 108, 114–16, 118–19
possession of fullness 113–14
to *qi*, priority 99–102
rational investigation 101
role of 98
as unitary universal/collection of universals 109–14
Lokuang, Stanislaus 107
Lowe, EJ 92

Markosian, Ned 139, 188 n.20
non-mereological universals 139–40
Marmadoro, Anna 175 n.27
Martin, C.B. 29
material composition, problems 5, 7, 12–13, 32–3, 40, 45, 61, 80, 131, 149, 159, 165, 176 n.60. *See also* theory of material composition
Goliath and Lumpl, case 7–8, 12
parts and wholes, persistence conditions 8
Tibbles, cases 8–10
materiality, principle of 122, 158–9

material nature (*li* and *qi*) 110–12, 115–18
material object(s) 1, 7, 10, 18, 28, 68, 76–7, 81–2, 95, 97, 122, 130, 134, 139, 157. *See also* genuine material objects
  composition 124, 132, 139–40
  cross-cultural recognition 4
  electrons 130, 173 n.2, 173 n.6
  formal principles of 20–1
  identity of 8, 14, 129, 133–4, 137–9, 144, 146–9, 155
  matter and form 2–3
  metaphysics of 4, 7, 128
  monstrous 20
  as proper parts 9, 54–5
  substance as 66
  unity of 13, 31–2, 128, 150, 166
material substance 12, 64, 66–71, 73–4, 76–8, 105, 138, 179 n.60
material things 1, 16–18, 41, 43–5, 60, 73, 77, 82, 99, 102–3, 107–8, 118–19, 125–6, 137–40, 144, 153, 158–9
material whole 9, 29, 34, 40, 44–6, 48, 51, 53–6, 61, 63–4, 66, 73, 80, 84, 92–3, 97, 126–7, 130, 138, 159, 161–2
McDaniel, Kris 95
McKenzie, Kerry 180 n.79
Mencius 114
Mereological Analysis of Constitution (MAC) 21
Merricks, Trenton, overdetermination 160–2
metaphysical part 15, 64, 66, 73, 79, 82, 92, 124, 162, 180 n.67
  forms as 91–5, 180 n.67
  li as 114–18
  material thing 123
  prime matter 68, 82, 158
  substantial form 162
metaphysics 3–4, 7, 40, 65, 69, 78, 81, 83, 90, 94, 98, 119, 177 n.6. *See also* hylomorphism
  Buddhist 148, 154
  hylomorphic 123–4
  Neo-Platonic 120
  participation and hylomorphism 118–23
  relational 126
Mou Zong San 184 n.39

Neo-Aristotelian Thesis (NAT) 21
Net of Indra 152–3
non-particularist process ontology 103

On the Divine Names 120
ontological relativism 17
ontology, process 103, 123
  constituent and relational 103–4
  non-particularist 103
  particularist 103
  pure process 178 n.32
  relational 181 n.100
operation of composition 15–16, 18, 129, 131, 171 n.50
  mind-dependent 130, 134
  primitive 129
overlap 9, 92–4, 181 n.94, 181 n.100, 182 n.104
oxyhemoglobin 86, 89, 90–1

Pace 86, 177 n.10, 179 n.65
Paoletti, Michele Paolini 176 n.46
paraconsistent entities 146–7, 152
parthood relations 12, 15, 42–3, 92–3, 135, 159, 161, 181 n.95
  multiple primitive 181 n.96
particularist process ontology 103
particular parts 113, 116, 118, 125, 127, 150–1, 161–2
Pasnau, Robert 80, 89
Plato 108
Platonic Idea 100
power-property 175 n.27
Priest, Graham 128, 146–55, 189 n.38, 189 n.43, 190 n.49. *See also* gluons, theory of
  forms 189 n.46
  objects and other things 156
primary actuality 75, 80
prime matter (*materia prima*) 31, 66, 69, 76–7, 80, 88, 94, 109, 116, 158
  characterization 68
  metaphysical part 68
  primary approach to 66–8
  and proximate matter 82
  pure potentiality 77
process ontology. *See* ontology, process
proper parts 1, 8–9, 24, 42, 55, 93, 136–7, 175 n.27, 192 n.88

baseball as 160–1
H_2O molecule 36
improper *vs.* 9
of living organism 192–3 n.90
structures (considerations) 21–3
substances as 19, 25, 27, 29–30, 32–3, 35, 37–40, 42, 46, 70, 95, 125, 127, 158, 161, 164
whole and 23, 153
property-powers 28–9, 31
identity theory of 30
structures as 31, 46–53
proximate matter 67, 69, 80–2, 88–90, 109
pseudo-objects 41, 62, 86, 97, 163

qi (Zhu Xi's principle) 98–9, 111–12, 114, 118, 122, 127, 156, 158, 182 n.8, 187 n.94. *See also li* (Zhu Xi's principle)
determination 102
as difference maker 106–9
priority of *li* to 99–102
pure potentiality 117
pure/turbid 112, 114, 117–18
qi-of-a-particular-quality 186 n.70
speciation and individuation 107

radical monism 104–6, 111
Rea, Michael 175 n.27
relational ontology 181 n.100
constituent and 103–4
qi as difference maker in 106–9
Restricted Composition Principle (RCP) 20–1
restricted theories of material composition 4–5, 11–12, 17, 20, 33–5, 43, 47, 62–4, 81, 95, 97, 123–8, 141, 142, 155
coherent 157–63
grounding problem 40, 61
hylomorphic 167
kinds and 46, 54
meaningful 132–7, 145
pseudo-objects 41, 62

Scaltas, Theodore 179 n.65
secondary actuality 75, 84
Ship of Theseus (example) 1, 7
Sidelle, Alan 57–8
Socrates 37, 83, 89–90, 108

spatial parts 27, 77
Special Composition Question (SCQ) 1–3, 7, 9, 13, 20, 28, 32, 40, 75, 95, 139, 142, 167, 169 n.2
hylomorphic 167
"Nihilism" 9–11
standard mereology 12
structural hylomorphism 2–3, 26, 31, 33, 35
grounding problem (SPP) (*see* grounding, problem for SPP)
"structural" aspect of 3
structures 20–1, 28, 44, 65, 125, 129, 173 n.3
as causal power 129, 161
individual-making 28–9, 31, 46, 48, 51, 173 n.3
kinds of 44, 126
as objects 23–4
as proper parts/relations 53–60
as property-powers 31, 46–53
Stump, Eleonore 80–1, 192 n.81
Aquinas 179 n.60
substance(s) 13, 15–16, 26, 34, 36, 41, 48, 65, 83–5, 90–1, 155, 175 n.27, 177 n.3, 177 n.5
actualized thing 69–71, 74–5, 79, 92
Aquinas' characterization 73
as emergent 81
as material object 66
member of kind 42, 81, 83, 86, 108, 166
and parts 4, 49–50, 84 (*see also* substance-parts)
and power 48, 51
as proper parts 19, 25, 27, 29–30, 32–3, 35, 37–40, 42, 46, 70, 95, 125, 127, 159, 161, 165
property-bearers 73–4, 77–8, 87
simpliciter 25–6, 69, 173 n.4
substancehood 25–6, 34, 37
Substance-Part Principle (SPP) 35, 49, 57, 173 n.6
characterization 35
class membership in kind 37–8
grounding problem for 39–46
H_2O case 36
interpretations 38–9, 42, 148–9, 173 n.11
rejecting 61–2, 83–4
same substances/substances 36–7

substance-parts 4, 33, 35, 40, 46, 50, 53–4, 59, 61, 63–4, 125–6, 128, 138, 158, 166
substantial changes 30–1, 81, 84, 92, 165
   account for continuity in 88
   denial of possibility 105
substantial forms 5, 65, 83, 93, 97, 104–5, 118, 129, 141, 144, 146–7, 159, 161, 181 n.97
   actuality of matter 80–2
   actual substances 69–71
   causal agent 71
   causal powers 66
   as common part 93–4, 109
   as essentially actuality 71–6
   existence (*esse*) 4, 70, 78–80
   intrinsic 70–1, 79, 82
   matter, material parts, and property bearers 76–80
   overlap 92–4
   pluralism 70, 76, 144
   primary approach to "prime matter" 66–8
   Socrates 89
   substance 66
Summa Contra Gentiles (SCG) 178 n.34
Super-Humean position 190 n.49
"supplementation" principles 12
Suzie (parrot) 93, 141–2

Taiji 110–11, 119, 121–2, 187 n.93
theory of material composition 4, 12, 33–4, 65, 85, 94, 125, 127–8, 131, 134, 136, 146, 159
   entirely mind-dependent 136, 153–4
   hylomorphic 66, 94, 97
   non-Thomistic 83
   oxygen atoms 85–7, 90–1
   as "restricted" theories (*see* restricted theories of material composition)
   theoretical structure of 160
third factor 134, 136
Thomasson, Amie, *Ontology Made Easy* 188 n.20
Thomistic analysis/thesis 65, 82, 109
   puzzle of parts 65, 85–91
      H_2O molecules 87–8
      oxygen atoms 85–7, 90–1
   substance 84–5

substantial forms 66
Thomistic/Confucian theory 166
Tibbles, case 8–10, 12, 41, 46, 48, 50, 57, 60
   Body-minus 8–10
Tien, David 113
trout-turkeys (pseudo-objects) 10, 20, 41, 56, 62, 164
Turner, Jason 147, 189 n.44

unitary universal 109–14
Universalism 10–11, 13, 16–17, 20, 40–1, 60, 97, 126, 129–30, 132, 135–6, 141, 159, 164
universals and particulars 29, 60, 82, 92, 95, 103–4, 108–14, 126–7, 138, 173 n.6, 174 n.14, 181 n.100, 189 n.38, 189 n.46
unrestricted composition, principle 10, 20, 33, 56, 142, 164

van Inwagen, Peter 3, 7, 12–13, 20, 32, 34, 40–1, 45, 62, 95, 126–7, 130, 139, 142, 163. *See also* Special Composition Question (SCQ)
   lives/life 46–7, 56, 174 n.15, 182 n.104
   Material Beings 1, 9, 169 n.8, 181 n.94
   metaphysical simples 47–8
   Universalism (*see* Universalism)
van Norden, Bryan 107, 111, 158

Wang Fuzhi 187 n.94
Weak Supplementation (WS) 12, 22
Whitehead, A.N. 103

Yang Shi 106, 110
Yogācāra 152, 157–8
Youlan, Feng 187 n.93

Zhang Liwen 183 n.17
Zhu Wengong Wenji 182 n.8
Zhu Xi 4, 97–8, 103, 112, 126, 128, 155–6, 158, 163, 166, 182 n.1, 183 nn.16–17, 183 n.27, 184 n.34, 184 n.37, 184 n.39, 187 nn.93–4, 191 n.70. *See also li* (Zhu Xi's principle); *qi* (Zhu Xi's principle)
   Huayan Buddhism and 146–57
   material nature 115

metaphysical landscape 98–9
metaphysics 98, 103–4, 119, 123
radical monism 104–6
Renshuo 106

theory of material objects 98
Zhuzi Yulei 182 n.1
Zimmerman, Dean W. 188 n.16, 192 n.78

www.ingramcontent.com/pod-product-compliance
Lightning Source LLC
Chambersburg PA
CBHW062228300426
44115CB00012BA/2264